PUBLIC ADMINISTRATION
IN BRITAIN

PUBLIC ADMINISTRATION IN BRITAIN

JOHN R. GREENWOOD
DAVID J. WILSON

Principal Lecturers in Public Administration
Leicester Polytechnic

London
GEORGE ALLEN & UNWIN
Boston   Sydney

George Allen & Unwin (Publishers) Ltd,
40 Museum Street, London WC1A 1LU, UK

George Allen & Unwin (Publishers) Ltd,
Park Lane, Hemel Hempstead, Herts HP2 4TE, UK

Allen & Unwin, Inc.,
9 Winchester Terrace, Winchester, Mass. 01890, USA

George Allen & Unwin Australia Pty Ltd,
8 Napier Street, North Sydney, NSW 2060, Australia

First published in 1984
Second impression 1984
Third impression 1986

British Library Cataloguing in Publication Data

Greenwood, John R.
　　Public administration in Britain.
　　1. Great Britain – Politics and government –
　　1979–
　　I. Title　II. Wilson, David J.
　　350′.000941　　　　　JN309
　　ISBN 0-04-352109-6
　　ISBN 0-04-352110-X Pbk

Library of Congress Cataloging in Publication Data

Greenwood, John R.
　　Public administration in Britain.
Bibliography: p.
Includes index.
1. Administrative agencies – Great Britain.　2. Great
Britain – Executive departments.　3. Great Britain – Politics
and government.　4. Local government – Great Britain.
I. Wilson, David J. (David Jack)　II. Title.
JN318.G73　1984　　　350′.000941　　　83-25671
ISBN 0-04-352109-6
ISBN 0-04-352110-X (pbk.)

Set in 10/11pt Bembo by Graphicraft Typesetters Limited
and printed and bound in Great Britain by
Biddles Ltd, Guildford and King's Lynn

CONTENTS

PREFACE

This book is primarily aimed at meeting the needs of degree level students in public administration, government and politics. It should, however, be of use to a much wider clientele, notably students studying for post-experience and professional examinations, as well as those registered on relevant BTEC and 'A' level courses.

British public administration is a far more complex subject than is often realised. It is not simply the study of government. The failure by teachers and writers to appreciate this has often presented enormous difficulties for students, particularly those new to the subject. In this text the complexity of British public administration is an underlying theme, and an attempt is made to confront, rather than evade, problem areas. Material is presented in a logical, straightforward manner without distorting reality. While separate sections deal with the various sectors of the subject – enabling students to concentrate on those areas in which they are most interested – the book nevertheless provides an analysis of British public administration *as a whole* (unlike many competing texts which ignore or 'skate over' everything other than central government and elected local authorities).

Throughout, emphasis has been placed on actual working relationships within a wider political environment rather than on the formal, legal/constitutional position which some textbooks still depict. Obviously not all topics can be treated with equal depth, but we have attempted to provide adequate coverage of the *totality* of British public administration. At the risk of interrupting the 'flow' of our own remarks, extensive cross-referencing has been included in the text in order to emphasise the interlinkages which give the administrative system its coherence and flexibility. We have also attempted to explain British public administration as far as possible through the words and ideas of official reports and authoritative writers. Over 300 sources are cited or quoted, at least some of which we hope will be utilised by readers whose appetites are sufficiently whetted to want to study the subject at a more advanced level.

In bringing together and synthesising much of the published work on British public administration we have obviously been dependent on a large number of authors, both academics and practitioners. More specifically, however, we are indebted to numerous friends who have read substantial parts of the original drafts and made many useful comments which have helped to shape the finished product. The text was prepared for publication by March 1983 but, where necessary, amendments have been made in the light of changes following the June 1983 General Election.

Professor Andrew Dunsire of York University, Professor Roy Gregory of Reading University and Professor David Regan of Nottingham University have been particularly helpful in providing detailed comments on substantial parts of the early drafts. Leonard Tivey, Head of the Department of Political Science at Birmingham University, was a tremendous resource in the area of public ownership. Dr. Paul Cousins of Kingston Polytechnic provided some very precise and helpful advice on several chapters, and Dr. Bob Borthwick and Robert Pyper from Leicester University read and commented upon the original version of Chapter 13. Peter Hennessy of *The Times* kindly read the sections on the CPRS and Cabinet, and provided much 'real' information which we hope has enriched our final offering. Colleagues at Leicester Polytechnic have also been particularly helpful in looking at specific material. Our thanks are owed to: Merrill Clarke, Martin Davis, Alan Fletcher, Roger Hall, Neil Hawke, Ian Macleod, Pat Mounfield, Gerry Stoker and Tony Stott.

A text such as this could not be produced without assistance from practitioners of public administration. We are both fortunate that our long association with public administration courses at Leicester Polytechnic has brought us into contact with public administrators at all levels and in all parts of the public sector. Their many conversations with us over the years have, we hope, enabled us to capture something of the 'real world' of public administration. We are indebted to many, but space and confidentiality permit us only to acknowledge by name those who read and commented on particular parts of the text; namely, Roger Powling of the Thames Water Authority, and Ken Webster, former Treasurer of Leicester City Council, who guided us carefully through the minefield of local authority finance.

Last, but absolutely not least, our wives Sue Wilson and Pam Greenwood checked much detailed material but, above all, endured (with our children) more than a year of relative solitude while the book was written. Our debts are, therefore, immense but responsibility for any errors, omissions and inaccuracies remains ours alone.

JOHN R. GREENWOOD
DAVID J. WILSON
Leicester Polytechnic
August 1983

1 THE CONTEXT OF BRITISH PUBLIC ADMINISTRATION

What is Public Administration?

Any attempt to produce a simple definition of public administration is doomed to failure. As Waldo (1955, p. 2) has observed: 'The immediate effect of all one-sentence or one-paragraph definitions of public administration is mental paralysis rather than enlightenment and stimulation'. This is because the *complexity* of the field belies simple generalisations. Is there, for example, a single 'public' or various 'publics'? Whatever formal institutional descriptions might imply, there is, in reality, nothing simple about the *practice* of British public administration. Organisation charts in governmental institutions invariably present a neat, ordered universe, but nothing could be further removed from the actuality of public sector administration. The major theme of this book is that 'the ambiguity, confusion and complexity' which Rhodes (1981, p. 28) maintains characterises central/local government relationships in fact typifies the whole of British public administration.

At a basic level misunderstandings occur because the term 'public administration' is used in a number of different ways. As Fletcher (1967, pp. 53–4) explains, it can be used to denote:

1 The *activity* of public servants.
2 The *structure* of executive government: that is the institutions and patterns of relationships through which the activity of public servants is carried on.
3 The study of 1 and 2.

Put another way, public administration is 'an activity, a set of institutions and a subject of study' (Stanyer and Smith, 1976, p. 11). As a subject it 'focuses pre-eminently on the institutions, organizational structures and decision/implementation processes of government. It is largely a "formal" field, concerned with arrangements and procedures for making decisions, rather than with the substance or impacts of these decisions' (Dunleavy, 1982, p. 215). This text aims to provide a comprehensive analysis of British public administration, putting between the covers of one book material hitherto at best scattered amongst a variety of sources or at worst totally ignored. The extensive bibliographical references will, hopefully, lead students towards greater in-depth reading in what is a fascinating, if ever-changing, field of study.

The Policy/Administration Dichotomy

Confusion about definitions is compounded because the term 'administration' is not at all straightforward. Dunsire (1973) has argued that there are at least fifteen different meanings of the word, ranging from carrying out decisions to initiating policy. A distinction is sometimes made between 'policy' or 'politics' (which it is suggested is the work of elected politicians) and 'administration' or 'execution' (which is the work of officials or administrators). Under scrutiny, however, this distinction breaks down, for two main reasons:

1 Policy and administration are largely indistinguishable. All policy decisions are to some extent predicated upon considerations about implementation. No government, for example, could realistically take a policy decision to put a man on the moon until the means of its implementation were known to be available. More than this, administrative decisions – about how a policy should be implemented – themselves require implementation, and as such often take the form of another policy decision. For example, a decision to reduce inflation might be implemented in a number of ways: controlling prices and incomes, tax changes, controlling money supply, etc. Assuming the first of these is chosen, this in effect will become a policy – a prices and incomes policy – which will itself require decisions regarding implementation. Should, for example, *all* wages and prices be controlled or just some; should special machinery be established to monitor price and income movements; what penalties, if any, should be imposed upon unions or companies breaking the law? As these examples show, there is a 'seamless web' of policy and administration. Precisely where 'policy' ends and 'administration' begins is impossible to determine.

2 It is too simplistic to argue that the role of politicians is to

determine policy while that of officials is confined to implementing political decisions. Indeed, even if 'policy' and 'administration' could be clearly defined, the respective roles of politicians and officials would still be difficult to demarcate. Because administrative considerations bulk large in policy-making, and because in the modern world much policy-making requires specialist advice along with professional analysis, politicians in practice rely heavily on their officials when formulating policy. The distinction between policy determined by politicians and administration carried out by officials has little credibility in the real world of British public administration.

Environmental Influences

Public bodies do not exist in a vacuum but are closely related to the broader environment which they inhabit. They are both influenced by, and themselves influence, that environment.

ENVIRONMENTAL INFLUENCES UPON ORGANISATIONS

A number of external influences serve to both assist and constrain public administrators. The *political* dimension is particularly important. As Ridley (1979, p. 3) explains, public administration

is unavoidably a subsystem of the political system, not just related to it through inputs and outputs but dependent upon it for its basic structures and influenced by it in its values. If administrative systems cannot be understood except by reference to their political environment ... political systems cannot be understood without study of the administration. The administration not only forms the largest part of government, it lies at the centre of the policy-making process.

The close inter-relationship between politics and public administration is a practical reality whatever legal textbooks might indicate to the contrary. Public administration cannot be abstracted out of its social, political and economic environment; it needs to be considered as *part* of that complex environment.

Environmental factors help to determine the choices made by politicians and administrators. The prevailing social and political culture provides a framework within which administrative action occurs. Pitt and Smith (1981, p. 25) show, for example, how organisational life in government departments 'is affected by the rules and pressures generated by the political environment'. While recognising the importance of environmental factors it is, however, unwise to ignore the role played by key personnel, especially those with strong ideological predispositions. The relationship between an organisation and its environment is never purely mechanistic; the importance of *choice* within an organisation must always be recognised.

ORGANISATIONAL INFLUENCES UPON THE ENVIRONMENT

Public authorities are not simply passive systems upon which external forces impact; they themselves can affect the environment in which they operate. Civil servants, for example, can manipulate the environment in which they work by selecting the pressure groups which are admitted into departmental policy-making processes. Likewise, ministers can often manipulate public opinion by carefully timed 'leaks' of information to the media, or through speeches which set the subject and tone of public debate.

ORGANISATIONAL INTERDEPENDENCE

Organisations do not simply face complex environments but are themselves dependent upon elements in that environment. Organisational interdependence is an important element of contemporary public administration. Rhodes (1981, p. 87) illustrates this in the context of central/local government relationships: 'Local authorities are not "mere agents" of central government. They are political systems in their own right with the capacity to resist central demands. Moreover, central government is dependent upon local authorities for information, for expertise and for the implementation of policy.' Similar reciprocity is replicated at all levels of public administration.

The Extent of Public Administration

As Stanyer and Smith (1976, p. 21) observe, 'Many past studies have made the mistake of confusing public administration with the civil service and central departmental administration. Several books whose titles would lead one to expect a discussion of the whole system of public administration are found to have omitted local government, public corporations, field administration and bodies with uncertain or unusual status.' For example, one recent text states: 'By public administration, then, we mean the machinery of central and local government, the process of implementing political decisions, and the body of people involved in that process' (Derbyshire with Patterson, 1979, p. 3). To limit public administration simply to central and local government, however, is to omit from analysis roughly half the public sector (Wilson and Woodhead, 1982, p. 210). Only half of the 7.4 million public service employees in mid-1980 worked for the civil service or local authorities; the rest were employed by public corporations (e.g. Post Office), the National Health Service, or one of many non-departmental public bodies such as the Arts Council (Briscoe, 1981, p. 94).

An approach which ignores half the public sector leads, as Stanyer and Smith (1976, p. 22) comment, to a failure to appreciate that there exists a *system* of government, of which central administration is only part. 'The pattern of interactions and relationships between separate elements – the structure of the system – can never be studied properly from the point of view of only a small part with highly specialised characteristics.' It is important to recognise that the 'system' of public administration is linked in a variety of ways with the rest of government and with society as a whole. Public bodies, in other words, are part of a complex environment.

Complexity is compounded, moreover, by the tremendous diversity *within* parts of the public sector. With nationalisation, for example, Rolls Royce is a very different organisation from the British Steel Corporation and the National Bus Company. Formally, all have been nationalised, but their operating procedures, financial turnovers and commercial outlooks are quite distinctive. Likewise, West Midlands County Council with 2,700,000 inhabitants, is worlds apart from a tiny parish council (such as Walton-on-the-Wolds in Leicestershire with an electoral roll of 193 in 1982). Statutorily, both are 'local authorities' but in practice they are as different as chalk and cheese. Similarly, there are major differences between central government departments in terms of size, internal structures, and operating styles. The 'typical' government department does not exist, and this makes the administrative environment at the core of central government particularly complex.

Most complex of all, perhaps, is the world of quasi-government (see Chapter 10). Contrast, for example, the United Kingdom

Atomic Energy Authority, employing 13,919 staff and spending £251.2 millions in 1979/80 with the Apple and Pear Development Council employing just seven staff and spending £344,000. The presence of such diverse bodies within a single category is an indication of the complexity which characterises British public administration both *between* and *within* the various organisational categories.

Further ambiguity and confusion stems from the blurred terminology which besets public administration. Many of Britain's political institutions have evolved slowly over long periods and – although the terms used to describe them have been retained – the institutions themselves have changed markedly. For example, the designation 'government department' now covers so many organisational forms that it is almost incapable of precise definition. As Hood *et al.* (1978, p. 22) have observed: 'Every public administration *student* (not to mention teachers), it might innocently be thought, ought to know what a "Government Department" is. But we came to realise that the question is a deep, indeed a philosophical one, and that there is certainly no single and all-encompassing definition of such agencies.' A similar lack of clarity surrounds the term 'civil service', one consequence of which, as Wood (1981, p. 480) points out, is that 'even the question of total numbers is difficult to answer'. Apparently simple issues are invariably far from straightforward.

Public and Private Administration

Public administration is undertaken in a political setting, which is often highly partisan. Stated simply its broad focus is the activity of the state. This contrasts to some extent with private sector administration where the goals are those of non-state organisations. Whereas public administration is broadly concerned with the formulation and implementation of public policy, private sector administration has a more restricted set of aims and is often motivated by practicalities such as profit margins. One difficulty, however, is that whenever comparisons are made between public and private administration the impression is frequently given that each is opposed to the other and occupies a separate and distinct field. In practice, much of what takes place in public administration is accomplished with the collaboration of numerous private groups and individuals; 'indeed, the line between "private" and "public" has now become so blurred that it is difficult to tell where government leaves off and private business begins' (Nigro and Nigro, 1973, p. 17).

Private organisations such as political parties and pressure groups are, for example, intimately involved with public administration, setting the parameters and the 'political agenda' within which public policy is formulated. No less obviously, public bodies make great use of private contractors to build offices, houses and hospitals, etc. Such contractors spend many millions of pounds of public money and employ large numbers of workers who, while technically not government employees, are in many respects a real part of its workforce. Equally, private business depends heavily upon public authorities to supply a host of services, some of them essential for economic performance (roads, airports, gas, water, electricity, etc.) and others fundamental to the maintenance of an effective workforce (health, education, social services, housing). The interdependence of the two sectors quickly becomes apparent.

As Dunsire (1973, p. 179) reminds us, it is a mistake to draw too firm a line between public and private administration. Often the internal distinctions between different public sector bodies are much more significant than contrasts with the private sector. Dunsire recommends: 'step back a pace and look at both public and business administration in the West together, in contrast to another culture ... and they are seen as inter-twined parts of the same system, inseparable from one another, the values of the one dependent upon the values of the other'. Today, in fact, many economists maintain that public sector efficiency can be adequately assessed with tools originally designed for private sector analysis. Likewise, many public sector organisations – particularly national-ised industries – produce and market products in a manner not dissimilar from private companies. Public and private enterprises, while legally distinguishable, are less clearly disentangled in prac-tice. Did, for example, the purchase by the state of a majority shareholding in British Leyland transfer it overnight from the private to the public sector and turn its 'managers' into public administrators?

As Dunsire (1982, p. 15) has argued, the boundary between what is 'state' and what is 'non-state' is increasingly 'seen as a distraction and an irrelevance'. In many key policy areas 'the policy commu-nity' comprising not only officials but 'businessmen, academics [and] spokesmen of various interests' is crucially involved in initiating or implementing a programme. Consultative committees and advisory councils proliferate and as Dunsire (1982, p. 16) has shown, 'Institutionalised traffic across the state/non-state boundary is heavy'. In certain contexts it is even appropriate to recognise the 'colonisation of the private sector by government' (Pitt and Smith, 1981, p. 39). Policy communities, of both a formal and informal nature, incorporating both public and private interests, illustrate the difficulty of separating state from non-state organisation and management. There must inevitably be an element of artificiality associated with any such exercise. Public administration does, nevertheless, have certain distinctive features:

PUBLIC ACCOUNTABILITY

Probably the main distinguishing feature of public administration lies in its accountability to the public. As Stanyer and Smith (1976, pp. 30–1) observe: 'At its most elementary, public accountability simply requires that public bodies give an account of their activities to other people and provide a justification for what has been done in terms of other people's values, in a way that private bodies do not'. In other words public bodies are subject to external checks and oversight (e.g. ministers are accountable to Parliament for the conduct of their departments by the convention of ministerial responsibility) from which private companies are relatively immune. The nearest analogy in the private sector is the ultimate accountability of a company board to shareholders, although this rarely involves the same degree of external checks and oversight as in the public sector.

The *accountability* of public bodies *for* their actions should not be confused with the *control of* them by politicians. Nevertheless, the two concepts are closely linked: ministers, for example, cannot be held accountable for the actions of their departments unless they have the means to control those actions. In Britain politicians have traditionally exercised constitutional control over public bureaucracies, and been held accountable for their stewardship to Parliament (in the case of central government) and to elected local councils (with local government). Of course, one effect of this is that public administrators are obliged to pursue aims determined by people other than themselves. This is fine in theory for accountability reasons, but in practice aims determined by outsiders may be vague and even contradictory. As Stanyer and Smith (1976, p. 31) conclude: 'Public bodies are expected to pursue multiple goals and meet multiple standards; hence the problem of distinguishing good and bad is particularly acute and hard to solve'.

EQUITY

Administrators are expected to treat members of the public fairly without showing partiality to one at the expense of another. While there is often ambiguity about precisely what this means, at some levels it is relatively easy to determine. With social security, for example, where entitlement to benefits, exemptions, services etc. is laid down quite precisely in law, it follows that claimants in identical circumstances should receive identical treatment – even though they may be dealing with different local offices. As Stanyer and Smith (1976, p. 31) comment, this has important administrative implications 'in that it puts a premium on stability, consistency and accuracy, which are less important values in many private enterprises'. Discretion must obviously be used by public administrators on occasions but, in the interests of fairness and equity, is rarely encouraged, whereas in the private sector companies can show favour to certain customers by, for example, providing discounts or preferential treatment where appropriate.

LEGALITY

Another principle of public administration is that the decision and actions of officials must never be *ultra vires* (or beyond their legal powers). Whereas private individuals and companies are generally free to perform any act not prohibited in law, public authorities can do only those things which they are specifically empowered by law to perform.

DIVERSITY

The fact that public administration takes place within the constraints of equity and legality does not mean that policy outputs and implementation are both uniform and standardised throughout Britain. Public administration must respond to diverse pressures, needs and circumstances, and most governmental systems are flexible enough to allow this. In Britain, for example, there are major variations in the standard of provision by local authorities (see Chapter 9). A common legal framework does not automatically produce common policy outputs and implementation patterns; hence, the importance of analysing administrative *processes* rather than simply the formal legal/constitutional framework within which public administration occurs.

The Expansion of British Public Administration

The size and complexity of British public administration has increased enormously over the last century. Underpinning this has been a vast expansion of the state's role in social and economic matters. In the mid-nineteenth century there was a very restrictive view of government with foreign affairs and the maintenance of law and order being the dominant interests. Today, despite a retreat in areas such as housing, education and transport, the state still provides a comprehensive range of social services; additionally it seeks to 'manage' the economy and run major public industries.

As the scope of government has developed, so the numbers of people in public employment have expanded from 3.6 per cent of the working population in 1891 to some 30 per cent in 1980. The civil service alone expanded from 16,000 in 1868 to 745,000 in 1975, albeit declining to 642,800 in July 1983. Likewise, the amount of the Gross National Product consumed by the public sector, which stood at less than 15 per cent in 1900, had grown to around 50 per cent by the late 1970s. As Table 1.1 indicates, public expenditure is still enormous despite the Thatcher government's attempt to cut back the public sector.

Table 1.1 *Public Expenditure in Britain, 1981–2*

	£ billion
Central government	83.4
Local authorities	28.2
Nationalised industries	2.4
Other public expenditure (mainly certain public corporations)	1.5
Adjustments	1.4
Round total	117.0

Source: HM Treasury, *Economic Progress Report*, September 1981.

During the twentieth century the work of government has increased in *complexity* as well as in scope. Consequently, public administrators today frequently require a technical orientation – with appropriate skills and equipment – which was unimaginable in the nineteenth century. One hundred years ago any literate person with reasonable intelligence and education could make a competent administrator. Many of today's public administrators have to perform functions (e.g. economic planning) and use techniques (e.g. cost-benefit analysis, economic model building, management techniques) which were unheard of a century ago. There have also been institutional changes of unforeseen dimensions. Institutions formed to perform functions in the pre-twentieth century state, such as the Cabinet, government departments, and local authorities, have had to adapt to new and more exacting circumstances. Other institutions such as public corporations have been added piecemeal as the state has acquired new functions. At the same time the *political environment* of public administration has undergone major changes. For example, the rise of disciplined parties, which has given ministers in normal circumstances the ability to control Parliament, has strengthened the position of civil servants by giving them the means, through their political 'masters', to turn their policy proposals into legislation. In other respects, however, the civil servant's position has been weakened. Not only has the development of universal adult suffrage reinforced the concept of accountable public administration, but the rise of the mass media, and the proliferation in the twentieth century of pressure group activity, has introduced new external constraints to which public administrators must respond.

These important changes present two main problems:

1 The institutions, personnel and techniques of British public administration must be seen within the context of adaptation to changing circumstances. Despite substantial change, much of the past has been retained. The legacy of the past cannot be ignored if we are to fully understand the institutions, techniques and personnel of contemporary British public administration.
2 At the same time, however, new governmental forms and administrative processes have developed such as accountable units, departmental agencies and quangos. Additionally, a host of new and sometimes perplexing terms have emerged: ombudsmen, PESC, PAR, hiving-off, etc. British public administration has to some extent become 'jargonised', creating obvious difficulties, especially for students new to the subject.

This book sets out to examine British public administration, not from a formal, legal standpoint but by explaining what actually happens. The extent and scope of British public administration is, of course, enormous, and given the 'ambiguity, confusion and complexity' which it exhibits, the reader cannot expect to find neat, definitive conclusions. The subject, moreover, is continually changing; models or generalisations are liable to prove inaccurate or misleading within even a short passage of time.

Inevitably in a book such as this the complex administrative network has to be divided up into a number of constituent parts for the material to be manageable. While, for example, there are sections on government departments, the Cabinet, the civil service and so forth, these should not be regarded as neat, self-contained compartments operating in isolation from each other. Extensive inter-relationships occur both formally and informally. Informal relationships, not easily charted, are particularly important in keeping the wheels of administration satisfactorily oiled. Common backgrounds and educational experiences between ministers and civil servants, for example, can result in working relationships which are far removed from any formal 'position statement' or chain of command. Likewise, common membership of social or professional organisations may facilitate co-ordination both within Whitehall and between Whitehall and individual local authorities. Formal hierarchies reveal little about actual working relationships, which are invariably much more ambiguous than boxes on neatly designed organisational wall charts would indicate. In the final analysis public administration responds to many values – efficiency, rationality, equity and so forth – and thus defies neat labels.

2 DEPARTMENTS AND DEPARTMENTALISM

Although central administration accounts for only about one-tenth of public sector employment, the British political system is highly centralised. It is largely within central administration that public policy is formulated, and although many services are provided by subordinate agencies (such as local authorities and public corporations) fundamental decisions about standards and machinery of provision are usually taken at the centre. It is to central administration, therefore, that we now turn, commencing with government departments, the main components of the central administrative machine.

What Is a Government Department?

Traditionally government departments have been distinguished from other kinds of organisation 'mainly on the grounds that they alone face control by society generally' (Pitt and Smith, 1981, p. 61). However, there is no clear definition of the term 'government department', and no such thing as a 'typical' department (see Hood and Dunsire, 1981, esp. ch. 3). It is, however, possible to identify three broad types:

(i) *Ministerial departments*. The key departments which operate under the direction of ministers.

(ii) *Non-ministerial departments* under non-political executives: e.g. Department of Inland Revenue, Board of Customs and Excise. Although formally headed by Boards, departmental administration and policy is usually answered for by ministers.

(iii) *Semi-autonomous agencies*. A miscellaneous group exhibiting some of the features normally associated with departments, but generally operating independently of ministers unless major political questions are involved. They may nevertheless be thought of as departments in their own right through being staffed by civil servants, being in receipt of budgetary estimates, or being classified as a Crown body (e.g. British Museum, National Gallery). Included within them are *departmental agencies* (such as the Defence Procurement Executive within the Ministry of Defence) – a fast growing organisational form which in the mid-1970s employed about 26 per cent of the civil service (Pitt and Smith, 1981, p. 65) – and, more problematically, 'hived-off' *non-departmental agencies* such as the Manpower Services Commission.

This ambiguity surrounding the term 'government department' presents difficulty in delineating the boundaries of central administration. Whether, for example, the British Museum or the Manpower Services Commission should be seen as part of central administration depends largely upon the criteria used for defining government departments. Indeed, the position has become more confused in recent years through the proliferation of new organisational forms such as departmental and 'hived-off' agencies, and by the occasional wholesale removal of departmental functions and status. In 1969, for example, the functions of the Post Office – a ministerial department – were transferred to the Post Office Corporation, a public corporation (see pp. 184–96); while in 1980 Her Majesty's Stationery Office, a non-ministerial department, was officially reclassified as a public corporation. Bodies of this kind – departmental agencies, 'hived-off' units, public corporations – now exist in quite large numbers, often performing functions similar to those previously carried out by departments. As Richardson and Jordan (1979, p. 57) observe, recent years have witnessed a 'Disintegration of the Centre', and there is now 'no reasonable means of distinguishing between "central administration" and bodies outside' the perimeter.

Because of such problems even a count of government departments is difficult. As Hood and Dunsire (1981, esp. pp. 41–51, and 257–69) show, within government itself several different 'official' lists of departments are in use. Hood and Dunsire themselves settle on the sixty-nine departments 'which accounted for a vote in the budget estimates in ... 1976–77' (a definition inclusive of the British Museum, the National Gallery, and the Wallace Collection). These sixty-nine departments cover a multitude of functions and are organised on a variety of principles. Perhaps only two generalisations can safely be made about them: (i) most, if not all, have some links, however tenuous, with ministers; (ii) the most politically salient are usually ministerial departments (Hood and Dunsire, 1981, pp. 143–63). These ministerial departments represent the most recognisable inner core of central administration, and (in January 1982) the most important and best known were the eighteen listed in Table 2.1.

Table 2.1   *Major Government Departments (and Staff in Post)*[1]
January 1982

Ministry of Agriculture, Fisheries and Food (MAFF)	12,502
Ministry of Defence (MOD)	201,665[2]
Department of Education and Science (DES)	2,477
Department of Employment	30,596[3]
Department of Energy	1,153
Department of the Environment (DOE)	9,697[4]
Department of Health and Social Security (DHSS)	96,849
Department of Industry	8,414
Department of Trade	6,883
Department of Transport	13,191
Foreign and Commonwealth Office	11,194
HM Treasury	2,582
Home Office	34,856
Law Officers' Department	20
Lord Chancellor's Department	9,893
Northern Ireland Office	201
Scottish Office	10,581
Welsh Office	2,263

[1] Full time equivalents including Industrial Civil Servants.
[2] Excludes Royal Ordnance Factories.
[3] Excludes Manpower Services Commission; Health and Safety Commission/Executive; Advisory Conciliation, and Arbitration Service.
[4] Excludes Property Services Agency.
Note: In June 1983 the departments of Trade and Industry were merged to become a new Department of Trade and Industry.
Source: Civil Service Statistics (HMSO, 1982), Table 1.

Departmental Organisation

Although departments vary widely in internal organisation, reflecting differences in the volume and complexity of their work, three important features common to many, if not most, departments can be identified: Size; Decentralisation; and Bureaucratic organisation.

SIZE

As Table 2.1 shows, departments vary markedly in size, although almost all major departments are large organisations. This has a bearing on the way in which departments operate. Pitt and Smith (1981, p. 63) explain: 'Larger size increases the complexity of organizations. There is greater division of labour . . . The range and frequency of repetitive occurrences increase. This requires the development of rules and procedures as an alternative to personal control by superiors of their subordinates.' In other words, thé bureaucratic characteristics of government departments – written rules, codified procedures, hierarchic structures, etc. – are partly a product of size, and are usually most marked in the larger departments. Larger departments, in fact, generally present greater managerial problems than smaller ones. Internal communications are usually more formalised, effective ministerial control is more difficult, and problems of 'specialization, line management, co-ordination and planning' are more likely to be encountered.

While size is related to organisational complexity it is not, however, an indicator of departmental influence. (The Treasury, for example, is one of the smallest departments.) Essentially, size reflects the nature of departmental work: departments concerned mainly with policy formulation, or supervisory functions, are usually smaller than those providing services direct to the public. Thus the DES with around, 2,500 civil servants is relatively small: it employs no teachers itself, its main responsibility being to advise, and to monitor, local education authorities which do. The DHSS, by contrast, which has some 800 local offices handling benefit claims, employs almost 100,000 officials.

DECENTRALISATION

Although their precise geographical jurisdiction varies, most departments administer services over large areas. Some provide services exclusively for constituent parts of the United Kingdom (Northern Ireland, Scottish, Welsh Offices); others on a British basis (Employment); others still on a United Kingdom (Customs and Excise) or world (Foreign and Commonwealth Office) basis. To discharge functions over such wide areas many departments operate through local or regional 'field offices'. This process, known as *territorial decentralisation*, 'involves the . . . delegation of authority' to departmental field officers on an area basis and is a 'very familiar' feature of British government departments (Pitt and Smith, 1981, p. 68). (Functional, as opposed to territorial decentralisation, where the basis of delegation is not primarily areal, also occurs within government departments – see pp. 26–30.)

Despite their extensive use there is little standardisation in the distribution of departmental field offices. Traditionally each department has developed whatever local pattern best suited its own tasks, despite the problems of inter-departmental co-ordination which this often creates. Indeed, single departments sometimes have different field networks for different functions: for example, in 1971 the Environment Department had fourteen 'separate out-stationed organisations', many with different boundary patterns (Draper, 1977, pp. 51–2). Likewise, there is little standardisation of field office functions. Some have executive functions; others are concerned with inspection, regulation, planning, or a mixture of functions. Usually, however, because effective decentralisation can only be achieved by weakening central control, the amount of authority delegated is limited, inviting the description 'pseudo-decentralisation'.

Decentralisation should not be confused with the location in Belfast, Edinburgh and Cardiff of the headquarters of the Northern Ireland, Scottish and Welsh Offices; nor with the deconcentration from London of headquarters units of other departments, such as DHSS headquarters divisions in Lytham and Newcastle. Nevertheless, the combined effect of these factors is striking, with 76 per cent of civil servants being employed outside London in 1983.

BUREAUCRATIC ORGANISATION

Government departments are organised according to the bureaucratic pattern familiar in large organisations, particularly public bodies. Fundamentally, bureaucratically organised bodies exhibit a hierarchic structure. Each official has clearly defined duties within specified limits, and operates under the supervision of a higher officer within a 'line' command structure. This organisational pattern is particularly appropriate for public agencies given the constraints within which they typically operate. As far as government departments are concerned three such major constraints are identifiable: (i) Public accountability; (ii) Equity; and (iii) Specialisation.

(i) *Public accountability* (see p. 8) requires departments to conduct their work in a manner acceptable to Parliament. In most departments – and in *all* ministerial departments – ministers are constitutionally responsible to Parliament for every aspect of departmental work. Consequently, departmental officials must act in accordance with ministerial instructions and statutory powers.

Bureaucratic organisation, by allowing detailed control of subordinates within a hierarchic command structure, offers perhaps the only means by which large government departments can discharge their functions consistent with public accountability requirements.

(ii) *Equity* (see p. 9) requires departments to treat citizens equally in identical circumstances. This presents considerable managerial problems, particularly for large departments with staff widely dispersed in field offices. Once again, bureaucratic organisation offers an apparent solution, enabling departmental rules to be enforced through a line management system extending from the highest departmental levels, through the local controllers of field offices, down to officials in contact with the public.

(iii) *Specialisation*. All departments are to some degree multifunctional: at the very least they have to perform not only 'housekeeping' functions – e.g. finance and personnel management – but also 'operating' functions related to the laws and policies which they administer. To perform a range of functions effectively large organisations usually allocate work to different groups and individuals according to their skills and abilities. Typically the organisation is divided into segments, each being given responsibility for specialised tasks under the supervision of a director. To inter-relate the work of the various segments the directors themselves are within the 'control' of the overall organisational hierarchy. In this way government departments can perform a variety of functions, without undermining either internal cohesion or their ability to provide accountable and equitable administration.

Of course, bureaucratic organisation has some disadvantages (hence, the pejorative use of the term 'bureaucratic'). The limited responsibility afforded to each official, for example, may stultify initiative; the constant reference upwards and downwards through a hierarchy may cause delay; and strict application of rules may make officials inflexible and insensitive. While bureaucracy, however, is 'antithetical to some human values' it is nevertheless 'supportive of others such as accountability, rationality and equity, [which are] of central significance' to democratic governmental systems (Pitt and Smith, 1981, p. 139). For this reason it is probably unavoidable as a feature of government departments.

Bureaucratic organisation is evident from even a brief glance inside government departments. Usually, the basic organisational unit is the division, each division being responsible for particular areas of departmental work. (In 1980, for example, the Department of Employment had twelve main divisions: Industrial Relations I, Industrial Relations II, Research and Planning, Economic Policy (Manpower), Overseas, Incomes I, Incomes II, Statistics, Finance, Establishments, Manpower (General) and the Solicitor's Office.) Divisions are normally broken down into branches – the Statistics Division in the above example had branches dealing with Earnings, Prices, Unemployment, Employment and Price Surveys – and branches, in turn, into sections. In larger departments related divisions may be formed into 'groups', 'units', 'directorates' etc., precise arrangements varying between, and sometimes within, departments. Built into the departmental structure will be the minister's *Private Office*. Run by the minister's *Private Secretary* – usually a young civil service 'high flier' – the Private Office deals with the minister's correspondence, keeps his diary, and handles his communications with departmental officials.

Departmental Organisation and Civil Servants

Departmental organisation is closely linked with civil service career grades (which are unified throughout the service), particularly the grades of generalist civil servants who have traditionally held the key departmental posts (see Chapter 6). Each policy section is typically headed by an officer at Principal level, a branch by an Assistant Secretary, a division by an Under-Secretary, and a group of divisions by a Deputy Secretary (or in larger departments perhaps by a Second Permanent Secretary). Finally there is the Permanent Secretary (or a designated Permanent Secretary if there is more than one) who is the senior departmental manager and the adviser and confidant of ministers. He is also the designated accounting officer for his department and the department's Finance Division usually operates under his personal control.

This congruence of departmental and civil service hierarchies arguably exacerbates some of the problems inherent within bureaucratic organisations. Because civil service career patterns are involved, gradings may determine the allocation of tasks within departments, rather than vice versa. For example, if departmental work does not really require an Assistant Secretary, an appointment will nevertheless usually be made at this level, otherwise career prospects would differ between departments, undermining the uniform grading which is the essence of civil service organisation. This, of course, creates possible extra delay and inefficiency;

not only may appointments and promotions not be justified by departmental work, but the number of hierarchical grades through which communications must pass is unnecessarily extended.

Of course, many departments require specialist skills and employ appropriate staff (scientists, engineers, doctors, etc.). Such specialists have traditionally had their own separate career and grading structures (see Chapter 6), and their own specialist branch and divisional hierarchies. Under this system of *parallel hierarchies*, a generalist policy formulator requiring technical advice would typically refer to a specialist of similar rank. This arrangement, a legacy from periods when government required less technical information, not only placed specialists in subordinate positions (as technical advisers to the generalists who formulated policy and briefed ministers) but required continual cross-referencing between specialist and generalist hierarchies. Under modern conditions this often produced confusion and delay, and led, perhaps inevitably, to demands for changes in patterns of departmental organisation.

Reforming Departmental Organisation

One of the most authoritative demands for the reform of departmental organisation came from the Fulton Report on the Civil Service (1968). This made two particularly important recommendations:

(i) *Integrated hierarchies.* Fulton (I, para. 162) recommended the creation, 'under a single head', of 'unified hierarchies' consisting of both 'administrators and specialists'. This followed earlier experimentation within a small number of departments, notably the Ministry of Technology, part of which operated with 'a unified hierarchy incorporating . . . technical, financial, administrative and other specialist staff'.

(ii) *Functional decentralisation.* Fulton envisaged an element of functional decentralisation, a process whereby 'a special body is set up to assume responsibility for . . . [specified] functions, usually . . . on a national basis' (Steel, 1979, p. 30). Fulton recommended:

(a) the establishment of *departmental agencies* within departments. Although remaining *within* the department, and operating 'under the direction of a Minister . . . answerable for its activities to Parliament' (Brown and Steel, 1979, p. 301), normal lines of departmental organisation would be relaxed, leaving managers considerable autonomy in managerial and budgetary matters.

(b) 'Hiving-off' departmental functions to autonomous *non-departmental agencies* established outside departments. Wholly responsible for work delegated to them, they would not normally be subject to direct ministerial control, their relationship with government and Parliament being similar to that of public corporations and other *ad hoc* agencies (see Chapters 10 and 11).

Fulton believed that such arrangements could be applied quite extensively. The idea was to transfer to such agencies largely self-contained functions where performance could be measured in financial or quantitative terms, and managers held accountable for standards of achievement. This was expected to provide both greater efficiency and more effective accountability than orthodox departmental arrangements. Managers would largely be freed from the bureaucratic constraints inherent in departmental procedures, and agency costs could be budgeted for separately (instead of being 'lost' in wider departmental accounts). This would present the opportunity for enhanced budgetary control in line with 'output budgeting' techniques pioneered in *Programme, Planning and Budgeting (PPB)* systems in the USA. In contrast with conventional departmental accounting, which is geared to 'inputs' or subjects of expenditure (e.g. wages), PPB accounting relates to 'outputs' or objects of expenditure. This enables expenditure on specific programmes or services to be costed, costs to be analysed against benefits, and the efficiency of agencies administering them to be assessed (see Bourn, 1979, esp. ch. 3; and Garrett, 1972, pp. 115–49 and 1980, pp. 88–98).

Progress with introducing these more business-like arrangements, despite strong support from the 1970–4 Conservative government, has been somewhat limited. Most departments, for example, were reluctant to change to integrated hierarchies, and apart from minor exceptions – notably the Ministry of Public Building and Works, which merged higher professional and managerial hierarchies in 1969 – there were few significant moves in this direction. One reason is that integrated hierarchies arguably threaten the continued dominance of the generalist administrators within departments – the very officials who, ironically, were charged with effecting their introduction. Organisational structures often reflect the interests and attitudes of the staff within them.

According to Garrett (1980, p. 65) 'the idea of ... integrated hierarchies was ... buried by the Civil Service'; consequently, most departments have retained their parallel hierarchies, even though as an organisational arrangement it is almost unique among Western bureaucracies.

With the establishment of 'hived-off' and accountable units there was rather more progress (see pp. 13–14; and Jordan, 1976; and Pollitt, 1980). Major departmental functions have been allocated to accountable units within, for example, the Ministry of Defence (Defence Procurement Executive) and the Environment Department (Property Services Agency), while the Department of Employment was largely dismembered through major functions being 'hived-off' to bodies such as the Manpower Services Commission, the Health and Safety Commission, and the Advisory, Conciliation and Arbitration Service. Elsewhere 'equivalent developments' have occurred by establishing 'trading funds' for 'quasi-commercial activities' (e.g. ordnance factories) which have not been 'hived-off', while new forms of management accounting have been used 'increasingly to supplement traditional ... accounting' in departmental fields where activities are measurable 'in quantitative or financial terms' (Brown and Steel, 1979, p. 302).

Nevertheless progress has probably been less than Fulton hoped. Again, there is evidence of civil service resistance: in 1977 the Expenditure Committee reported (HC 535, 1976/7, I, para. 94) 'that the Fulton proposal of accountable units [had not] been taken sufficiently seriously' by civil servants. More importantly, it has proved difficult to isolate self-contained functions appropriate for transfer to accountable units. In central administration few services produce profits, and cost/benefit calculations must usually include political and social, as well as financial, factors. Commercial companies can close costly services, or cease supplying unprofitable customers, relatively easily. Government departments, however, must maintain costly services and administer them equitably so long as the law requires their provision. Such factors make the concept of autonomous managerial and budgetary units of limited applicability to many parts of the public sector. Significantly, even where accountable units have been formed they have often been less autonomous in practice than in theory. As Pitt and Smith (1981, p. 65) observe, 'In government the practice of management ... reflects political compromises and objectives. Degrees of managerial autonomy do not ... correlate neatly with managerial structure.'

This is not to suggest that commercial management practices are irrelevant to public administration. Accountable units do have numerous advantages; and in some cases their greater managerial flexibility has been used to good effect. Significantly, some of the most striking progress in developing integrated hierarchies has occurred within the Property Services Agency, while the 'hived-off' Manpower Services Commission demonstrated much imagination ('facelifting' Labour Exchanges into relatively attractive Job Centres, for example) which arguably would not have occurred within an orthodox department. No less impressively Sir Derek Rayner, of Marks and Spencer, who from 1979 to 1982 acted as efficiency adviser to Mrs Thatcher, identified potential savings of £275m a year on the basis of 135 scrutinies within government departments.

The constraints of accountability and equity within which public administrators typically work and their overall goal – public interest (rather than private profit) – usually require organisational arrangements different from commercial enterprises. Where the work of public administrators can be measured in financial or quantitative terms (as with quasi-commercial activity), or where overmuch political control may be undesirable (as with regulatory agencies), departure from orthodox departmental arrangements may be desirable (for other examples see Chapters 10 and 11). Most of the work of central administration is not, however, of this kind. Hence, while the search for greater efficiency will undoubtedly continue, the traditional government department seems destined to remain the basic component of British central administration.

Advisory Machinery

A further important feature of departments is the advisory committees (or councils) which enable civil servants and ministers to ascertain informed opinion before arriving at decisions. Consisting of outside 'experts' and pressure group representatives, as well as departmental officials, they are normally formed at ministerial discretion (although in a few cases Parliament has given advisory bodies statutory rights of consultation). Their existence is largely a response to two developments: a) As government work has become more technical, departments have increasingly needed advice from outside experts; b) As governments have become more interventionist, departments have increasingly consulted affected interests, both because they are felt to have a 'right' to consultation, and because their co-operation is often essential to policy implemention. Most departments are keen to establish close relations with client groups – the DHSS with the British Medical Association, for example – while pressure groups themselves welcome the access to departmental personnel which such relationships provide.

Although rarely 'hitting the headlines', advisory bodies are an important element in central policy-making, enabling departmental officials and client groups to achieve consensus in private before submitting an 'agreed policy' to ministers. These formal channels, of course, are often supplemented by informal consultations and negotiations, attesting that in Britain the most influential groups usually concentrate their pressure upon the departmental civil servants (Eckstein, 1960), and to the fact that such officials play a crucial part in the policy-making work of central administration.

The Departmental Pattern

While the efficient allocation of work is important in all organisations, in central administration it is especially so. Ministerial responsibility (see pp. 226–34) requires a designated minister to be answerable for every aspect of government work; consequently, any confusion about work distribution between departments will blur ministerial responsibility. The ultimate decisions about the number and jurisdiction of departments – the departmental pattern – rest with the Prime Minister; indeed, Heath took the 'key decisions' personally with the advice of a very limited circle of people (Pollitt, 1980, p. 98). Nevertheless, in reality the Prime Minister's choice is subject to serious constraints. In fact the tendency at any one time is for the departmental pattern to reflect three main influences: a) The role of the state; b) Political factors; c) Administrative considerations.

(A)   THE ROLE OF THE STATE

The mid-nineteenth century state had a minimalist role: the government was more concerned with foreign affairs and defence than domestic politics, and the departmental pattern reflected this. In 1851, for example, the main departments were: the Treasury, Customs and Excise, Inland Revenue, Board of Trade, Post Office, Home Office, Irish Office, Lord Chancellor's Office, Privy Council Office, Admiralty, War Office, Ordnance Board, Foreign Office, and Colonial Office. A century later the pattern was very different. The state had lost its 'caretaker' role, and was now interventionist in both social and economic fields. Technological and industrial developments also had an influence on the departmental pattern, which in 1951 embraced thirty major ministries. Of the 1851 departments the Irish Office and Ordnance Board had disappeared and the Privy Council Office was no longer of major importance. To the remaining eleven, however, had been added nineteen 'new' ones: Commonwealth, Defence, Materials, Civil Aviation, Labour, Transport, Works, Local Government and Planning, Health, National Insurance, War Pensions, Education, Air, Supply, Scottish, Fuel and Power, Scientific and Industrial Research, Agriculture and Fisheries, and Food.

Since 1951, although the state's role has remained relatively stable, governments have faced further new problems which have been reflected in the departmental pattern: technological changes (Ministry of Technology, 1964–70); decline of Empire (Colonial and Commonwealth Offices merged with Foreign Office); economic decline (Department of Economic Affairs, 1964–9); inflation (Department of Prices and Consumer Protection, 1974–9); national minorities (Welsh and Northern Ireland Offices, 1964 and 1972); environmental problems (Department of the Environment, 1970). As these examples show, the departmental pattern changes as governments respond to new circumstances. The cumulative effect of these changes by early 1983 had been to reduce the number of major departments to twenty (the eighteen ministerial departments listed in Table 2.1 plus the Inland Revenue and Customs and Excise). This reduction, however, was not due to any decrease in governmental functions, but to prime ministerial attempts to redistribute departmental work in a manner more accurately reflecting political priorities and the demands of administrative efficiency.

(B) POLITICAL FACTORS

The departmental pattern is inevitably influenced by political considerations. A new department, for example, may reflect a policy shift (e.g. the Northern Ireland Office created in 1972 after the introduction of 'direct rule'); a response to new problems (e.g. creation of the Energy Department in 1974 following fuel crises); an attempt to reassure the public that 'something is being done' about pressing problems (e.g. creation of the Department of Prices and Consumer Protection, 1974); or a political appeal to important electoral or client groups (e.g. creation of the Welsh Office, 1964). Again, a departmental reconstruction may be related to political tensions within government. A department might, for example, be created to accommodate a particular politician, or a departmental reconstruction used as an excuse for a ministerial re-shuffle. Given, moreover, that 'administrative gains' usually 'take some time to [reach] fruition' and are 'subject to [considerable] uncertainty', prime ministers are often 'tempted to design changes that ... maximize the shorter term benefits', such as political gains, 'rather than administrative efficiency' (Pollitt, 1980, pp. 96–7).

Because of such influences the departmental pattern may become administratively untidy, but most prime ministers apparently feel that the 'right' political image brings greater electoral rewards than considerations of administrative efficiency. Consequently, while long overdue administrative reforms might be 'ignored' – producing a 'freezing' of outdated departmental structures – shifts in public opinion and political circumstances may produce sudden and frequent alterations to departmental boundaries, and a consequential destabilisation of the departmental pattern.

(C) ADMINISTRATIVE CONSIDERATIONS: THE ALLOCATION OF FUNCTIONS

The development of the departmental pattern has been largely haphazard. Broadly speaking, as new governmental functions have appeared, they have been allocated either to existing departments or, where existing departments were overloaded or political considerations dictated otherwise, to newly-created ones. As Hanson and Walles (1980, p. 135) put it, the departmental pattern has been shaped by 'a continuous process of creation, fission, fusion and transfer, rapid at some times, slower at others'.

Administrative considerations, however, have not been totally ignored. As long ago as 1918 the Machinery of Government Committee (Haldane Report, 1918) identified two main principles for allocating functions between departments: 'distribution according to the persons or classes to be dealt with, and distribution according to the services to be performed'. The former, the clientele principle, was rejected. Although clientele-based agencies (such as Poor Law Boards in Haldane's day) are not unknown in British public administration, as a guiding principle for allocating all central administrative functions the outcome would be massive duplication of provision: for example, hospitals for the old, for students, for the unemployed etc., an arrangement described by Haldane as 'Lilliputian administration'.

The alternative, which Haldane recommended, was 'distribution according to ... services ... performed', with departments providing a comprehensive service to the whole community. Application of this principle, usually known as the 'functional' principle, would, Haldane argued, produce 'the minimum amount of confusion and overlapping'. Ten services, he believed, could be identified, each of which could be placed 'under separate administration': Finance, National Defence, External Affairs, Research and Information, Production, Employment, Supplies, Education, Health, and Justice. This was not a plea for just ten departments to be established, because some of the services would probably need to be administered by more than one department.

Haldane's recommendations can be questioned on two main grounds:

(i) Haldane ignored two other principles of allocation: *process* and *area*. The omission of *process* (kind of work) is understandable – not until much later was it seriously considered as a possible principle for allocating functions. Moreover it is unlikely that all central administrative functions could be distributed on this basis. Although not entirely absent from the departmental pattern – the Public Record Office, and some accountable units (e.g. Defence Procurement Executive) offer examples – the comprehensive allocation of functions by process would cause innumerable administrative problems (especially inter-departmental co-ordination), and would seriously blur the policy-making process.

The omission of *area* is more surprising, for several departments with territorial responsibilities existed in Haldane's day: the Colonial, Irish, India, and Scottish Offices. The latter, together with the Welsh and Northern Ireland Offices, still exists, and the problems of constituent minorities within the UK are likely to present a continuing need for such departments into the foreseeable future. Nevertheless, the area principle could not provide a basis for allocating all central functions, for certain of them, such as defence, diplomacy, economic affairs, and transport, have a national dimension not easily divisible on an area basis.

(ii) A more serious charge against Haldane is oversimplification (see Johnson, 1971). The functional principle is not always distinguishable from process: Research and Information, and Supplies, from Haldane's list could both be regarded as processes. Likewise, the functional/clientele distinction is not always clear: a department administering the 'function' of education, for example, serves a specific clientele (pupils and students). The functional principle, moreover, does not always indicate clearly to which departments particular services should be allocated. Thus Aviation, just emerging in Haldane's day, could be placed with Research and Information on Haldane's list, with Production, or even Defence. The functional principle, in short, offers little guidance about which functions should be grouped together. Discussion about appropriate functional groupings has usually in Britain been conducted 'by taking the then present as the starting point and proposing marginal changes – amalgamations and splitting-offs' (see Pollitt, 1980, p. 95).

Although Haldane's recommendations were never consciously implemented, the functional principle has nevertheless provided the main basis of the subsequent departmental pattern. Indeed it was reaffirmed, without acknowledgement, in the White Paper *Reorganisation of Central Government* (1970). This specifically endorsed (paras 8 and 11) 'the application of the functional principle as the basis for the allocation of responsibilities' and called for 'the grouping of functions together in departments with a wide span', an approach which foreshadowed the creation in 1970 of two 'giant' departments, Trade and Industry, and Environment.

GIANT DEPARTMENTS

The process of merging smaller departments with related functions into larger 'giant' departments is not new. The 1970 'giants' were, in fact, the final stage in a process which started in the 1950s, and gathered pace in the 1960s when three major mergers occurred (creating the Department of Health and Social Security, the Foreign and Commonwealth Office, and the Ministry of Defence). The rationale for such mergers was largely administrative. Sir Richard Clarke (1971, p. 3) explains:

> The 'giant' can develop its own strategy and decide its own priorities; it can settle problems itself instead of lengthy discussion in interdepartmental committees; it is big enough to have specialised services; it can support a clearer strategy at the centre.

A further advantage was a reduction in the number of departments requiring Cabinet representation, thereby limiting the Cabinet's size in accordance with administrative thinking which sees smaller Cabinets as more efficient than larger ones.

These 'giant' departments were not supposed to be federations of ministries, but were unitary departments in their own right. In practice, however, many failed to develop real cohesion. The

Environment Department (DOE) according to Painter (1980, p. 142) 'resembled a conglomerate rather than an integrated coherent whole'; while the DHSS, despite having a 'common' Secretary of State and some common support services, operated essentially as two distinct wings corresponding to the separate ministries which had been merged. In 1973 each of these wings had its 'own' permanent secretary, finance division, and funds (Brown, 1975, pp. 53–4). 'Giant' departments, moreover, were difficult to manage. Teams of ministers were necessary to run them – the DOE had nine ministers at one stage – and formal machinery was often necessary to effect internal communications which previously had been conducted informally (see Draper, 1977, p. 97). Because of such problems, as well as through political expediency, during the 1970s the process of merging departments was reversed. Although the Ministry of Defence and DHSS remained unscathed, other major 'giants' all underwent some unscrambling. In 1974 Energy was detached from the Department of Trade and Industry following a fuel crisis, and a few months later the remnants were formed into three new separate departments: Trade, Industry, and Prices and Consumer Protection. In 1983, however the departments of Trade and Industry were yet again merged to form a single Department of Trade and Industry. In 1976, likewise, Transport was detached from the DOE.

HALDANE IN THE 1980s

No one organisational principle underlies the development of the post-Haldane departmental pattern. Pollitt (1980, pp. 95–6), in fact, identifies four main influences which have been at work:

(i) General preference for organizing by 'function'...

(ii) An upper limit to the number of important ('main') departments set by the traditional, political need for the ministers of all those departments to have seats in the Cabinet ...

(iii) A lower limit ... set by the requirement that any given department must not be so large or so heterogeneous as to [be unmanageable] ...

(iv) The political need of Prime Ministers to find [senior] posts ... for his most important party colleagues

Elsewhere Pollitt (1982, pp. 73–4) shows that changes in the departmental pattern occur frequently (with a peak following elections – the 'New Broom' effect). Between 1960 and 1979 thirty-one ministerial departments disappeared and twenty-eight were born. Many of the new creations had a short existence; indeed, thirteen of them had disappeared by 1981. As these figures show, the departmental pattern is *dynamic*, not static. Given the scale, complexity and political environment of public administration today, searching for one universal principle for allocating functions is doomed to failure. While Haldane's list of functions, despite its shortcomings, foreshadowed later developments quite well – reflecting a general preference for the fewest possible combinations of functionally coherent departments – political and administrative exigencies have continued to intrude. As Brown and Steel (1979, p. 291) suggest, 'departmental structures' reflect contemporary 'needs and political preferences ... rather than abstract principles'.

The Dynamics of Departmental Work

The role of departments is theoretically to advise ministers about policy and implement ministerial decisions. Departments, however, are not neutral in policy matters. They are part of a complex policy community, embracing client groups, media correspondents, outside 'experts', informed MPs and so forth, within which many policy attitudes are generated and developed. Much policy is also initiated within departments themselves, arising from perceived defects in existing arrangements, changing circumstances, and so on. Moreover, although most important policy decisions require ministerial approval, implementation is largely left to departmental officials. Departments thus stand at the 'cross-roads' of the policy-making process, as well as being the main agency of policy implementation.

Departments, it should be stressed, are not monolithic: they contain a myriad of personnel hierarchies, organisational units, client groups and so forth, each with their own distinctive perspectives and influence. One important internal division is that between ministers and top departmental officials (see Chapter 5). Differences, however, can also arise between specialists and generalists, between headquarters and field offices, between one division (or group of divisions) and another, within or between advisory committees, and between departmental client groups (e.g. between county and district councils in the case of the DOE). Departments, moreover, are dynamic, living organisms: officials within them each have their own perspectives, rivalries, career aspirations, values and experiences, which are all brought to bear in making decisions. Many departments, moreover, as Griffith (1966, p. 515) writes, are 'split amongst many different buildings and, as in every organization, the smaller separate groups acquire their own characteristics'. Consequently, within most departments, there is enormous heterogeneity, which manifests itself in differences over resources, structure, and policy. Thus Griffith found 'differences in the attitudes of the Ministry of Health to health services and to welfare services, in the Ministry of Housing and Local Government to housing and to planning, in the Home Office to children and to police'.

Differences within departments are sometimes related to the departmental pattern. If a department's scope is too wide it may become split by deep divisions; if it is too narrow it may be 'captured' by a client group (the Ministry of Agriculture with the National Farmers' Union is one possible example). Again, departmental size may affect the relative influence of ministers and civil servants: for example, transport was detached from the giant DOE in 1976 partly through a belief that transport policy was not adequately under ministerial control.

Just as sections within departments develop distinctive attitudes, so might departments themselves. In Shirley Williams' view (1980, pp. 92–3), 'the extent to which departments have characteristics and indeed even characters' of their own is 'often underestimated'. As an example she cites the contrast between the Departments of Employment and Industry. The former – which works closely with unions, and often participates in 'urgent' talks concerning industrial disputes – has a 'twenty-four hour time-scale', and 'many' of its 'senior officials work in shirtsleeves'. In the latter – which is more concerned with industrial investment and which works closely with the CBI – senior officials 'dress differently' and have a 'slightly longer time-scale'. Departments, moreover, operate from their own buildings, and their staff interchange little (other than at top levels). Consequently, each department tends to develop what Griffith (1966, p. 515) describes as 'a philosophy, an ethos, and an atmosphere which is peculiarly its own'. Departmental officials also develop loyalty towards their department. As Crossman (1975, p. 31) observed, though 'civil servants ... respect ... the Minister, they have a much stronger loyalty to the Ministry'.

Out of this individualism a distinctive departmental approach to policy and administration often emerges. In Shirley Williams'

(1980, p. 92) view, departmental attitudes are 'coloured ... by the last major reform that they undertook' or by past achievements. (Thus the DHSS instinctively tends to defend the integrity of the National Health Service.) In some cases ministers may be at odds with departmental policy. When this happens, Crossman (1975, p. 31) observed, the minister meets 'quiet resistance ... a great deal of it'. Even if departmental policy is ignored or overturned by a minister, it may be successfully 'imposed' upon successors. To quote Crossman again, departmental 'policy goes on while Ministers come and go'.

Sometimes, inevitably, departments compete with each other. Spending departments, for example, are often in competition with one another, as well as with the Treasury, for finance. Departments also fight over territory. Crossman (1975, pp. 24–5) observed how his permanent secretary 'waged ... battle' for four days 'to save her Department' from losing functions to a new department. New departments, in fact, often have difficulty establishing themselves in the face of 'suspicion and distrust' from 'elderly and well-established' departments (Williams, 1980, p. 93). The Department of Economic Affairs, an innovation of Wilson's first government, survived only five years. Its first ministerial head explains: 'Our success meant a tremendous threat to half a dozen old-established departments' (Brown, 1972, p. 112). Sometimes territorial battles are fought over many years. The Civil Service Department, for example, was never popular with the Treasury, out of which it had largely been carved. In 1981, four governments later, it was abolished, and many of its functions returned to the Treasury.

Departmental competition also occurs over policy. Some departments are almost permanently in conflict: for example, the Department of Trade 'has traditionally been a free trade department' while the Industry and Employment departments 'have a considerable tendency towards protectionism' (Williams, 1980, p. 89). Departmental policy battles may be fought both outside and inside Whitehall: outside, for example, through departmental 'leaks' to MPs, pressure groups, the media and so forth; inside through inter-departmental and Cabinet discussions. Before such meetings departments will brief minister against minister. As Barbara Castle observed (*Sunday Times*, 10 June 1973) shortly after joining the Cabinet, 'I suddenly found I wasn't in a political caucus at all. I was faced by departmental enemies.'

Departmental influence is, therefore, considerable, although obviously there are variations from issue to issue. Departments may ally on one issue, but disagree or remain neutral on others. On other occasions there will be unanimity. Whatever the line-up, however, 'central policy-making' is usually the product of what Richardson and Jordan (1979, p. 26) describe as 'a process of departmental pluralism'.

This analysis, however, should not be carried too far. Many policy initiatives occur outside central administration, and even within it departmental influences are not always decisive. Not all ministers tamely endorse departmental policy, and even when they do their arguments may not prevail. In particular they may be defeated in the various supra-departmental agencies within central administration, agencies which not only resolve departmental disputes but seek to forge a collective governmental view from the disparate pressures emanating from within and without central administration. These agencies are examined in the following two chapters.

3 CO-ORDINATING CENTRAL ADMINISTRATION

The differences which often exist within and between departments can be minimised or reconciled by co-ordinating mechanisms. This chapter focuses on the most important such mechanisms operating within central administration.

What is Co-ordination?

Stanyer and Smith (1976, p. 157) define co-ordination as 'the controlling of activities and decisions of individuals or agencies so that they are harmonized in the pursuit of some stated common goal or objectives'. As this definition implies, two broad aspects can be identified: (i) the co-ordination of *decisions*; and (ii) the co-ordination of *activities*.

(i)   *The co-ordination of 'decisions'*   is broadly synonymous with the *co-ordination of policy-making*. In central administration different sections or departments frequently have responsibility for closely related functions and, if incompatible policies are to be *avoided*, co-ordination has to take place at an initial stage. If compromise cannot be reached, or if initial co-ordination fails, any ensuing inconsistencies must subsequently be *resolved*. Co-ordination thus involves both the *avoidance* and the *resolution* of conflict.

Policy co-ordination has both a *preventative* and a *strategic* function. Preventative co-ordination primarily involves preventing (or resolving) policy conflict; strategic co-ordination is more concerned with relating particular policy decisions to overall goals, and in this sense is closely allied to *planning*. Although planning need not involve co-ordination – an individual may plan his own actions without reference to others – in central government, because decisions often involve several parts of the administrative machine, co-ordination is usually an integral part of effective planning. Strategic co-ordination may involve just a few organisational units, or an entire organisation (as with *corporate planning*). It invariably also involves *forward planning* (either short or long-term), in which case the co-ordinator may be concerned with a variety of tasks: forecasting, budgeting, goal identification and so forth. The wider the policy range and the longer the time scale, the more difficult strategic planning is likely to be. Nevertheless, strategic co-ordination is fundamental to public administration; without it policy-making could easily become a piecemeal, incremental process conducted without reference to overall goals.

(ii) *The co-ordination of 'activities'* is essentially concerned with the *co-ordination of administration*. Here, too, both conflict *avoidance* and *resolution* can be distinguished, as well as *preventative* and *strategic* aspects. With administrative co-ordination, however, a further distinction can be made: that between *procedural* and *substantive* co-ordination. With the former the co-ordinator, usually for reasons of efficiency and consistency, seeks common administrative procedures and methods (e.g. accounting procedures). Substantive co-ordination, by contrast, is concerned with harmonising the acts of individual persons or units to obtain efficient policy execution. As such it involves the allocation of functions and resources, as well as performance review and monitoring tasks.

In practice, it is often difficult to distinguish between these various forms of co-ordination. Many central administrative agencies co-ordinate both administration and policy, while the distinctions between preventative and strategic co-ordination, and between the procedural and substantive, are not always clear cut. Nevertheless, co-ordination is essential to efficient administration. As Stanyer and Smith (1976, p. 157) explain, co-ordination 'is the essence of organizational decision making and permeates the whole administrative process ... [It is] almost ... synonymous with management'.

While co-ordination is important in all organisations, it is particularly so in central administration – for four main reasons:

(A) SIZE AND COMPLEXITY

In small organisations co-ordination is relatively simple: in a two-man shop, for example, each partner observes the other and regulates his own work accordingly. In government departments, however, the number of employees, and the diversity of functions, make the harmonisation of work difficult without formal machinery. These problems multiply when co-ordination *between* departments is involved. However carefully tasks are allocated, the possibility of functional overlap always exists. Indeed, so wide is the scope of central administration that the most disparate units may sometimes find themselves with common interests. For example, the Sports and Recreation Unit of the Department of the Environment and the Soviet Department of the Foreign and Commonwealth Office may have largely separate interests, and yet their work must be co-ordinated at any point where it may impinge (e.g. over the proposed boycott of the 1980 Moscow Olympics). Its sheer size and diversity makes central administration heavily dependent upon co-ordinating mechanisms: without them its numerous departments and divisions would be unable to work in unison at any of the almost infinite number of points at which their work overlaps.

(B) EQUITY

The need for equity also makes co-ordination necessary within central administration. Effective co-ordination, for example, facilitates equitable treatment of clients by departmental field offices, and by different departments where several have responsibility for a particular service. (The DES, and the Welsh, Scottish, and Northern Ireland Offices, for example, all have education responsibilities.)

(C) ACCOUNTABILITY

Ministerial Responsibility (see Chapter 13) also provides a stimulus for co-ordination within central administration. In ministerial departments each minister has *individual responsibility* to Parliament for all his department's work. Consequently, unless all departmental divisions are working in harmony, a minister may find himself defending incompatible actions and decisions. Under the convention of *collective responsibility* ministers are responsible, not only for their own department, but also for the work of all other departments. Although today often interpreted rather loosely, this convention nevertheless requires a measure of consistency between departments, further reinforcing the importance of co-ordinating mechanisms.

(D) POLITICAL FACTORS

As undue favouritism to one client or electoral group (e.g. unions, tenants) runs the risk of alienating others (e.g. employers, landlords), most governments try to maintain a balanced programme. Policy co-ordination is thus important in central administration for political as well as administrative reasons.

While such factors make co-ordination important in central administration, the problems presented are considerable. Central administration is not only bigger and more multi-functional than other organisations, it also lacks coherent goals against which alternative courses of action might be assessed. (For example, in private companies, conflicts can often be resolved through profit and loss calculations.) As Simon *et al.* (1971, p. 435) observe, usually only in wartime is there an overriding goal (winning the war) sufficient to impose coherence at governmental level; consequently, in normal circumstances goal co-ordination has to be secured largely by mechanisms within central administration itself.

Informal Co-ordinating Mechanisms

In many organisations, particularly in small ones, co-ordination is achieved informally. Even in large organisations, however, there can be a good deal of informal co-ordination: for example, by conversation or memoranda. That this is so in central administration is evident from Painter's description (1980, p. 148) of the Department of the Environment:

> Minutes and memos, per medium of the xerox machine and the internal delivery system, flowed constantly from directorate to directorate ... Copies of everything would be sent to anyone who might conceivably be interested.

In fact, aspects of British central administration are particularly conducive to informal co-ordination, even at the highest levels. Ministers, for example, frequently have informal links with one another, usually having worked together for many years in political circles and sharing broadly similar political attitudes. Thus ministers in different departments will invariably be on the same 'political wavelength' and will feel able to contact one another informally should the need arise.

Informal co-ordinating mechanisms also exist among civil servants. For example, the common grading system used throughout the service (see Chapter 6) facilitates identification by officials of their 'opposite numbers' in other sections or departments. It also encourages a willingness to communicate: officials not knowing each other may nevertheless talk frankly if their grades – and hence their status and responsibilities – are similar. This tendency is reinforced by the similar social and educational background of many top civil servants, and their movement between departments (see Chapter 6). Senior civil servants develop a common 'culture' and 'language'; 'so many assumptions are shared' that discussion is often unnecessary (Kellner and Crowther-Hunt, 1980, pp. 272–3). Consequently a measure of unconscious co-ordination occurs, with civil servants tending to 'work and think in similar ways' (Baker, 1972a, p. 109).

Of course, not all 'assumptions' within the civil service are shared. Differing perspectives, new ideas and circumstances can often divide opinion. It is helpful here to bear in mind the *negotiated order* model of Strauss *et al.* (1976). Co-ordination within and between groups involves a multitude of linkages between individuals and agencies, usually with a wide variety of interests and views. While largely governed by formal rules, as well as informal conventions and understandings, the actors in each linkage have considerable autonomy. Each linkage is in a sense unique, being built around individual perceptions and interests of the actors concerned. As circumstances change these actors adapt by a process of bargaining and negotiation. Sometimes one party will give way as a reward for past favours by the other, or simply to maintain a relationship which may prove valuable in the future. The effect is that co-ordination within central administration – and within any large organisation – does not occur between monolithic blocs, but by a process of interpersonal interaction. It is a product of a multiplicity of individual decisions, each one of which affects the overall order. As a result relations between, as well as within, departments are not static, but are an ever-changing pattern of negotiation, bargaining and compromise by individuals at many levels and points of contact. Interestingly this model is also applicable to policy-making and implementation (see Richardson and Jordan, 1979, pp. 101–3; and Barrett and Fudge, 1981, esp. pt 3), emphasising the diffusion of power among a multitude of semi-autonomous individuals and agencies rather than the master/subordinate relationship often portrayed in formal organisation charts.

While informal co-ordination is important, the size and complexity of central administration necessitates the existence of formal co-ordinating mechanisms – both *within* and *between* departments.

Co-ordination Within Departments

Nominally, at least, co-ordination within departments is the responsibility of the permanent head who acts, as necessary, in consultation with the minister. In small departments 'where all the senior staff are accommodated in close proximity and are frequently in contact with each other and with the permanent head', this function may be discharged largely without 'formal arrangements' (Walker, 1982, p. 259). While even in large departments there will be some informal co-ordination (see previous section), most also need formal mechanisms. At least three such mechanisms normally exist within departments:

(i) *Common service divisions*, such as Finance and Establishments, whose horizontal links throughout the department usually enable them to perform a central co-ordinating role.

(ii) *The hierarchic structure* also assists intra-departmental co-ordination. Painter (1980, p. 137) explains:

> The conventional Whitehall department is offered as the organizational solution, with its centralization of authority, upward flow of advice through regular hierarchical channels, and common frame of policy guidelines and traditions to provide coherence for policy.

(iii) *The functional principle of work allocation* (see pp. 26–8), which is applied widely inside departments, locates related functions within the same departmental divisions.

Despite the existence of these 'traditional' co-ordinating features in most departments, intra-departmental co-ordination frequently exhibits serious shortcomings. This is especially so with *strategic co-ordination*, which is often crowded out from the attention of ministers and top civil servants by immediate policy pressures. Indeed, from the 1960s there were a number of developments which, although concerned mainly with expenditure planning, policy analysis, and efficient management, if fully implemented would nevertheless have vastly improved intra-departmental co-ordination. The most significant of these were:

PESC AND PAR

The 1961 Plowden Report, *The Control of Public Expenditure* (Plowden Committee, 1961) led to the establishment of annual governmental reviews of public expenditure co-ordinated by the *Public Expenditure Survey Committee* (PESC). As these exercises normally incorporate five years' 'look-ahead' projections for each department, with each department having *relative* freedom to determine priorities within global expenditure totals agreed by the Treasury, one effect was to stimulate the development of departmental machinery for co-ordinating future policy, programme and resource needs. To assist with this a system of *Programme Analysis and Review* (PAR) was established in 1970, designed to enable departments 'to determine' their 'own priorities' within their departmental PESC allocation (Heath and Barker, 1978, p. 372). Each department was to organise itself to produce 'PARs as well as ... PESCs' (Clarke, 1971, p. 7). Thus, by the early 1970s, most departments had special machinery for conducting annual exercises in forward planning, programme analysis, and policy co-ordination. This departmental machinery, Brown and Steel (1979, p. 241) explain, often resembled a small-scale PESC 'analysing needs and allocating resources within a PESC programme for which the department was responsible'.

PLANNING UNITS

A further stimulus was provided by the Fulton Report recommendation that departments should establish 'planning and research units' to be responsible 'for major long-term policy-planning' (1968, I, para. 173). Fulton envisaged that such units, headed by a Senior Policy Adviser and containing outside experts on temporary contracts as well as civil servants, should identify future needs and problems and ensure that 'day-to-day policy decisions' were taken with due recognition of 'likely implications for the future'. Ten years after Fulton, Macdonald and Fry (1980) identified 'policy planning units' or similar bodies in at least thirteen departments. While their structure and functions varied widely, most had responsibility for co-ordinating departmental policy. They concluded (pp. 421, 432):

> Policy planning units are a familiar feature of British central government ... What seems to be happening is that all the various elements of forward policy consideration are co-ordinated, the co-ordination produces a capacity for oversight, and the oversight makes possible a limited degree of central direction.

MANAGEMENT INFORMATION SYSTEMS FOR MINISTERS

In 1980 MINIS, a management information system for ministers, was introduced into the Department of the Environment. Its purpose was to provide 'information primarily for Ministers and senior officials ... about activities, past performance and future plans for each part of the Department ... It shows how the work is organised and who is responsible for doing what' (*Efficiency and Effectiveness in the Civil Service*, 1982, para. 27). Essentially a management tool, its implications for co-ordination are considerable: when fully operational it should enable ministers and senior officials to maintain ongoing prioritisation 'of the different tasks to be performed and ... to decide how resources can best be allocated between them'. Any duplication of effort, or failure to meet departmental goals, should be identified, and corrective action taken. In 1982 the Commons Treasury and Civil Service Committee recommended that MINIS or its equivalent should be adopted in all departments (HC, 236 1981/2, recommendations iv and v), and the government generally endorsed this view (*Efficiency and Effectiveness in the Civil Service*, 1982, para. 29).

The impact of these developments should not be exaggerated. Economic problems in the 1970s made forward expenditure projections and planning increasingly speculative. By the 1980s PAR had largely been abandoned (Gray and Jenkins, 1982), while PESC had changed 'from a mainly planning system to one in which short-term cash control predominated' (Hood and Wright, 1981, p. 23; see also Wright, 1977 and 1980). Even the Planning Units, which apparently flourished in the 1970s, were not the kind envisaged by Fulton. No 'Fulton-type' Senior Policy Advisers were appointed, few specialists from outside the civil service were recruited, and most Planning Units were as much concerned with short-term problems as with long-term policy co-ordination (Macdonald and Fry, 1980; and Garrett, 1980, pp. 101–9). MINIS, moreover, despite strong support from Mrs Thatcher, met considerable resistance and indifference within Whitehall, and less than two years after its introduction Likierman (1982, p. 141) concluded that 'the chances of widespread adoption must be slight'.

The increasingly speculative nature of long-term planning was not the only reason why some of the anticipated improvements in internal co-ordination failed to materialise. Co-ordination often restricts the independence of organisational sub-units; consequently, individual policy divisions and officials were sometimes reluctant to see their freedom threatened by the introduction of departmental planning mechanisms. Some of these mechanisms, notably Planning Units and Senior Policy Advisers, also conflicted with traditional Whitehall practice (whereby policy divisions led by generalist civil servants monopolised policy advice at higher levels). MINIS, likewise, may be seen as a threat to senior officials fearful that it provides ministers with 'a much better understanding of what is going on in ... [departments] and a greater degree of control' over their activities (Likierman, 1982, p. 138).

At the best of times, therefore, one might expect new internal co-ordinating mechanisms to be coolly received by departmental officials. In a recession, however, with governments committed to retrenchment in Whitehall, they might additionally threaten civil service jobs, careers, and even whole sections. (Several DOE divisions 'disappeared' as a result of the MINIS exercise: Lee, 1981, pp. 42–3; see also Likierman, 1982, p. 138.) It is not, therefore, surprising that attempts to improve intra-departmental co-ordination have generally had limited success. By the early 1980s PESC, PAR and Planning Units had all failed to meet initial expectations, and MINIS was receiving a cool reception within Whitehall.

Co-ordination Between Departments

Co-ordination *between* departments is not unrelated to co-ordination *within* them. Blocks of work in one department requiring co-ordination may, following changes in the departmental pattern (see pp. 24–30), be relocated in separate departments and thereafter require co-ordination by inter-departmental machinery. Indeed changes in the departmental pattern are often influenced by co-ordination considerations. For example, the creation of giant departments was partly designed to alleviate the burden upon inter-departmental machinery by transferring large amounts of work to the intra-departmental plane. In practice, however, many of the anticipated improvements failed to materialise: internal co-ordinating machinery within these larger departments frequently became overloaded, and real 'integration' often never materialised. In any event the drift back towards smaller departments after 1970 (see pp. 28–9) largely reversed the process, and led to much co-ordinating activity being returned to the inter-departmental sphere.

Co-ordination *between* departments generally poses greater problems than co-ordination *within* them: there are more functions, more personnel, and the co-ordinated units – government departments – are often strongly placed to challenge 'unsympathetic' co-ordinators. Moreover, the hierarchic pattern of organisation which enhances vertical co-ordination *within* departments (see previous section) is usually absent at the inter-departmental plane. As no department is officially 'superior' to any other, inter-departmental co-ordination is largely conducted through horizontal channels, by a process of discussion, negotiation and adjustment between theoretically equal departments.

While much horizontal co-ordination of this kind occurs informally, considerable use is also made of formal channels. These include:

COMMON MACHINERY

Administrative co-ordination is greatly facilitated where different departments utilise common machinery. The Departments of Industry and Trade, for example, before being merged in 1983, maintained a common network of regional field offices, as well as some common headquarters service divisions. Obviously, the scope for such arrangements depends largely upon the departments' functions. (Industry and Trade worked in similar fields, had similar service needs, and similar regional client groups.) Where, however, departments have little in common, administrative alignments of this kind are less appropriate.

COMMON SERVICE ORGANISATIONS

These have 'horizontal' links between departments, and also an important co-ordinating role, especially with regard to procedural co-ordination. The National Audit Office, for example, which audits the accounts of all departments, influences the standardisation of accounting procedures throughout Whitehall. 'Common service' bodies may also co-ordinate particular governmental activities; thus the Central Office of Information supplies publicity services to government departments, and the Property Services Agency provides common services relating to government property, land, buildings and furnishings.

THE TREASURY

This is the most important 'common service' organisation within central administration. It has long been recognised 'as the leading department, controlling the departments' expenditure and staff and appointments, besides its function as the central economic and financial department' (Clarke, 1975, p. 69). Particularly important is *Treasury control*: the Treasury's role in co-ordinating financial, manpower, and economic resources.

Financial control includes the Treasury's right to vet departmental estimates before presentation to Parliament, a right which enables the Treasury to identify any overlap of departmental functions, to ensure that departments are spending (and acting) according to agreed policies, and to influence procedural co-ordination in financial matters. Financial control also involves policy co-ordination. As Treasury control extends to virtually all government expenditure, departments wishing to embark on new policy (requiring expenditure) must first bargain with it. Lord Bridges (1964, p. 41) explains:

> One of the main tasks of the Treasury ... is to examine the stream of proposals submitted to it so as to provide material for a judgement of their comparative merits. Given that there can never be enough money ... which are the most deserving? And as between approved objects of expenditure, how much should be spent on each to retain right priorities?

As central departments, moreover, have increasingly provided funds for local authorities, nationalised industries, and numerous other non-departmental bodies, so the Treasury's financial control has extended beyond central administration to the wider public sector.

Manpower control involves the Treasury's responsibilities for civil service manpower, pay and superannuation. This enables the Treasury to monitor manpower throughout central administration, and requires departments to bargain with the Treasury for extra manpower resources.

Economic control, the significance of which has increased with greater governmental intervention in the economy, also enhances the Treasury's co-ordinating role. This involves financial and manpower management in support of national economic targets (reducing inflation or unemployment, stimulating investment, improving productivity and so forth). As economic control involves future as well as current expenditure, the Treasury's role also extends to forward planning. Since the mid-1970s, moreover, as governments have placed increasing emphasis on cash-limited central and local government expenditure (and tighter borrowing controls on nationalised industries), so the significance of the Treasury's economic control function for public sector co-ordination has also increased. (For wider discussion see Hood and Wright, 1981.)

Of course, the Treasury's co-ordinating role varies with political and economic circumstances, and with changes in the departmental pattern. Between 1964 and 1969 it lost, nominally at least, economic co-ordination functions to the Department of Economic Affairs, while between 1968 and 1981 manpower control was lost to the Civil Service Department. (Control over manpower numbers, administrative costs, pay, and conditions – but not personnel management, recruitment, and training – were regained by the Treasury in 1981.) For most of the postwar period, however, economic and manpower functions have been exercised by the Treasury, and even when they have not the Treasury's financial control has assured it of a central co-ordinating role. To quote Lord Bridges (1964, p. 41), the Treasury's 'business' leads it 'to concern itself with every important aspect of government policy'.

INTER-DEPARTMENTAL COMMITTEES

These further facilitate co-ordination within central administration. Some, being serviced by the Cabinet Office, are technically Cabinet committees (see pp. 62–5) although unlike the most important Cabinet committees they usually consist only of civil servants. The number of inter-departmental committees fluctuates with changing political and administrative circumstances, although one survey in the early 1950s revealed 'at least 700 inter-departmental committees, of which more than 100 were technically Cabinet committees' (Daalder, 1975, p. 247). Some inter-departmental committees are *ad hoc*, formed to co-ordinate specific parts of central administration as and when necessary; others are permanent. Examples are the *Public Expenditure Survey Committee* (chaired by a senior Treasury official and containing the principal finance officers of the main spending departments) which co-ordinates the annual PESC exercise, and the *Regional Economic Planning Boards* (containing senior officials from departmental field offices) which help co-ordinate the work of departments with planning functions in the regions.

While the importance of inter-departmental committees varies enormously, at the highest level their influence is considerable. This is particularly true of those 'official' committees (usually consisting of Permanent Secretaries or other top departmental officials) which 'shadow' ministerial Cabinet committees. Cross-man (1975, p. 198) felt that these enabled civil servants to 'pre-cook' ministerial decisions, while Haines (1977, p. 16) described the committee of 'first' Permanent Secretaries which meets weekly to discuss forthcoming Cabinet business as an additional 'Cabinet ... that very few people outside Whitehall know anything about'. Such committees usually meet more frequently than, and in advance of, ministerial committees; consequently, they may 'de-velop inter-departmental loyalties, and even commit their depart-ments ... without ministerial authority' (Wilson, 1977, p. 127). While, clearly, inter-departmental committees cannot be dis-regarded as a source of civil service influence (see Headey, 1975, pp. 119–21), they are nevertheless indispensable to central adminis-tration. A response to the growth of government, and to the devel-opment of government activity across departmental boundaries, they provide an essential instrument for horizontal co-ordination between departments, leaving only the most intractable and politi-cally sensitive issues to be resolved at ministerial level. Without them central administration would grind to a halt, and ministerial workloads become even more unbearable.

CO-ORDINATING MINISTERS

Where major inter-departmental co-ordination is required, special co-ordinating ministers have sometimes been appointed. In 1936, for example, a Minister for the Co-ordination of Defence was appointed to integrate the work of the three service ministries, an arrangement reinforced in 1940 when the Prime Minister, Chur-chill, took over the role. Churchill experimented along similar lines in 1951 by appointing a number of co-ordinating ministers (or 'Overlords'). For example, Lord Woolton (Lord President of the Council) was made responsible for co-ordinating the Ministries of Food and Agriculture; and Lord Leathers for co-ordinating Trans-port, and Fuel and Power. Departmental ministers retained respon-sibility to Parliament for their departments, but their work was co-ordinated by the 'Overlords' who represented the departments in the Cabinet. These arrangements, however, effectively ceased in 1953, mainly because they were felt to blur accountability. While departmental ministers retained constitutional responsibility to Parliament, policy for their departments was largely determined by the 'Overlords'. (Controversy was further heightened because the main 'Overlords' were peers and could not be questioned in the House of Commons.) Consequently prime ministers since Churchill have used co-ordinating ministers more sparingly. Unlike the 'Overlords' such ministers have rarely had powers of direction, and have usually been appointed either:

(i) To co-ordinate activities or policies cutting across several departments (such as Michael Heseltine's responsibilities for co-ordinating government action in Merseyside following the 1981 riots); or

(ii) To act as 'neutral' chairmen of Cabinet committees on which representatives of co-ordinated departments also sit.

CO-ORDINATING DEPARTMENTS

The co-ordinating department is, in theory, more sound constitutionally than the co-ordinating minister because there is usually a clearly defined 'division of responsibility' between the co-ordinating department and the departments 'which it co-ordinates' (Mackenzie and Grove, 1957, p. 346). It is also more effective administratively because, whereas 'Overlord-type' co-ordinators, having no department, usually 'operate with a small office of civil servants', often drawn from the Cabinet Office (Jones, 1975, pp. 42, 51), the ministerial head of a co-ordinating department has full departmental resources to support and advise him or her. An obvious example is the Ministry of Defence, which from 1947 to 1964 had statutory responsibility for co-ordinating the three service departments in specified areas (a task which was formerly done by an 'Overlord-type' minister). Similarly, between 1964 and 1969 the Department of Economic Affairs held responsibility for long-term economic planning, which involved co-ordinating the related activities of various departments such as the Treasury, Employment, and Trade.

Despite these theoretical advantages, however, most co-ordinating departments have been barely more effective than 'Overlord-type' co-ordinators. Co-ordinating departments are no less likely to meet resistance from the departments which they co-ordinate, particularly as their respective responsibilities cannot in practice always be clearly delineated. (Those between the Treasury and the DEA, for example, were not always 'meaningful'.) Moreover, co-ordinating departments are usually dependent to some degree upon the co-ordinated departments to implement their decisions. The DEA failed, partly at least, because the 'execution' of its economic plans rested with the Treasury. Similarly

Defence ministers between 1947 and 1964 were often unable to develop coherent defence policies: they could only 'negotiate compromises and allocate "fair shares" between the Services' (Clarke, 1975, pp. 70, 75). Significantly, in this case, the co-ordinating and co-ordinated departments were amalgamated in 1964 to form the 'new' Ministry of Defence – again illustrating the value of combining administrative as well as co-ordinating powers through departmental mergers. Undoubtedly this logic was not lost upon those prime ministers who between the mid-1950s and 1970 instituted numerous such mergers culminating in the creation of giant departments (see pp. 28–9). This process has, of course, gone into reverse since 1970, a development which highlights an important point: valuable though co-ordination usually is, other criteria – political as well as administrative – may sometimes be more important, and necessitate organisational structures which may impede efficient co-ordination.

Central Policy Review Staff (CPRS)

Most co-ordinating mechanisms so far discussed concern specific departments or fields of activity. Most, also, concern preventative co-ordination rather than strategic co-ordination. Theoretically, in central administration, ministers are responsible for defining strategic objectives: in reality day-to-day pressures often prevent this. The White Paper *Reorganisation of Central Government* (1970, para. 45) observed: 'Governments are always at some risk of losing sight of the need to consider the totality of their current policies in relation to their longer term objectives; and ... of evaluating ... the alternative policy options and priorities open to them'. To rectify this deficiency it proposed (para. 46) the creation of a 'small multi-disciplinary central policy review staff in the Cabinet Office'. Working under the Prime Minister's supervision, but serving all ministers collectively, its tasks were to enable ministers 'to work out the implications of their basic strategy in terms of policies in specific areas, to establish the relative priorities to be given to the different sectors of their programme as a whole, to identify those areas of policy in which new choices can be exercised and to ensure that the underlying implications of alternative courses of action are fully analysed and considered' (para. 47). The CPRS, as its creator, Edward Heath, explained (Heath and Barker, 1978, p. 382), was formed primarily so that 'government strategy could be continuously reviewed and regularly reported upon'. Starting work in

February 1971 the CPRS (or, as it was popularly known, the 'Think Tank') performed a major role in central government co-ordination until its disbandment in July 1983. Its work during this period can be examined under several headings:

COMPOSITION

The CPRS was intended to provide a counterweight to departmental interests and civil service advice; consequently, its composition was untypical of central administration. Its members were temporary (some were from outside the civil service), there was no internal hierarchy, and there was a mix of specialist and generalist skills. Usually about eighteen strong, CPRS staff were drawn about equally from inside and outside central administration. Those from inside were usually 'high flier' civil servants seconded from departments; outsiders came mainly from business, banking, and universities. This diversity was reflected in the backgrounds of the four CPRS directors. Lord Rothschild (1970–4) was a former head of research at Shell; Sir Kenneth Berrill (1974–80) was an academic economist and former Treasury official; Sir Robin Ibbs (1979–80) was a former ICI director; and John Sparrow (1982–3) a merchant banker.

In other respects, however, the CPRS was more typical of British administrative practice. Members were recruited primarily for their intellectual qualities and although empowered to commission research from outside consultants, the CPRS essentially relied upon its members' intellect 'to assess the arguments of experts' (Brown and Steel, 1979, p. 334). In this respect there were close parallels with the generalist tradition inherent in British central administration.

ACTIVITIES

CPRS activities varied according to differing personalities, political circumstances and levels of prime ministerial support. Plowden (1981), however, identified five main activities.

(i) *Strategy discussions.* During the Heath government (1970–4) strategy discussions with ministers – at which the government's progress in attaining strategic objectives was reviewed – were regular occurrences. Heath found such strategy sessions useful (Heath and Barker, 1978, esp. p. 382) but they were abolished after 1974.

(ii)   *Contribution to day-to-day issues.*   Housed in the Cabinet Office, the CPRS was able to contribute to briefing documents prepared by the Cabinet Secretariat (see p. 66) which form the basis of Cabinet and Cabinet committee discussions. Normally its contribution was limited to issues which it felt were 'not being properly presented' or 'thought through' (Plowden, 1981, p. 66). Consequently, the CPRS was able to inject strategic considerations – including views which interested departments might not put – into the policy-making process.

(iii)   *In-depth studies.*   Each year the CPRS mounted in-depth studies. (About half a dozen a year were produced as reports, although not all were published.) Most studies *crossed departmental boundaries*: for example, energy conservation, scientific research and development, the British motor industry, central/local government relations, race relations. Often, also, they were of *long-term relevance*: the implications of population changes, for example. Occasionally, administrative questions are also examined. The 1975 report, *A Joint Approach to Social Policies (JASP)*, highlighted the need for greater inter-departmental co-ordination in formulating and administering social policies. Another, in 1977, recommended improved machinery for co-ordinating UK representative agencies overseas. While similar studies could be – and sometimes were – performed by departments, the CPRS's freedom from day-to-day pressures and vested departmental interests enabled it to engage in more wide-ranging analyses than might otherwise have been possible. As Mackintosh (1977, p. 518) explained, the CPRS operated rather 'like a standing, all-purposes, fast-moving royal commission'.

(iv)   *Co-ordinating inter-departmental activities.*   The CPRS sometimes had a 'troubleshooter' role, chairing and/or providing the secretariat for sensitive inter-departmental committees. According to Plowden (1981, p. 67) this usually happened when 'no major department could be relied upon to produce a disinterested chairman and . . . the Cabinet secretariat, concerned to be neutral, might not do the job purposefully'.

(v)   *Intra-departmental co-ordination.*   The CPRS policy review function sometimes occurred at the intra-departmental plane. For example, it was closely involved with departmental PAR exercises (see pp. 39–40), assisting in the choice of programmes for review, and to some extent in the conduct of reviews themselves.

THE CPRS: AN ASSESSMENT

When the CPRS was formed there was speculation that it might be a 'forerunner of a new Prime Minister's department taking over the co-ordinating functions of the Treasury, Civil Service Department and ... Cabinet Office'. Others, however, felt it would be 'reduced to impotence by the unwillingness of departments to supply it with information' (Bourn, 1979, p. 35). The first possibility, although Heath reportedly favoured it, never materialised. According to Rose (1980, p. 31) 'the collective weight of jealous departments' and influential ministers 'squashed' the idea. Consequently, the basic ingredients for such a development were lacking from the start: the CPRS served all ministers collectively, had no permanent members, no executive functions, and few independent information-gathering and research resources. Heath's successors, moreover, never harboured the same ambitions for the CPRS. Indeed, Wilson and Callaghan established in No. 10 a small *Policy Unit*, headed by Dr Bernard Donoghue, which met for them 'some of the needs that the CPRS had met for Mr Heath' (Plowden, 1981, p. 81). Mrs Thatcher, likewise, relied heavily on her own policy unit, initially headed by (Sir) John Hoskyns, and on other personal advisers.

Lacking the resources to develop into a Prime Minister's department, civil service opposition to the CPRS was less than might otherwise have been expected. Other factors also minimised potential opposition: the high proportion of CPRS members drawn from the civil service, and the heavy dependence on departments for information. According to Plowden (1981, p. 81) the CPRS enjoyed 'good access' to departmental information, and 'close working relationships with officials'. Rothschild and Berrill also made considerable efforts to consult Permanent Secretaries and 'carry them' on major issues. Indeed, the relationship may have been too close, for after 1974 there were repeated suggestions that the CPRS had been 'captured' by the civil service (Benn, 1982, p. 60; Haines, 1977, p. 37; Plowden, 1981, p. 81).

Whatever the precise relationship with officials, the CPRS undoubtedly improved co-ordination in central administration. Pollitt writing in 1974 (p. 390) claimed that close relations with ministers enabled the CPRS to detect 'changes in political mood'; its 'central position' enabled it to 'see the big picture'; and its 'freedom from executive responsibilities' allowed it the escape from 'pressure of day-to-day events'. Its successes, moreover, were considerable. Its contribution to the development of a joint approach to social policies (JASP) was, according to Plowden (*The Times*, 23 July 1983) decisive; it successfully completed a project which would otherwise have foundered under the weight of extra work involved for the department mainly concerned – the DHSS – and the resistance and relative lack of concern of other departments. It also alerted Heath's government to 'the enormous increase in raw material prices which was coming' and to the need for a 'bold departure on incomes policy' (Heath and Barker, 1978, p. 383). Its briefings to ministers, according to Wilson (1977, p. 125), were invaluable, and many of its published studies were widely acclaimed. Its (1975) report on the motor industry, although implicitly rejected by the government, subsequently became 'basic to much informed thinking about the problems of British manufacturing industry', and its (1977) review of overseas representation, although criticised by the Foreign Office and other affected interests, was some years later emerging in policy (Plowden, 1981, p. 89).

By the late 1970s the CPRS had established itself within central administration as a strategic policy unit capable of relating departmental programmes to long-term and corporate objectives. It supplied to ministers, and especially the Prime Minister, a strategic policy and information service that was not departmentally oriented. Sir Harold Wilson's view in 1977 (p. 125) was that the CPRS had 'come to stay', as 'an integral part of the decision-making centre of government'. Six years later, however, in July 1983 it was abolished by Mrs Thatcher on the grounds that 'the purposes for which [it] was set up [were] now being met satisfactorily in other ways': for example, by 'the increased role for Cabinet Office secretariat in preparing issues for collective ministerial discussion, and the Prime Minister's own policy unit' (*The Times*, 17 June 1983). Undoubtedly the establishment of the policy unit in 1974 did diminish the CPRS's role and Mrs Thatcher's subsequent consolidation of personal policy advisers within No. 10 (see p. 69) further accelerated this trend. Whereas the CPRS, housed in the Cabinet Office, served the Cabinet collectively, the No. 10 policy unit provided the Prime Minister with her own personal 'think tank'. As such, the rise and fall of the CPRS has to be seen within the context of the contemporary debate about Cabinet and prime ministerial government (see pp. 62–72).

Other factors also influenced the CPRS's disbandment. Within Whitehall enemies were undoubtedly made of departments, civil servants, and ministers in disagreement with CPRS advice. Relations with Mrs Thatcher, moreover, were never easy; the CPRS had been established by her political rival, Heath, upon whom it is widely thought to have urged economic policy changes in 1972 which were anathema to Mrs Thatcher's wing of the party. There were also problems of secrecy, highlighted before the 1983 Election by the publication of several politically embarrassing 'leaks' from confidential CPRS reports (including one in 1982 setting out options which included radical changes in financing welfare services). Analysing policy options may be a sound feature of rational decision-making, but can be politically embarrassing when possible shortcomings in government policy become public knowledge. There is evidence also that the CPRS suffered from the increasingly speculative nature of strategic planning in a period of rapid economic change. By the 1980s the CPRS was continuing 'to do good work on specific issues' but, as Lord Hunt put it (*The Times*, 10 June 1983), 'had lost the strategic oversight of policy for which it was designed'.

That there is a need within central administration for strategic policy analysis across inter-departmental boundaries is beyond dispute. What is less clear is whether such a role can be performed better by a body such as the CPRS, relatively free from departmental pressures and the everyday exigencies of government, than by other agencies more firmly rooted in the political and administrative system. The dominant view is probably that it can, but only if firm support from the Prime Minister is forthcoming. By 1983 the CPRS had clearly lost prime ministerial support and its disbandment consequently caused little surprise.

Most of the co-ordinating mechanisms so far examined have only limited jurisdiction: they secure co-ordination within a relatively small part of central administration. Where, however, disagreements cannot be resolved by such mechanisms, or where co-ordination across the whole sphere of government is required, other agencies, with power to impose solutions upon competing factions, are necessary. This requirement is largely filled in Britain by the Cabinet, which Steel (1979, p. 23) describes as 'the ultimate forum for the co-ordination of all the activities of government'. As such it requires detailed treatment in a separate chapter.

4 THE CABINET SYSTEM

At the apex of central administration lies the *Cabinet*, consisting of the Prime Minister and twenty or so of his or her most senior ministerial colleagues. In 1867 Walter Bagehot wrote that Britain enjoyed 'Cabinet government': the Cabinet was the instrument of 'fusion' between the executive and legislative branches of government, the body which effectively ruled the nation (Bagehot, 1963 ed., pp. 65–9). Developments since then have greatly increased the Cabinet's significance. Modern Cabinets normally consist of leading members of the majority party and, so long as party discipline is maintained, can control the legislative as well as the executive branches of government. At the same time the expansion of state activity has vastly increased the significance of Cabinet decisions. It has also increased the volume and complexity of Cabinet work, necessitating changes in its composition, organisation, and procedures.

Some of these changes have arguably strengthened the Prime Minister at the expense of Cabinet colleagues, leading to suggestions that Cabinet government has now been replaced by prime ministerial government. No less important to public administration students, however, is the issue of whether the Cabinet system has adapted sufficiently during the twentieth century to provide for the efficient direction of central administration. Both these issues are discussed in this chapter.

Cabinet Functions

The Cabinet lies at the apex of both central administration and the wider political system. Within central administration its main task is 'to co-ordinate the work of the various departments and committees and thus ensure that the activity of the government has a certain coherence' (Mackintosh, 1977, p. 413). Within the political system it is the *ultimate* target of the host of extra-governmental pressures which make demands upon government. Modern Cabinets, to up-date Bagehot's terminology, are the final point of 'fusion' between central administration and the wider political community, their role being to ensure that the former remains aware of, and responsive to, legitimate demands of the latter.

While technically the Cabinet determines its own functions, administrative and political demands necessitate the performance of several broadly identifiable tasks. Essentially there are three main functions: Policy-making; Administrative control; and Co-ordination and delimitation.

POLICY-MAKING

The Cabinet is the ultimate policy-making body within central administration. However, meeting as it usually does for only a few hours per week, it cannot take *all* government policy decisions. Less important decisions are normally taken within departments or, where several departments are involved, by inter-departmental or Cabinet committees. Urgent decisions may be taken by the Prime Minister alone or in consultation with key ministers, or by an inner or partial Cabinet (pp. 60–2). Even when Cabinet discussion does occur, however, it may be superficial, and decisions often merely ratify conclusions reached elsewhere. The main participants in Cabinet discussions, for example, are frequently ministers with departmental interests, who speak to briefs prepared by their civil servants. Skilful timing and presentation by influential ministers, especially the Prime Minister, may also inhibit Cabinet discussion. Bruce-Gardyne and Lawson (1976, p. 28), for example, explain how, following extensive behind-the-scenes discussions, Macmillan steered the decision to build Concorde through his Cabinet:

> The Prime Minister ... told his colleagues about his great aunt's Daimler, which had travelled at 'the sensible speed of thirty miles an hour', and was sufficiently spacious to enable one to descend from it without removing one's top hat. Nowadays, alas! people had a mania for dashing around ... He thought they all really agreed. No one seriously dissented. It was all over in a few minutes.

Despite these limitations, 'for the most politically important issues the Cabinet is the effective decision-making body' (Jones, 1975, p. 31). Although technically the Cabinet agenda is drawn up by the Cabinet Secretary in consultation with the Prime Minister, in practice most important issues have to be included for discussion at some point. For example, decisions concerning all, or nearly all, departments – such as a public expenditure 'package' – usually 'go direct to the Cabinet' as do those which 'are too big, too urgent or too secret' to be resolved elsewhere. Usually departmental ministers, or the Prime Minister, decide which issues come into this category, although some are 'blown on to the Cabinet by their suddenness and importance' (Gordon Walker, 1972, pp. 117–21). For example, the 1982 Argentine invasion of the Falkland Islands led to the summoning of an 'emergency Cabinet meeting', attended by the Joint Chiefs of Staff, to decide the government's response (*The Times*, 3 April, 1982).

Many issues also reach the Cabinet as a matter of routine. Usually all important *Foreign and Commonwealth items* and all *White Papers* are automatically reported to it. The Cabinet also considers the Chancellor's *budget proposals*, although normally only a day or so before they are presented to Parliament. However, Cabinet disagreement over the 1981 budget led to prime ministerial assurances that, in future, budget strategy would be discussed by the full Cabinet before, and not after, the Chancellor's proposals were finalised.

Forthcoming parliamentary business also receives regular Cabinet consideration. As a major element in the initiation of legislation, the Cabinet spends much time considering bills emanating from departments for inclusion in the government's legislative programme. As parliamentary time is a scarce resource, this involves considering not just the merits of proposed legislation, but also the priority that it should receive. Of course, in 'normal' circumstances most Cabinet legislative proposals are subsequently endorsed by Parliament; consequently, modern Cabinets usually function, not just as the final determinant of government policy, but as the ultimate determinant also of *public* policy and legislation.

ADMINISTRATIVE CONTROL

The Cabinet not only takes policy decisions, but also bears ultimate responsibility for their implementation. In most cases Cabinet decisions are simply communicated to the departments for implementation. Occasionally, however, the Cabinet's role is more positive. A serious breakdown in administration, for example, would almost certainly be discussed by Cabinet. Sometimes in such circumstances the Cabinet may decide to maintain direct oversight and control of administrative work – for example by authorising a Cabinet committee or group of ministers to exercise control – or it may establish new administrative procedures or machinery. Consequently, while most administrative work occurs below Cabinet level, the Cabinet bears ultimate responsibility and 'takes the lead in initiating most ... administrative action' (Steel, 1979, p. 23).

CO-ORDINATION AND DELIMITATION

The Cabinet also bears ultimate responsibility for co-ordination within central administration. The Cabinet's primacy in policy determination gives it final responsibility for both preventative and strategic policy co-ordination (see pp. 34–5). It also has an important role in administrative co-ordination. The Cabinet, according to Mackenzie and Grove (1957, p. 360), is 'the court of last appeal for disputes between Departments about jurisdiction' and thus bears *ultimate* responsibility for the departmental pattern. As they observe (p. 359), 'effective "co-ordination" requires power to decide who is to be responsible for action. The "sovereignty" of the Cabinet includes power to shape the machinery of government.'

Influences Upon the Cabinet

Cabinet decisions are not taken within a vacuum. The Cabinet responds to issues, problems, and opinions emanating from within central administration, as well as to environmental influences (economic factors, social forces, international tensions, and so forth) and a host of other extra-governmental pressures. Some of the latter, like Royal Commissions and public inquiries, advisory committees, quangos, and public corporations, may have been established by central administration to perform advisory or executive functions. Other pressures will be generated independently of central administration. In addition to parliamentary influences, and pressure from foreign governments and international agencies such as the EEC and NATO, such influences include: a) electoral factors, b) party pressures, c) the media, and d) pressure groups.

(A) ELECTORAL FACTORS

The Cabinet's authority in normal circumstances stems from its electoral mandate; consequently, it will to some extent be influenced by election commitments. As these, however, are invariably broad statements of intent, often drawn up in opposition, the Cabinet still has a significant role: for example, making decisions about the details, priority, and feasibility of commitments as well as about issues unforeseen in the manifesto.

(B)   PARTY PRESSURES

Modern Cabinets are usually *party Cabinets* and, as Rose (1980, pp. 312–13) observes, 'rely upon a majority in ... Parliament to sustain [their] existence'. The maintenance of a parliamentary majority is essentially the responsibility of the *Government Whips* who, while able to exert considerable pressure upon MPs to support government proposals, also communicate backbench views to the Cabinet. Norton (1981, pp. 29–30) quotes one Conservative whip: 'if the Chief Whip comes to the conclusion, on the basis of sounding out the parliamentary party, that something cannot be done, then, as a general rule, that is that: it cannot be done'. Views are also transmitted to the Cabinet through the parties' organisations. Both main parties are highly organised in Parliament (Norton, 1979 and 1983), with regional and subject committees of MPs, and regular meetings of the full parliamentary party – machinery which provides an important, and private, channel through which backbenchers can exert pressure on their party leaders.

The Cabinet must also respond to pressures from its extra-parliamentary supporters. These may be transmitted either informally, through exchanges between ministers and party members, or through formal organisational channels (party conferences, committees and so forth). While their effect will vary according to issue and circumstance, the Cabinet must nevertheless at all times seek 'to carry the party with it'. Failure to do so may not only sap party morale, with ultimate electoral repercussions, but, more immediately, may breed disaffection among backbenchers and make the work of the Whips more difficult.

(C)   THE MEDIA

The Cabinet is also influenced by the media, which transmit public opinion and report, comment upon and interpret happenings of political significance. As a result the media help to 'set the agenda' of political debate. Issue emergence through the media is an important source of public policy, and when salient issues develop the Cabinet must usually respond. At times the media may become all important. Lord Boyle has commented (Boyle and Crosland, 1971, p. 109), that 'The Cabinet increasingly, as the years go on, tends to be most concerned with the agenda that the press and media are setting out as the crucial issues before the nation at any one time'.

The media, of course, transmit opinions in two directions: from ministers to the public as well as vice versa. Most departments have press offices, including No. 10. The latter is particularly significant: busy journalists all too often faithfully reproduce the material it supplies, leading to suggestions that the media is manipulated into setting the political agenda desired by the government. More negatively information flowing out of central administration is restricted by the Official Secrets Acts, which prevent disclosure by civil servants of even the most trivial official information. Although difficult to enforce, the effect is to make British central administration perhaps the most secretive in the Western world (see Michael, 1982).

(D)   PRESSURE GROUPS

Pressure groups represent another major influence upon the Cabinet; indeed, their influence upon both policy-making and administration has increased considerably during the twentieth century as the expansion of state activity has made central administration increasingly dependent upon group co-operation and advice. Generally the most influential groups are *sectional groups* (like the CBI and TUC) which defend important sectional interests. Many such groups – like public sector unions – provide essential public services or possess the power to cause social and economic disruption. They often also possess other significant resources: organisation, wealth, status, large or influential memberships, expertise, and so on. Inevitably such groups often command considerable political 'muscle'. This is most evident in fields such as industrial relations and prices and incomes, where the policy initiatives of successive governments during the 1960s and 1970s were frustrated largely by opposition from powerful trade unions.

Not all groups, of course, possess such influence. For example, *promotional groups* which (like CND or the League Against Cruel Sports) promote a particular cause, usually possess fewer resources: smaller memberships, less expertise and wealth, and relatively little disruptive capacity. Nevertheless, some promotional groups have campaigned with great success. Environmental groups, for example, have presented a considerable challenge to perceived threats to the environment (Kimber and Richardson, 1974; Lowe and Goyder, 1983); while CND during the early 1980s focused mounting public attention on the Cabinet's decision to site nuclear cruise missiles in Britain. Often using the media with effect, such groups usually try to force on to the 'political agenda' issues which the Cabinet might otherwise ignore.

While pressure groups, by seeking (often conflicting) concessions from government, make the work of central administration more difficult, in other respects they make it easier. They provide information essential for policy formulation, assistance with implementation, and a means of consulting sections of the community about policy proposals. Indeed, since the war Cabinets have tended increasingly to look to groups (rather than Parliament) to 'legitimise' policies. A 'voluntary' prices and income policy, for example, supported and 'policed' by the CBI and TUC, is more likely to prove effective than one imposed by legislation. So interdependent at times are key producer groups and government that some writers claim to detect in Britain the emergence of *corporatism* – a system in which, stated simply, major functional groups are incorporated into state decision-making in return for policy concessions (see Newman, 1981).

As already observed (pp. 23–4) the main focus of pressure group activity in Britain is at the departmental level. Consequently, the Cabinet tends to become involved only when group pressures are too intractable to be resolved by departments, or where client groups of different departments make conflicting demands. As this implies, Cabinets frequently reject 'unacceptable' group demands, and indeed possess formidable resources – the armed forces at one extreme to the claim to represent the national interest at the other – with which to resist. Nevertheless, the cumulative influence of group pressures upon Cabinet decision-making is considerable. As Richardson and Jordan (1979, p. 3) observe, 'a proper understanding of the ways ... issues arrive on the political agenda, ... the way in which policies are decided, their actual content, and subsequent implementation, can only be reached by reference to the group system'.

As should be clear, the Cabinet is the *ultimate* target of pressures emanating both from within and without central administration. While the source and strength of pressure will vary from issue to issue, whenever pressures conflict the Cabinet will have to calculate relative costs and benefits of different courses of action. The Cabinet, in short, must try to balance incompatibles, or as Jones (1975, p. 40) puts it, 'to make unity out of diversity'.

Cabinet Composition and Size

The Cabinet's composition is itself a source of diversity. Although its members normally belong to the same party, they are also ambitious politicians often representing different factions and 'wings' within the party. Most, moreover, are departmental ministers whose policy perspectives invariably reflect departmental attitudes. Consequently, participants in Cabinet discussions themselves reflect diversity, and their decisions often represent compromises rather than outright victory or defeat for one or other competitor.

Ironically, it is the need to produce unity which largely explains the Cabinet's diverse composition. Because of its co-ordinating role all major departments – as well as any co-ordinating ministers (see pp. 46–8) – are usually given representation. Departments and their client groups, moreover, are likely to feel loss of prestige and influence without Cabinet representation. Patronage and party considerations also intrude: most prime ministers use Cabinet posts to reward supporters, 'neutralise' rivals, and to represent all strands of party opinion. Indeed, while the Cabinet's composition is theoretically a matter of prime ministerial discretion, in practice administrative and political factors seriously restrict his or her freedom of choice. They also tend to exert pressure for large Cabinets, pressure which has increased over the past century as the size of the central administrative machine has expanded.

Surprisingly, in view of such pressures, the Cabinet was barely larger in 1983 (21 members) than in 1900 (19). One reason is that large Cabinets usually take longer to reach decisions than smaller ones: more members want to speak and more views must be reconciled. Other than in wartime, most twentieth-century Cabinets have numbered about twenty: since the war, for example, most Cabinets have had between sixteen and twenty-four members. Despite the vast increase in government work, therefore, the Cabinet's size during the twentieth century has remained surprisingly stable. Prime ministers have balanced the need for Cabinets large enough to allow effective co-ordination, and adequate patronage, with the requirement to keep them below the level – just over twenty – beyond which they become too unwieldy for effective decision-making.

Even with Cabinets around twenty, modern prime ministers have often formed inner Cabinets which they have consulted more regularly than the full Cabinet. Usually, the term *inner Cabinet* denotes an informal grouping of 'friends or confidants of the Prime Minister drawn from members of his Cabinet' (Gordon Walker, 1972, p. 37). While they may carry considerable political weight, such bodies have no official status and their decisions do not bind the Cabinet. In 1968 Wilson, departing from this informal model, established a Parliamentary Committee of the Cabinet.

Comprising senior ministers, and serviced by the Cabinet Secretariat, it functioned in some respects as a formalised inner Cabinet. However, it disappeared in 1970, and has had no lasting effect on central administration.

Different from an inner Cabinet is what Gordon Walker (1972, pp. ·87–8) describes as a '*partial Cabinet*' – 'a number of Ministers who constitute part only of the Cabinet but act for a time as if they were the Cabinet'. Sometimes these are technically Cabinet committees (see next section), at other times not. Usually concerned with 'matters of great moment and secrecy' they 'prepare policies ... and ... take decisions without prior consultation with the Cabinet' although the Cabinet 'is in due course informed and consulted'. According to Gordon Walker (pp. 89–90), partial Cabinets took the decision to manufacture the atom bomb in Attlee's government, and drafted plans to invade Suez in 1956. Similar arrangements existed during the 1982 Falklands dispute when an inner group of Cabinet ministers, chosen and chaired by the Prime Minister, was entrusted with the day-to-day handling of the crisis.

By utilising inner and partial Cabinets, prime ministers, with the assistance of senior colleagues, have been able to discuss issues more thoroughly, swiftly, and urgently than would otherwise be possible given the size of modern Cabinets. It is in the same vein that the establishment of a Cabinet committee system should be seen.

Cabinet Committees

Cabinet Committees offer a classic example of the ambiguity and complexity which characterises public administration. Technically these comprise all committees serviced by the Cabinet Office, but as the composition, terms of reference, and number of these (usually above 150) varies widely this definition has little practical value. Some of these committees, moreover, consist of ministers, others of civil servants, and others still of both; some are permanent standing committees and others temporary or *ad hoc*. The picture is further confused because information about Cabinet committees is shrouded in official secrecy. For students of public administration, therefore, Cabinet committees present many problems. One, for example, is that a distinction between inter-departmental committees (see pp. 45–6) and Cabinet committees, and between official (civil service) and ministerial committees, cannot always be clearly drawn.

Despite occasional prior use of committees, it was not until the First World War that a Cabinet committee *system* came into being. Under war pressures vast amounts of work had to be delegated to newly-created Cabinet committees, of which 165 were in existence by 1918. Between the wars these committees were largely unscrambled (see Gordon Walker, 1972, p. 39). However, similar arrangements were re-introduced during the Second World War, following which Attlee's government – with a heavy programme of social and economic reconstruction – retained them as a permanent peacetime structure, as they have remained ever since. As a minute by Prime Minister Callaghan in 1978 stated, 'The Cabinet committee system grew up as the load on the Cabinet itself became too great' (Sedgemore, 1980, p. 77).

Two main types of Cabinet committee can broadly be identified: *standing committees* (which may form sub-committees) and *ad hoc committees*. Most postwar governments have had standing committees covering defence, economic policy, home affairs, social services, legislation, and future legislation (Mackintosh, 1977, p. 528). Consisting essentially of ministers (Cabinet Office officials may also attend), chaired by senior Cabinet members, and each covering broad policy fields, committees of this kind are now a permanent feature of central administration.

Many *ad hoc committees*, by contrast, are either temporary – being formed to deal with particular problems – or are for long periods inactive. The temporary committees are often entitled Misc (short for miscellaneous) followed by a number, a title which conceals the influence which many of them wield. In 1981/82, for example, Misc 7, consisting of the Prime Minister and four Cabinet colleagues, was effectively responsible for the decision to replace Polaris with the Trident missile system. Of those inactive for long periods some recur: Mackintosh (1977, p. 528) cites the Agriculture Committee revived annually for price reviews. Others are resurrected to deal with particular crises: examples are the Transition to War Committee, chaired by the Cabinet Secretary (responsible for planning mobilisation in the event of war between NATO and Warsaw Pact countries); and the Civil Contingencies Unit, chaired by the Home Secretary (responsible for planning to 'break strikes' and keeping 'essential industries going') (Hennessy, *The Times*, 10 February 1981).

The *composition* of Cabinet committees is determined by the

Prime Minister, although usually representatives from all 'interested' departments are included. On average each Cabinet minister attends three or four committee meetings each week, and usually spends more time (four to six hours) in committee than in full Cabinet (three to five hours) (Headey, 1974, p. 36). Partly to ease the burden upon Cabinet ministers, junior ministers and civil servants often represent their departments on committees, especially on less important ones. Civil servants also sit on the 'official' committees which 'shadow', and often influence, the ministerial Cabinet committees.

Cabinet committee *functions* are also technically a matter of prime ministerial discretion, although essentially they perform a twofold role: a) they enable problems to be delegated for detailed consideration and resolution on the Cabinet's behalf. This allows matters to receive the attention they require, and saves Cabinet time. b) They allow less important items to be resolved without involving the Cabinet. Normally a policy initiative emanating from a department is sent by the Cabinet Office to the appropriate standing or sub-committee for a decision. (Usually, it will also be discussed beforehand by the shadowing official committee or, if the Cabinet Office feels much more work is required, an *ad hoc* official committee may be formed.) As a rule, appeals against committee decisions to the full Cabinet are not allowed without approval from the committee chairman concerned. This arrangement, although not always rigidly applied (Jones, 1975, p. 48), has, since its introduction in 1967, greatly enhanced the importance of Cabinet committees, giving their decisions virtually the same authority as the Cabinet itself.

Cabinet committees undoubtedly improve the efficiency of the Cabinet machine, keeping the Cabinet agenda free from all but the most important and controversial issues. They are the means by which the Cabinet machine has adapted to the twentieth-century increase in the volume and complexity of government business, producing a Cabinet *system* of government in place of the nineteenth-century 'Cabinet government' described by Bagehot. Significantly, however, they have also altered the decision-making process within central administration in a manner which arguably strengthens the Prime Minister at the expense of his or her Cabinet colleagues. The structure, composition, remit, and chairmen of Cabinet committees are determined by the Prime Minister. Sometimes committees have been established 'to by-pass ... a particular minister' (Mackintosh, 1977, p. 521); at other times their decisions – and even their existence – have allegedly been concealed from other Cabinet members (Benn, 1982, p. 29; Sedgemore, 1980, pp. 14–15). Several issues of fundamental importance, in fact, have allegedly been decided in committee without full Cabinet knowledge: Crossman (1963, pp. 54–6), for example, cites the Attlee government's decision to manufacture the atom bomb and Eden's decision to invade Suez in 1956. One conclusion drawn by some observers (Benn, 1982; Crossman, 1963; Mackintosh, 1977; and Sedgemore, 1980) is that Cabinet committees (as well as partial and inner Cabinets) have resulted not simply in the demise of Cabinet government, but in its replacement, effectively, by prime ministerial government.

Not all observers accept this analysis. Gordon Walker (1972, pp. 85–91), for example, rejects Crossman's interpretation of decisions such as manufacture of the atom bomb and Suez. Jones (1975, p. 49) argues that committees and partial Cabinets are subordinate to the Cabinet which 'is a constant restraint on them and whose reactions they anticipate'. They also include influential ministers whose support the Prime Minister must retain. Significantly, Crossman, a leading member of the prime ministerial school, argued while a member of Wilson's Cabinet for the establishment of an inner Cabinet to restrain the Prime Minister from making policy through private consultations with departmental ministers (Jordan, 1978).

While the contribution of Cabinet committees to the capacity for prime ministerial government is a matter for argument, their effect upon the efficiency of central administration is not. To quote Sir Harold Wilson (1977, pp. 86, 89), Cabinet committees 'make the whole government more effective ... If the system had not existed, it would have had to be invented.'

The Cabinet Office

The business of the Cabinet and its committees is co-ordinated by the Cabinet Office. Formed in 1916 to enable the Cabinet to operate under war pressures, it has, during the twentieth century, developed into 'the "nerve-centre" of British Government' (Jones, 1975, p. 50). By the 1970s it comprised some 700 staff, many of whom were senior civil servants seconded from departments. Its head, the Cabinet Secretary, is one of the most influential figures in Whitehall, and also holds the post of Head of the Home Civil Service.

In 1983 the Cabinet Office comprised five main components:

(i)   *The Cabinet Secretariat* is the original and most important component. Its work is closely linked with the Cabinet: it assists the Prime Minister in preparing the Cabinet agenda, keeps Cabinet minutes, transmits Cabinet decisions to departments and monitors their implementation. It performs similar functions for Cabinet committees and sub-committees, also providing a 'neutral' chairman for them when necessary.

(ii)   *The Central Statistical Office*, added to the Cabinet Office in the 1940s, by the mid-1970s accounted for about half of total Cabinet Office staff. It prepares and interprets statistics for use in policy-making, and co-ordinates government statistical work.

(iii)   *The Historical Section,* which is responsible for the preparation of official histories.

(iv)   *The Government's Chief Scientific Officer* has been housed in the Cabinet Office since 1966.

(v)   *The Management and Personnel Office* responsible for civil service personnel management, training and recruitment was established in 1981 following disbandment of the Civil Service Department. Although having departmental status, the M and PO is housed within the Cabinet Office and operates under the Cabinet Secretary's supervision. Ministerial responsibility for the Office rests ultimately with the Prime Minister, although day-to-day work is usually delegated to a subordinate minister. These arrangements, when introduced, were widely interpreted as an attempt by Mrs Thatcher to secure greater central direction over civil service management and efficiency.

The Cabinet Office, clearly, is more than just a secretariat. It is today 'the main co-ordinating office' within central administration (Mackintosh, 1977, p. 519). As the 'general administrative co-ordinator of Government' (Jones, 1975, p. 50) it monitors the implementation of Cabinet decisions by departments and acts as a 'clearing house' for inter-departmental communications. It also has a central role in policy co-ordination, invariably being involved in important initiatives emanating from departments. Normally a department wishing to raise an item in Cabinet (or committee) produces an advance paper. Other departments with an interest may also produce papers, the Cabinet Office's minimum role being to ensure that such papers are circulated in good time and that all appropriate departments are consulted. The Office may also produce a 'neutral' steering brief for committee chairmen. Its maximum role is to try to remove any apparent defects in proposals, and to resolve any inter-departmental differences. To quote Hennessy (*The Times*, 8 March 1976), 'whether it requires fine-tuning or knocking heads together, this is where policy is invariably handled in its final stages'.

To perform this role the Cabinet Office possesses considerable resources. Its prestige usually enables it to obtain advice and co-operation from departments and most Cabinet Office staff specialise in specific fields. Such are its resources 'that the most difficult problems of recent years – devolution, Northern Ireland and British policy towards the European Community – have all been handed to special units' within it (Mackintosh, 1977, pp. 519–20). By the late 1970s it had a clear internal hierarchy, 'with groups of functions organized around each of the deputy secretaries' and with 'second permanent secretaries' being appointed to head some of the new policy units (Editorial. *Public Administration*, vol. 60, no. 1 (1982), p. 8).

The Cabinet Office's development reflects the twentieth-century expansion of government activity and the increase in potential points of inter-departmental conflict. In the interests of co-ordination it has been necessary to strengthen the 'centre' against departments. Significantly, the Treasury – the original co-ordinating department – has long sought to absorb the Cabinet Office (see, for example, Hennessy, *The Times*, 8 March 1976). That it has failed is partly because the Treasury, as a department itself, cannot be neutral in inter-departmental battles; and partly because the Prime Minister – the minister closest to the Cabinet Office – has more control over co-ordination by having important functions performed there.

Although the Cabinet Office serves the Cabinet collectively, it operates under prime ministerial direction. Its development has greatly increased the Prime Minister's administrative support: it transmits his or her views throughout central administration, warns about problems 'looming up', and provides a mechanism for bringing particularly complex problems under closer prime ministerial control. Despite this the Cabinet Office is not *the* Prime Minister's department. It serves the Cabinet collectively, its responsibility being to execute the wishes, not of the Prime Minister, but of the Cabinet. Indeed, not having a department leaves the Prime Minister under-resourced relative not only to departmental ministers, but possibly also to the chief executives of most other

national governments. The implications of this are further discussed in the next section.

A Prime Minister's Department?

The Prime Minister is the focal point of the Cabinet. He or she
summons and chairs its meetings, appoints its members, determines its agenda, sums up discussion, appoints members and
chairmen of Cabinet committees, and supervises the Cabinet
Office. Thus, while subject, like other ministers, to the final
authority of the Cabinet, in practice the Prime Minister exercises
considerable influence over it.

The Prime Minister is heavily involved in the policy-making,
administrative, and co-ordinating work of central administration.
Major policy initiatives usually come to the Prime Minister's notice
before they reach the Cabinet, while subjects assuming major
importance within Parliament, the media, or the party, will usually
at some stage receive his or her personal attention. Once directly
involved in an issue, moreover, the Prime Minister is powerfully
placed to steer it through the Cabinet system. Of course, no Prime
Minister can deal personally with all policy matters. His or her
involvement is inevitably selective but, when it does occur, may
well be crucial to the outcome.

The Prime Minister also becomes involved in major administrative issues. While departmental ministers are primarily responsible
for policy implementation, the Prime Minister will usually react to
'danger signals' suggesting that departmental administration is
suspect. The Prime Minister, moreover, exercises substantial control over the government machine: he or she has considerable
control over the departmental pattern (see pp. 24–30) while
appointments to the most senior civil service posts usually require
prime ministerial approval. The Prime Minister also plays a crucial
co-ordinating role, having access to all ministers and – through the
Cabinet Office – communications with all departments. As Rose
(1980, p. 34) explains, his or hers is an ideal vantage point from
which 'to scan the horizon', to see the 'interconnections among
policies', and to 'steer policies toward certain broad political
objectives, and away from recognizable difficulties'.

Despite these responsibilities, only limited resources are available
directly to the Prime Minister (as opposed to the Cabinet collectively). These are mainly located in the *Prime Minister's Office*,

which usually contains around eighty full-time staff employed in four main groups (Jones, 1980). These are:

(i) *The Private Office*, staffed by civil servants, which keeps the Prime Minister's diary, deals with correspondence, and provides briefing material. It is headed by the Prime Minister's Principal Private Secretary who leads a small team of assistant private secretaries – normally 'high fliers' on secondment from departments – each covering broad policy areas.

(ii) *The Political Office*, usually consisting of political appointees chosen by the Prime Minister, has been an important feature of recent governments. It provides political advice, and help with constituency and party duties. Its members have sometimes allegedly exercised considerable influence, most notably Mrs Marcia Williams (Lady Falkender) who headed Wilson's political office (Jones, 1976, esp. pp. 34–6; and Williams, 1972).

(iii) *The Prime Minister's Press Office*, which handles public relations and acts as a link between the Prime Minister and journalists. It may be headed either by a civil servant or by a journalist with sympathies close to the Prime Minister (see Jones, 1976, pp. 34–6; and Haines, 1977).

(iv) *The Policy Unit*, created in 1974 by Wilson (see pp. 51–2), operates as a policy analysis unit capable of providing advice independently of the official machine. Acting on its own initiative, or at the Prime Minister's request, it is usually headed by a political sympathiser of the Prime Minister. Other members may include either political appointees or civil servants seconded from departments (Jones, 1980, pp. 12–14, 30; and Stephenson, 1980, pp. 32–4).

Collectively these resources are meagre, and leave the Prime Minister ill equipped 'to compete with the Cabinet Office or other departments' (Jones, 1975, p. 55). Significantly, by 1982 Mrs Thatcher had supplemented them by adding to the Prime Minister's Office special advisers in key policy areas such as the economy, foreign affairs, and defence. While by no means a new departure, the calibre of these appointees aroused 'speculation' that Mrs Thatcher 'was seriously contemplating the establishment of a prime minister's department to ... provide an alternative view of policy to that offered by the departments' (Peele, 1983, p. 103). Following the 1983 General Election such speculation was further reinforced by the removal of the 'Rayner' efficiency unit (see p. 23) from the Management and Personnel Office 'to become directly answerable to No. 10'. Although housed in the Cabinet Office, the Unit – headed from mid-1983 by Sir Robin Ibbs – was intended to 'be in effect an extension of the Prime Minister's Office', thereby providing Mrs Thatcher with a 'personal instrument' for promoting managerial efficiency throughout Whitehall (Hennessy, *The Times*, 19 July 1983). Developments such as these suggested to some observers that, despite 'formal protestations to the contrary . . . at the end of the Thatcher administration government centralisation will indeed have been reinforced and there may be a prime minister's department in all but name' (Peele, 1983, p. 104).

The case for a Prime Minister's department, in fact, has frequently been advanced, and rests on three main arguments.

(i) The Prime Minister requires briefing and policy options other than those presented by the departments. To some extent this facility is already provided by the Policy Unit and the Prime Minister's special advisers. However, a Prime Minister's department would be able to tap more expertise, present a wider range of options, and produce more thoroughgoing analyses than are presently available.

(ii) Prime ministers need staff commensurate with their range of functions. A former head of the CPRS has observed (*The Times*, 6 December 1980) that arguments for a Prime Minister's department are strengthened by the need for modern prime ministers 'to answer to Parliament and the press for virtually every government activity' and by 'the growth in contacts between heads of governments'.

(iii) The need to strengthen the Prime Minister's co-ordinating role. Sir John Hoskyns, former head of Mrs Thatcher's Policy Unit, has likened Whitehall to 'a "headless chicken" incapable of developing a central strategy for the government' (*The Times*, 8 November 1982). A Prime Minister's department could possibly fill this gap, assisting the Prime Minister to not only develop 'central strategy' but also to monitor its implementation throughout central administration.

Common to most such arguments is an awareness that, despite presiding over a highly centralised political system, British prime ministers lack the capability for central direction possessed by most other chief executives (Rose and Suleiman, 1980). Placing those functions performed by the Cabinet Secretariat, the former CPRS, and the public expenditure and manpower units of the Treasury and the Management and Personnel Office *directly* under prime ministerial control would 'make an effective equivalent of the White House Staff with the other agencies co-ordinating work for the President' (Mackintosh, 1977, p. 519).

There are, however, equally powerful *arguments against establishing a Prime Minister's department*. These include:

(i)   A Prime Minister's department is arguably unnecessary. Although the Cabinet Office serves the whole Cabinet, it gives considerable assistance to the Prime Minister and is 'the functional equivalent' of prime ministerial departments in other countries (N. Johnson, *The Times*, 17 November 1982). As Sir Harold Wilson (1977, p. 106) argues, a Prime Minister's department is unnecessary as 'everything he could expect to create is there already to hand in the Cabinet Office'.

(ii) A Prime Minister's department is not only administratively unnecessary, but arguably also undesirable. Such a department could impose serious administrative burdens upon the Prime Minister. It would also develop its own attitudes and tend to urge these upon the Prime Minister. Consequently, the Prime Minister's status as a 'neutral' Cabinet chairman, and his or her ability to help Cabinet colleagues reach unified decisions, would be seriously impaired.

(iii) A Prime Minister's department would downgrade other departments and increase the Prime Minister's capacity to impose his or her will on Cabinet colleagues. Such a development could not, therefore, be considered without reference to the debate about prime ministerial government.

To understand the force of this latter argument it should be stressed that control of the Cabinet and government machine (see previous section) forms only part of the potential for prime ministerial government. Alongside this must be seen the Prime Minister's role as *party leader*: not only does this confer influence in party manoeuvring, but the increasing focus on party leaders at elections (Seymour-Ure, 1974, pp. 202–39) enables a victorious Prime Minister to claim a personal mandate. The Prime Minister is also *the most important MP*, being able to dissolve Parliament and (through the whips) normally to determine how it votes. These powers are further strengthened by patronage. The Prime Minister appoints (and dismisses) ministers, and influences the conferment of knighthoods, peerages, and appointments to state bodies (Benn, 1982, pp. 26–8; and Sedgemore, 1980, pp. 57–63); hence, he or she can reward party workers, MPs, and ministers who show loyalty and overlook those who do not. The Prime Minister also hands in the government's resignation, which – like the dissolution power – might be used or threatened to bring rebels into line (Sedgemore, 1980, pp. 66–7). He or she is also the focus of the media, and thus well-placed to set the subject and mood of public debate.

This concentration of power in the Prime Minister is, of course, counterbalanced by important constraints. One is the amount of work, which limits the time that can be devoted to all but the most important issues. Another is the need to retain party and parliamentary support (p. 58) which may necessitate policy compromise and limit prime ministerial freedom with ministerial appointments. Because of the political damage that the resignation of key ministers might cause, the Prime Minister must carry ministerial and party colleagues with him or her. Numerous observers (Jones, 1965; Gordon Walker, 1972; Wilson, 1977) in fact reject the prime ministerial thesis, emphasising the collective role of the Cabinet and the constraints which make it difficult for prime ministers to act alone.

Whichever view is most accurate, the Prime Minister's bureaucratic resources are a factor in the equation, and the establishment of a Prime Minister's department would undoubtedly be seen as a further step towards prime ministerial government. The administrative gains of such a development are, moreover, also questionable. While a Prime Minister's department would undoubtedly enhance the potential for prime ministerial direction of policy and administration, it would also leave the Prime Minister with less time and detachment to devote to inter-departmental and strategic problems. According to Rose (1980, p. 321) a Prime Minister's primary concern is 'with meta-policy, that is, relationships between the particular policies of different ministries or sub-governments'. It is an open question whether a Prime Minister's department would impair, rather than enhance, the ability to perform this role.

5 CENTRAL ADMINISTRATION IN ACTION

In advanced political systems bureaucratic influence is inevitable. In Britain such influence is checked by constitutional restraints: civil servants work under the direction of ministers who are accountable to Parliament. This constitutional bureaucracy owes much to history, having evolved during the early nineteenth century (see Parris, 1969). Since that time, as governmental workload has increased, it is frequently alleged that civil servants – not ministers – effectively run central administration. This chapter focuses on central administration in the context of the complex relationships which exist between civil servants and ministers.

Key Personnel in Central Administration

There are two main types of personnel: ministers and civil servants.

(i) *Ministers*, who provide the political leadership. Normally drawn from the majority party in the House of Commons, most are MPs, although a minority – usually about 20 per cent – may be peers. During the twentieth century, as central administration has grown, so too has the number of ministers, from sixty in 1900 to 103 in 1983.

Today, most departments are headed by a small ministerial team, only one of whom – usually denoted by the title *Secretary of State* – sits in the Cabinet. Sometimes major departments, e.g. the Treasury, may have more than one Cabinet representative, as also, exceptionally, may other departments (see Jones, 1975, pp. 44–5). Below Cabinet rank are two subordinate ministerial tiers. First, full ministers not in the Cabinet: sometimes these may head small departments (e.g. Minister of Overseas Development), but more usually they are second-rank ministers – known as *Ministers of State* – in large departments (e.g. Minister of State, Home Office). Below these are *Parliamentary Under Secretaries of State*, sometimes colloquially known as junior ministers. (These should not be confused with *Parliamentary Private Secretaries*, who are unpaid ministerial aides and not officially members of the government.) Although the Secretary of State remains constitutionally responsible to Parliament for the work of his or her ministerial subordinates, in practice departmental business is usually allocated between members of the ministerial team. Indeed, in many cases junior ministers take the 'final' ministerial decision, leaving the Secretary of State free to concentrate on the most important matters. Non-Cabinet ministers also frequently sit on inter-departmental and Cabinet committees, and are thus a factor in relations between, as well as within, departments.

The most important member of a department's ministerial team is the *Secretary of State*: he or she represents the department in Cabinet and has overall control of its affairs. According to Headey (1974, chs 9–11) three broad ministerial roles are identifiable: *(a) Policy Initiators:* ministers making a significant contribution to departmental policy. *(b) Executive Ministers* who, while regarding policy formulation as important, also attach importance to departmental management: Denis Healey, for example, when Minister of Defence (1964–70), paid great attention to departmental organisation and use of resources. *(c) Ambassador Ministers* who, like Tony Benn as Minister of Technology (1966–70) and Secretary of State for Industry (1974–5), attach priority to publicising the policies and services of their department. While most ministers devote some attention to all these roles, as a rule their routine is so demanding that there is insufficient time to pursue all three simultaneously with any great effect.

Prior to taking office, most Cabinet Ministers have served a long 'apprenticeship', both in Parliament and in different departments, working their way up the ministerial hierarchy. Few, however, have specialised knowledge of their department's work (which can inhibit the 'policy initiator' role) or have prior experience of running large organisations (thereby inhibiting the 'executive minister' role). The background of British ministers, in fact, differs dramatically from their equivalents in many other countries: for example, Dutch ministers tend to be specialists in the work of their departments, while in the USA they are often experienced business executives (Headey, 1974, pp. 249–69). It is at least arguable whether the ministerial contribution to departmental policy-making and management would be greater if a different pattern of ministerial recruitment and career development was adopted in Britain.

(ii) *Civil servants.* The term 'civil servant' lacks precise definition, an ambiguity which is not just of academic significance. As the Expenditure Committee observed in 1977 (HC, 535, I, p. lxxvii), 'the vagueness of definition has given scope for a fruitless juggling of statistics in which numbers of "civil servants" are bandied about which are really almost meaningless'. Thus in 1974, officials in the Manpower Services Commission and associated agencies were excluded from official civil service statistics, but two years later were included in them. This imprecision, while sometimes politically convenient for ministers and civil servants, makes any attempt to interpret civil service statistics fraught with difficulty.

Notwithstanding such difficulties, the most authoritative definition is that used in the annual *Civil Service Statistics*. This essentially defines a civil servant as:

> A servant of the Crown working in a civil capacity who is not the holder of a political (or judicial) office; the holder of certain other offices in respect of whose tenure special provision has been made; a servant of the Crown in a personal capacity paid from the Civil List. (*Civil Service Statistics*, HMSO, 1982, p. 3)

This definition, while leaving ambiguity as to whom precisely it includes, nevertheless excludes ministers, judges, members of the armed forces, and employees of nationalised industries, local government, and the NHS. In January 1983 some 652,500 full-time equivalent civil servants were officially in post, of which 520,300 were non-industrials, and 132,200 industrials (*Civil Service Statistics*, 1983, p. 6).

As government work has expanded during the twentieth century, civil service numbers have increased sharply (see Table 1.1). This increase, however, has been at a vastly greater rate than has occurred with ministers. Kellner and Crowther-Hunt (1980, p. 220) have observed: 'In 1900, we had 50,000 civil servants controlled by about 60 ministers. Today we have some 700,000 civil servants with just over 100 ministers.' This relatively faster growth rate is not without significance for minister/civil service relationships.

Role and Characteristics of Civil Servants

In theory there is a clear distinction between the *political* role of ministers, and the *administrative* role of civil servants. The minister is politically accountable for departmental policy and administrative efficiency, while the civil servant serves the minister and implements policy on his minister's behalf. Several characteristics of the British civil service stem from this distinction between political and administrative roles, the most important being: (i) permanence, (ii) political neutrality, and (iii) anonymity.

(i) *Permanence.* Britain, unlike some countries (e.g. the USA) does not have a 'spoils system', where administrative posts are in the gift of politicians and the occupants usually change with each new government. British civil servants are permanent career officials who work with governments of all political complexions.

(ii) *Political neutrality.* Because British civil servants must serve ministers with differing views, they must observe strict political neutrality. This requires some restrictions on civil servants' freedom: for example, they must avoid partisan political activity, and the expression of views contrary to those of ministers.

(iii) *Anonymity.* Because too close an identification with particular policies or ministers might compromise political neutrality, British civil servants have traditionally enjoyed anonymity. Their relations with, and advice to, ministers, are confidential; and the convention of 'individual responsibility' (Chapter 13) normally ensures that ministers answer for their actions in public and in Parliament.

In recent years some of these traditional characteristics have been weakened as civil servants and their actions have become more open to the public gaze. Senior officials now frequently give evidence to parliamentary select committees (Chapter 13), and the actions of almost any civil servant can be investigated by the Ombudsman (Chapter 14). Some civil servants now even appear at press conferences and on television as departmental spokesmen. Some have also identified closely with particular ministers: Sir William Armstrong, when head of the Home Civil Service, had such a close relationship with Heath that he was nicknamed the 'deputy Prime Minister'. Most problematically, perhaps, the use in recent years of specialist advisers – political appointees who act as temporary departmental officials – has further blurred the traditional concept of a permanent, politically-neutral, and anonymous civil service (see pp. 84–6).

Under modern conditions, of course, the distinction between political and administrative roles is far from clear. It is blurred not only by the policy/administration dichotomy, but also because today ministers have to recognise the *administrative* implications of their policy decisions. Indeed, much ministerial time is devoted to discussions about resources (finance, manpower etc.) necessary to implement policy. Conversely, under modern conditions, civil servants not only take policy decisions but – as the size of the administrative machine makes ministerial control impossible – they must also bear some responsibility for administrative efficiency. In addition they must develop an awareness of their minister's *political* position – anticipating party reaction, parliamentary questioning/criticism, public opinion and so forth. Indeed, so narrow is the dividing line between political and administrative roles that, as Brown and Steel (1979, p. 131) observe, 'When the relationship between Ministers and civil servants is examined in detail the crude differences ... begin to melt away'.

Civil Servants and Ministers: Working Relationships

The constitutional distinction – between ministers who make policy, and civil servants who advise upon and administer it – bears little relationship to what actually happens. In practice, civil servants are far more influential than their constitutional position suggests. Their relationship with ministers, however, as Brown and Steel (1979, p. 127) observe, 'is a complex and subtle one, varying with different personalities and circumstances'. For convenience it can be explored in relation to six key factors.

(A)   TENURE OF OFFICE

Civil servants, once appointed, have tenure and cannot easily be removed. Although they frequently change jobs they are nevertheless 'able to develop an expertise within a particular area of policy and administration which the minister will find difficult if not impossible to emulate' (Pitt and Smith, 1981, p. 51). This permanence contrasts with the transitory nature of ministers, who spend a *relatively* short time in government and rarely remain in the same department for more than a few years before being moved on. In Conservative governments from 1951 to 1964 the median tenure of departmental ministers was twenty-eight months (Headey, 1974, p. 96). Under Harold Wilson's administration from 1964 to 1970 the median tenure for Cabinet Ministers was one year thirty-two weeks, while from 1974 to 1979 the median tenure was two years five weeks (Alderman and Cross, 1981, p. 428). The product of frequent ministerial 're-shuffles' – usually dictated by political rather than administrative considerations – the effect is often to leave ministers with insufficient time to acquire adequate expertise to enable them to formulate and implement key policies. As Anthony Crosland has commented, 'I reckon it takes you six months to get your head properly above water, a year to get the general drift of most of the field, and two years really to master the whole of a Department' (Boyle and Crosland, 1971, p. 43). The irony is, of course, that just as ministers begin to master their departmental work they are invariably transferred to another post. Consequently, as Kellner and Crowther-Hunt (1980, p. 213) observe, when ministers and civil servants disagree 'it is not an equal contest between two temporary incumbents, but an unequal match between a temporary minister and the permanence of the accumulated experience and policy of the department itself'.

(B)   EXPERTISE

Lack of specialist preparation for ministers (p. 74) is compounded by the absence of planned career development. Ministers move from department to department, often for pragmatic political reasons, as the Prime Minister directs, rarely having relevant expertise in their new policy areas. Headey (1974, p. 94) shows that in only twelve out of ninety-three Cabinet appointments between October 1964 and April 1971 was a minister appointed who had previous experience in the same department or in the same general policy area.

In this vein, Richard Crossman (1975, p. 23) ventilated his own anxiety on his appointment to the Ministry of Housing and Local Government in October 1964: 'It's amazing how in politics one concentrates on a few subjects. For years I've been a specialist on social security and I know enough about it. Science and education I had picked up in the months when I was Shadow Minister. But I've always left out of account this field of town and country planning . . . all this is utterly remote to me and it's all unlike what I expected.' In this context, the initial dominance of the Permanent Secretary, Dame Evelyn Sharp, was hardly surprising.

Anthony Crosland's career provides a good example of the difficulties facing ministers attempting to acquire and develop expertise in specific policy areas:

1964–5:   Minister of State, Economic Affairs
1965–7:   Secretary of State for Education and Science

1967–9: President of the Board of Trade
1969–70: Secretary of State for Local Government and Regional Planning
1974–6: Secretary of State for the Environment
1976–7: Foreign Secretary.

In nine years as a minister Crosland held six different posts with little logical progression from an expertise standpoint. 'Ministers do not serve a long apprenticeship in their departments in a junior position as do many managing directors in industry, but instead are catapulted into their offices with minimal preparation. Thus it is the rare exception to find a minister ... who has prepared himself for the burdens of the office which he assumes' (Pitt and Smith, 1981, p. 52).

Some ministers do, of course, stay in a single policy area/department for several years, e.g. Denis Healey (1964–70) was Minister of Defence and from 1974 to 1979 was Chancellor of the Exchequer. Additionally, of course, some departments are less specialised and technical than others, so at least some ministers can be expected to pick up departmental threads fairly quickly. Nevertheless, given the increase this century in both the scope and complexity of government, many policy decisions are inevitably made in areas where ministers are unlikely to have any expertise. The lack of career development for ministers plays directly into the hands of senior administrators who often have 'a near monopoly of knowledge relevant to policy-formation' (Smith, 1976, p. 102).

(C) DEPARTMENTAL SIZE

The growth of government, and the disproportionate increase of civil servants relative to ministers (see p. 75) has further tilted 'the balance of Whitehall power more in favour of civil servants and away from ministers' (Kellner and Crowther-Hunt, 1980, p. 220). Departmental management is theoretically the province of ministers, but the size and functional range of many modern departments – particularly those which came into being following mergers in the 1960s and 1970s – in practice makes this impossible. As Kellner and Crowther-Hunt (1980, p. 220) observe, four ministers in the Environment Department cannot realistically control 38,000 officials; likewise a massive department like Health and Social Security, with 96,850 civil servants in 1982, cannot be effectively controlled by a single Secretary of State, two ministers of state, and four under-secretaries. The growth of government, in short, has largely outstripped the capacity of ministers to control their departments. As Pitt and Smith (1981, p. 53) put it, 'increase in the size of organizational units has inevitably led to officials having the power to decide what issues will be referred to ministers and what can be resolved without ministerial intervention'.

(D) WORKLOAD

Just as the size and complexity of departments often strengthens the hand of civil servants, so likewise workload prevents ministers from dealing personally with more than a limited number of issues. Not only does the bulk of departmental work continue without ministerial involvement, but ministers have a wide range of duties *outside* their departments. Between 1964 and 1974, one survey found, ministers spent a minimum of sixty hours each week working; of this at least forty-five hours were spent in Cabinet and Cabinet committees, Parliament, interviews and discussions outside the department, receptions and lunches, official visits, as well as constituency responsibilities. 'In other words, every minister has a strenuous full-time job as politician and as ambassador for his department *before* he can deal with the direct task of running his department' (Kellner and Crowther-Hunt, 1980, p. 216). In these circumstances ministers inevitably become very dependent on civil service briefing papers presenting clear recommendations. As Smith (1976, pp. 105–6) explains, 'a minister's policy-making responsibilities are outnumbered by other tasks ... policy matters often appear to be dealt with in whatever time is left over from other commitments'.

Pressure upon time can sometimes be played on by civil servants: for example, by briefing ministers at the 'last minute' when there is insufficient time to search for alternatives to options recommended by officials; and by requesting 'urgent' approval of complex decisions when the minister is short of time. (For example, see Crossman, 1975, esp. p. 79.) As Norton (1982, p. 77) explains, 'A minister with a crowded diary, one organised for him by his officials, is not in the best position to maintain effective supervision of the empire under his nominal control'.

(E) INFORMATIONAL RESOURCES

Ministers depend heavily on civil servants for information. Issues working their way up through the Whitehall hierarchy are documented at every level in reports and minutes drafted by civil servants. Civil servants, likewise, filter the demands of client groups and determine the options to be presented to ministers. As a result, ministers on most issues take 'their' decisions on the basis of civil service briefs containing carefully sifted background information and official recommendations. 'Ministers', as Kellner and Crowther-Hunt (1980, p. 237) put it, 'confront problems on the basis of papers written by officials.'

The way information is presented, of course, may help to shape both the decision and its implementation. Benn (1980, p. 68) cites one interesting example of alleged bureaucratic manipulation of information. A draft Defence White Paper presented to one Cabinet meeting showed such a gap in the military balance between East and West as to arouse questioning:

> It turned out that in calculating the military strength of the West the Ministry of Defence had left out the French armed forces. When questioned the reason given was that NATO did not exercise the same operational control over the French forces as applied to the rest of the alliance ... [This] crude misinformation was designed to win public support for a bigger defence budget by suggesting a more serious imbalance than existed.

(F) IMPLEMENTATION

The implementation or execution of policy is an area where civil servants are particularly important. To a great extent politicians, once policy has been decided, leave implementation to the bureaucracy. Ministerial decisions, however, do not automatically take effect. Occasionally ministerial instructions will be unwittingly overlooked in the welter of departmental work, or will be nullified by the discretion allowed to departmental officials. (The discretion allowed to DHSS counter staff to deal with individual cases, for example, is sometimes considerable.) In addition, however, there are a variety of tactics civil servants may deliberately employ to thwart implementation of policies about which they are sceptical: procrastination, 'discovering' insurmountable obstacles, effecting unworkable solutions, even – according to Shirley Williams – 'losing things' (Norton, 1982, p. 87).

There are several well-documented examples of bureaucratic inertia successfully frustrating the expressed intentions of ministers. One is the 'implementation' of the Fulton Committee's proposals for civil service reform (see pp. 95–107). Another concerns the 1974–6 Labour government's education policy. Page

(1979) has shown how Labour's 1974 election manifesto undertook to 'withdraw tax relief and charitable status from public schools'. The Permanent Secretary at the Department of Education and Science, Sir William Pile, was 'wholly committed to the private sector' of education, and in 1975 he dispatched a memorandum to the Education Secretary displaying all the classic signs of delay: the term 'public school' could not be defined adequately, redefining charitable status was a matter for other departments, withdrawal of tax concessions was the Treasury's responsibility, and so on. Pile concluded:

> these nine words from the manifesto raise technical problems to which at present nobody knows the answers ... action in relation to them lies primarily not with you but with the Home Secretary, the Chancellor of the Exchequer and the Secretary of State for the Environment ... I cannot think of anything that we ourselves can usefully do in the interim.

Needless to say, the government's election commitment was never implemented.

A Ruling Class?

Senior civil servants, it seems, can often thwart ministers; their permanence, expertise, numbers, and the ability to manipulate informational and implementation processes equip them to challenge even the most forceful minister in defence of departmental priorities. That these powers are used, moreover, seems clear from the memoirs of ex-ministers and others with inside knowledge. Marcia Williams (1972), Wilson's political secretary, maintained that the civil service obstructed the policies of the 1964–70 Labour administration, while Benn (1980), Haines (1977), and Castle (1980) make similar points about Labour governments in the 1970s. Neither have criticisms come solely from the left: Mrs Thatcher, for example, was reported in 1980 to be 'highly critical of the influence wielded by officials over both ministers and the choice of where expenditure cuts were to fall' (Norton, 1982, p. 83). Indeed, as Shirley Williams (1980, pp. 92–3) argues, it has become almost standard for Labour politicians to allege that the civil service is Tory, and for the Tories to allege that it is tinged with leftist views. Whatever the true picture, many knowledgeable observers clearly feel that the civil service is not politically neutral, and that public policy is determined at least as much by civil servants as by ministers. Thus Brian Sedgemore depicts civil servants as 'politicians writ large' (Expenditure Committee (1977), I, p. 1xxix); and Kellner and Crowther-Hunt (1980) present them as 'Britain's ruling class'.

Despite these observations, several factors caution against too ready an acceptance of the 'dictatorship of the official' thesis. Much of the evidence on which it is based is anecdotal which, as Goodin (1982, pp. 37–8) observes, *proves* nothing. Allowance must be made, he argues, 'for the possibility that disparate intentions of the various political actions' recorded by 'memoir-mongers ... may aggregate into collective actions in a way that none of them properly understand themselves'. There is also the possibility that bureaucratic hostility may be a scapegoat for ministerial incompetence. Benn's criticism of the civil service, for example, is dismissed by Heseltine (Young and Sloman, 1982, p. 29) as 'one of the classic rationalisations of personal failure'. Benn himself (1980, p. 75), perhaps significantly, quotes a former senior civil servant, Lord Armstrong, who, while admitting that he 'had a great deal of influence', felt that this was partly because 'most ministers were not interested [and] were just prepared to take the questions as we offered them'. Even Sedgemore (1980, p. 103), an arch-critic of civil service influence, concedes that 'most ministers could do more to help themselves' and that their relative lack of influence is largely 'their own fault'.

A further factor is that not all ex-ministers accept the 'dictatorship of the official' thesis. In evidence to the Expenditure Committee (1977, II.2, para. 1877) Edward Heath observed that in his experience 'civil servants were ... clearly and definitely ... under Ministerial control'. Harold Wilson told the same committee (para. 1924) 'that if a Minister cannot control his civil servants, he ought to go'. During the Attlee government's massive nationalisation programme the civil service, according to Morrison (1959, pp. 335–6), was 'loyal to the Government of the day'. There is, in fact, convincing evidence (Headey, 1975, pp. 131–5) that most officials welcome ministers who are capable of taking decisions and who give a firm lead which they can follow. Even where civil servants have been sceptical of ministerial policy, some ministers have nevertheless successfully imposed their will. Barbara Castle, for example, overcame objections in the Ministry of Transport (1965–8) to her integrated transport plan (Pitt and Smith, 1981, p. 53), while Benn scored a 'personal victory' (Sedgemore, 1980, p. 122) against his Energy Department officials over the future development of nuclear power. Benn's victory, however, was short-lived, for the new government returned in 1979 provided civil servants with an opportunity to re-fight 'the battle' and ultimately to win 'the war' (Norton, 1982, p. 88).

If the evidence about civil service power is inconclusive, this is probably because the 'evidence' is 'patchy', and also because the minister/civil service relationship cannot easily be measured. As Smith (1976, p. 108) observes, the 'personalities, ideologies, and circumstances' around which the relationship is built vary considerably. Strong ministers, or strong ideological commitments to policies, inevitably reduce the influence of civil servants: the Thatcher administration, for example, appeared to secure a marked shift towards monetarist policies despite the Keynesian orthodoxy of many Treasury officials. Relationships will also vary with circumstances: for example, a radical policy change is more likely to be effected if ministerial and civil service attitudes coalesce than if they do not. Likewise, a minister is likely to encounter more resistance if his or her proposals threaten conventional departmental wisdom – or departmental ambitions over territory and resources (see pp. 32–3) – than if they do not. Civil servants and ministers, moreover, are not monolithic groupings. Sometimes civil servants will disagree and ministers will be caught up in the battle, perhaps being briefed against one another. At other times ministers may be in disagreement. According to Heseltine (Young and Sloman, 1982, p. 29), Benn achieved so little as a minister not because of civil service obstruction, but because the Prime Minister 'disagreed with Benn [and] stopped him pursuing his ideas'.

As these examples indicate, the minister/civil service dichotomy is too simplistic. That civil servants have more influence, and ministers less, than constitutional theory suggests is undeniable. But where the boundary is drawn is impossible to determine. As Norton (1982, p. 90) concludes, 'the argument ... is not ... an argument of extremes ... The extent to which officials will or will not enjoy a certain mastery over their minister's decisions will vary from minister to minister, depending upon the minister himself, his permanent secretary and other senior officials, the ethos of the department ... and the political conditions then prevailing'.

Special Advisers

As a tentative response to the growing awareness of civil service power, ministers since 1964 have adopted the practice of appointing special advisers to complement the advice supplied by their civil servants. This practice has developed gradually, albeit in a piecemeal manner. From 1964 to 1970 advisers such as Thomas Balogh at No. 10 were much involved in policy-making, but from 1970 to 1974 the Heath government made much less use of such partisan, non-civil service, advice. The 1974–9 Labour governments agreed that any Cabinet minister could appoint two political advisers, and in 1977, for example, there were twenty-six such advisers, six of them working in a Special Policy Unit in the Prime Minister's Office and the rest in thirteen other departments. Mrs Thatcher and her Cabinet employed 'at least twenty-two' policy advisers 'if members of her policy unit and advisers to ministers within departments are counted' (Peele, 1983, p. 100). Some of these appointments (e.g. Sir Anthony Parsons, Professor Alan Walters) were at a very senior level consisting of people well able to provide alternative sources of policy advice to that of civil servants.

Partisan advisers are designed to serve ministerial interests and in part at least are symbolic of the prevailing scepticism which exists – particularly within the Labour Party – towards the civil service. Dr Bernard Donoghue sees them as 'the most important development in modern government in Britain. The machine is now so powerful and the career civil service so big and so influential, and with the capacity effectively to control many ministers, that ministers need an alternative source of advice and information' (Young and Sloman, 1982, p. 88). Nevertheless they have always been appointed on too small a scale 'for the basic relationship between a Minister and his career officials to be altered' (Brown and Steel, 1979, p. 130). Most, moreover, hitherto seem to have been largely neutralised by the civil service. Kellner and Crowther-Hunt (1980, p. 209) maintain that most were 'shunted off into the relatively harmless pursuit of keeping ministers' lines open to Transport House and Labour MPs ... [and] were ... kept away from the very documents and discussions that would have allowed them to marshal information and advise *in time* to affect policy decisions'.

Nevertheless, considerable support for special advisers remains. In 1977 the Expenditure Committee argued that their appointment had merit (I, para. 148–50), and even the civil service appears to have accepted them (Young and Sloman, 1982, pp. 90–1). The apparent institutionalisation of such advisers could point the way towards the French 'ministerial cabinet' system whereby a minister appoints a personal staff of about a dozen members to assist him or her, although a serious attempt to examine such a proposal in the 1970s was dropped due to civil service resistance (Pollitt, 1980, pp. 88–9). In 1982 Sir John Hoskyns, Mrs Thatcher's former senior Policy Adviser, revived the debate by suggesting that between ten and twenty senior civil servants in each department should be replaced by politically appointed officers on contract. He added that such outsiders might initially serve with an opposition party and move into departments when that party won office (Hoskyns, 1983). An even more radical way forward would be the adoption of the US pattern, replacing, wholesale, one administration's top civil servants by those supportive of the incoming government. This would provide ministers with personnel inside their departments to formulate and administer policies in line with the minister's own sympathies. At the same time, however, it would reduce continuity and, probably, administrative expertise. Brown and Steel (1979, p. 332) add that a further difficulty in this context is that Britain 'has no "in-and-outer" tradition and a much less flexible career structure, both in government and in the universities'.

Overview

As this chapter has shown, there are major difficulties in determining the relative influence of ministers and civil servants. Measuring 'power' and 'influence' in any meaningful way is a difficult exercise. With ministers and civil servants, confidentiality presents added difficulties for researchers, as does the fact that relationships vary over time, and with issues, personalities, and circumstances. As Kellner and Crowther-Hunt (1980, p. 238) conclude, 'The exact balance between ministerial and civil service power will very much depend on what is being decided, the political circumstances surrounding it, and the relative abilities of civil servants and ministers'.

While the relative influence of ministers and civil servants is difficult to determine, collectively they wield considerable power. Indeed, it is unwise to distinguish too starkly between their respective roles. Ministers and senior civil servants are part of a relatively small 'Whitehall Universe'; they work together, dine together, sit together on committees, and so on. In Neustadt's view (1966, p. 57) there is an intimate collaboration between civil servants and ministers 'grounded in the interests and traditions of both sides. Indeed, it binds others into a Society for Mutual Benefit: what they succeed in sharing with each other they need share with almost no one else, and governing in England is a virtual duopoly.' However, despite this view, it needs to be remembered that ministers and civil servants are only two out of many constituent elements in the policy community. Most policy proposals in central administration also involve, for example: (a) discussions with interested pressure groups, often presenting conflicting demands to civil servants; (b) discussions with backbench party groups, particularly on contentious issues; (c) where appropriate, discussions with external bodies such as the EEC, NATO, IMF, and so forth.

Ministers and civil servants are obviously integral parts of the policy-making process but it is important to see their contribution alongside that of other groupings. Once again. complexity is the order of the day.

6 REFORMING THE BUREAUCRACY

As administrative and political roles have become blurred under modern conditions, the recruitment, training and management of civil servants has become increasingly significant. Such factors affect not only the policy outputs and efficiency of central administration, but also its capacity to respond to ministerial directions and to wider environmental pressures. Dissatisfaction with the bureaucracy and pressure for reform is, however, nothing new.

Nineteenth-Century Pressure for Reform

Until the nineteenth century there was no clear distinction between political and administrative roles. Recruitment was largely by patronage, and promotion by seniority. Although not conducive to efficiency, contemporary administration was relatively simple: specialised techniques were unnecessary, workload was relatively light, and departments generally were small. Nevertheless, from the late eighteenth century demands for reform began to appear, gathering momentum during the early nineteenth century as the state acquired new functions and administrative costs began to rise.

As the evolution of the civil service receives detailed coverage elsewhere (e.g. Brown and Steel, 1979, ch. 1; and Parris, 1969) this chapter concentrates mainly upon the two major official investigations into the civil service which produced a) the Northcote-Trevelyan Report, 1854, and b) the Fulton Report, 1968. Some contemporary proposals for reform are also examined.

The Northcote-Trevelyan Report

This made four basic main recommendations: a) Recruitment by open competitive examination; b) Promotion by merit; c) Unification of the service; d) A division between 'intellectual' work to be performed by graduates, and 'mechanical' work to be allocated to those of lesser ability. These were radical proposals for the nineteenth century and they were implemented only slowly. In 1855, following administrative shortcomings during the Crimean War, the Civil Service Commission was established to test candidates for recruitment, but not until the early twentieth century were all Northcote-Trevelyan's recommendations implemented.

Of Northcote-Trevelyan's recommendations, the last listed above was probably the most significant, for it influenced the creation of hierarchical class divisions which have survived to this day. It also entrenched the concept of the generalist administrator. In the 1850s, understandably, the efficient performance of administrative work was seen in terms of general ability. Specialist skills were unnecessary because – apart from surveyors and inspectors – there was little need for them. Hence, the argument ran, any able 'intellectual' could meet the demands of the service even at the highest levels. While the Northcote-Trevelyan Report itself noted the advantages of recruiting graduates in 'relevant' subjects – such as political economy – as time passed this was seemingly forgotten. As the Fulton Report (1968, 1, para. 3) observed a century later, 'There emerged the tradition of the "all-rounder" ... or "amateur"'. At lower levels this 'tradition' became equally entrenched: for more routine 'mechanical' tasks – copying, keeping diaries etc. – specialist qualifications were considered even less necessary.

Of course, with the subsequent increase in the volume and complexity of government work, the demands upon civil servants changed substantially. By 1968, when Fulton reported, the civil service was twenty times bigger than in 1854, departments were larger, and work immeasurably greater and more complex. Senior civil servants advised ministers on major policy, took many policy decisions themselves, implemented and co-ordinated complex administrative schemes, and managed large departments. Such tasks required not only high administrative skills, but also managerial ability. They also necessitated employment of a wide range of specialist personnel such as economists, engineers, and statisticians. Even at lower levels within the service mere 'intelligence' was no longer sufficient. Today, relatively routine tasks (e.g. information retrieval or data processing) may require competence in computer handling and quantitative techniques. Since the 1850s, then, the civil service has come to require vastly different skills. And yet, as Fulton observed (1968, 1, para. 6), Northcote-Trevelyan's influence, a century later, was still profound: 'The basic principles and philosophy of the Northcote-Trevelyan Report have prevailed: the essential features of their structure have remained'.

The Fulton Diagnosis

The Fulton Report (1968), the first major official inquiry into the civil service since Northcote-Trevelyan, contained both a detailed analysis of the civil service in the 1960s and major recommendations for improvement. Fulton's analysis clearly revealed the continuing influence of the Northcote-Trevelyan philosophy. *Six main defects* were outlined in the report:

(A) 'GENERALIST' DOMINANCE

The Service is still essentially based on the philosophy of the amateur (or 'generalist' or 'all-rounder'). This is most evident in the Administrative Class which holds the dominant position in the Service. (1, para. 15)

By a 'generalist', Fulton meant 'the gifted layman' who was capable of taking 'a practical view of any problem, irrespective of subject-matter'. Largely a product of historical development, the virtual monopoly of major policy and administrative work held by generalists was still widely justified within the service by the breadth of outlook – as opposed to the 'narrow' approach of specialists – which they arguably brought to the problems of government. They could also arguably communicate more easily with ministers who were themselves usually laymen in departmental matters. Generalists, the argument ran, were 'experts' in the workings of government able 'to synthesize the views of specialists . . . and to evaluate them in terms of what is feasible' (Kellner and Crowther-Hunt, 1980, p. 33).

(B) THE 'CLASS' SYSTEM

The system of classes in the Service seriously impedes its work. (1, para. 16)

Northcote-Trevelyan's division of the service into 'mechanicals' and 'intellectuals' developed during the twentieth century into a hierarchy of *general service (or Treasury) classes*. In 1966, when the Fulton Committee was appointed, these comprised three main classes containing 138,700 members (Clerical Class, 89,500; Executive Class, 46,800; and Administrative Class, 2,400), and each with its own internal grading structure. Found throughout central administration, and staffed essentially by generalists, members of these classes largely monopolised senior policy and administrative work. The most important was the Administrative Class: working closely with ministers its members' primary function was to examine policy options, prepare advice for ministers, and to take responsibility, on behalf of ministers, 'for the administration and control of government departments' (Kellner and Crowther-Hunt, 1980, p. 33).

In addition to the general service classes there was an extensive network of *departmental and specialist classes*. Some departments, because of their specialised work, developed their own variant of the general service classes (e.g. Customs and Excise, Inland Revenue). Some also employed staff with specialist skills, although until 1939 their numbers were so small that each department individually recruited and employed such specialists as it needed. The subsequent increase in specialist staff during and after the war, however, led to a number of separate 'service wide' specialist hierarchies being created (e.g. Accountants, Scientists, Economists, Statisticians and Medical Officers). By the 1960s, as a result, a chaotic structure existed. The service was divided *vertically* into different specialist, departmental, and general service classes; and usually also *horizontally* between higher and lower levels within each class. Altogether Fulton (1968, 1, para. 16) identified '47 general classes whose members work in most government departments and over 1,400 departmental classes'. This situation seriously impeded work: it produced a 'rigid and prolific compartmentalism' which led to the 'setting up of cumbersome organisational forms' and artificially limited 'the range of jobs' on which any individual official could be employed (1, para. 16).

(C) SPECIALIST SKILLS UNDERVALUED

> Many scientists, engineers and members of other specialist classes get neither the full responsibilities ... nor the opportunities they ought to have. (1, para. 17)

The corollary of generalist dominance was that specialists had a subordinate position within the service. Unlike many other countries (e.g. USA, France, Western Germany), where higher civil servants generally have expertise in fields relevant to their work, specialists in Britain were largely excluded from the top departmental posts. Traditionally organised in separate hierarchies parallel to those of generalists, their role was to give technical advice to

generalists who made the final policy recommendations to ministers (see pp. 19–20). So wedded, in fact, to the generalist philosophy was the service, that even in fields where the need for specialists was recognised, minimal numbers were often employed: for
example, in 1968 the Home Civil Service contained only 309
accountants, of whom sixty-four were temporary (1, para. 37).

(D)   LACK OF MANAGEMENT SKILLS

Too few civil servants are skilled managers. (1, para. 18)

Although the major managerial role within departments fell to the
Administrative Class, most of the members saw themselves as
policy advisers rather than departmental managers. Partly, Fulton
felt, this stemmed from inadequate training in management. Indeed, *training* generally within the service had a low priority. The
generalist ethos saw practical experience of departmental work as
the best way of 'learning' the job; consequently, formal training
usually involved only short departmental induction courses. Following the Assheton Report (1944), the Treasury was made
responsible for co-ordinating training throughout Whitehall, and in
1963 a Centre for Administrative Studies was established. Nevertheless, the situation, Fulton felt, was unsatisfactory: 'many administrators and specialists ... received inadequate training (or none
at all) in techniques of modern management' while training in
policy fields was devalued because of the frequent job changes
inherent in generalist career patterns (1, para. 97).

(E)   AN ISOLATED AND EXCLUSIVE SERVICE

There is not enough contact between the Service and the rest of
the community. (1, para. 19)

Fulton feared that civil servants, particularly at higher levels,
suffered from 'exclusiveness or isolation' from the outside world.
Partly this was because a career service allowed little opportunity
for familiarisation with other walks of life, but partly also because
recruitment to the Administrative Class had 'not produced the
widening of its social and educational base that might have been
expected'.

Recruitment to the highest administrative levels has since 1870
been by open competition. Although opportunities existed for
recruitment to the Administrative Class by transfer or promotion

from other classes – about two-fifths of its members in 1967 had formerly belonged to other classes (Brown, 1970, p. 46) – those reaching the top posts (Under Secretary, Deputy Secretary, Permanent Secretary) were overwhelmingly graduates recruited direct from university. Many had degrees in arts subjects – between 1957 and 1963 54 per cent had degrees in history and classics alone (Brown, 1970, p. 44) – producing at the top of the service a graduate elite overwhelmingly drawn from arts backgrounds. In 1967, for example, only 12 per cent of graduates within the Administrative Class had degrees in natural sciences, compared with 25 per cent in social sciences, and 63 per cent in arts (calculated from Brown, 1970, p. 47). These trends persuaded Fulton (1, para. 77) that the service was 'more concerned with the quality of a man's degree than its relevance to the work of government', an impression which 'discouraged applications from graduates whose interests and studies are focused on modern problems'.

Graduate recruitment also came from a relatively narrow social spectrum: between 1957 and 1963 85 per cent of direct graduate entrants were from Oxford or Cambridge, 37 per cent had been to boarding schools, and 46 per cent had fathers in social class I (Brown, 1970, p. 44). The causes of these trends have been a matter of considerable controversy. Partly, it may reflect a greater tendency for persons from such backgrounds to consider civil service careers; equally, however, it might reflect a social and educational bias in civil service selection methods. Although recruitment is the responsibility of the independent Civil Service Commission, former or serving Administrative Class officials are prominent upon it – in 1977 all four members were senior Administrative Class officials and three had been civil servants all their working lives. They also figure prominently in selection procedures conducted by the Civil Service Selection Board (CIZBEE), while some of the tests and interviews used may favour certain types of candidate. (For discussion see Kellner and Crowther-Hunt, 1980, ch. 6.)

Whatever the reasons, the higher civil service in the 1960s was not socially representative. What is less clear is whether this had any effect upon its efficiency and performance. It can be argued that a relatively homogeneous higher civil service promotes informal co-ordination (pp. 37–8), and that the recruitment of successive generations of officials from similar backgrounds is conducive to continuity and stability within central administration. On the other hand social composition cannot easily be divorced from attitudes. In Miliband's view (1973, p. 115), the civil service in advanced capitalist societies 'by virtue of its ideological dispositions, reinforced by its own interests ... is a crucially important and committed element in the maintenance and defence of the structure of power and privilege inherent in advanced capitalism', a view arguably reinforced in Britain by the increasing tendency of top civil servants to take up business appointments on retirement (Richardson and Jordan, 1979, pp. 61–70; and Sedgemore, 1980, pp. 154–61). Whichever analysis one accepts, today's higher civil servants are concerned increasingly with administering and making policy for sections of society – welfare recipients, racial minorities, manual workers, etc. – of whom usually they have little direct experience. This, in essence, was Fulton's point (para. 19): 'The public interest must suffer from any exclusiveness or isolation which hinders a full understanding of contemporary problems'.

(F) POOR PERSONNEL MANAGEMENT

Serious criticisms of personnel management. (1, para. 20)

Personnel management deficiencies identified by Fulton stemmed partly from the rigidity of the class structure: 'Each civil servant is recruited to a particular class; his membership of that class determines his prospects ... and the range of jobs on which he may be employed' (1, para. 16). While mobility across class lines was possible – and was increasingly encouraged prior to Fulton – for the majority of officials transfer to another class was unlikely to happen; and, even when it did, transferees usually faced competition for subsequent promotion from younger and better educated candidates who had entered the higher class direct.

These problems Fulton attributed largely to the Treasury which, since the beginning of the century, had generally been responsible for civil service matters. The Treasury's handling of personnel management could not easily be divorced from the primacy of financial and economic considerations, while its Pay and Management Group had 'too few staff and too little expertise' to perform an effective 'central management role'. Consequently, many managerial matters were either delegated to departments or simply discharged by the Treasury on a 'guiding and advisory' basis (1, paras 245–6).

Fulton's Recommendations

Fulton made 158 recommendations. Some were mainly concerned with departmental organisation and are discussed elsewhere (see pp. 20–3). Others, however, were more specific to the civil service, notably the following:

(a) 'All classes should be abolished and replaced by a single, unified grading structure covering all civil servants from top to bottom.'
(b) 'The service should develop greater professionalism both among specialists ... and administrators ... For the former this means more training in management, and opportunities for greater responsibility and wider careers.'
(c) '[When recruiting graduates] more account should be taken of the relevance of their university courses to the job they are being recruited to do.'
(d) 'A Civil Service College should be set up ... [to] provide major training courses in administration and management and a wide range of shorter courses. It should also have important research functions.'
(e) 'A new Civil Service Department be set up ... under the control of the Prime Minister ... The Permanent Secretary of the Civil Service Department should be designated Head of the Home Civil Service.'
(f) '[More attention to] career management.'
(g) 'Greater mobility [between the civil service] and other employments.' (1, pp. 104–6)

The significance of these proposals should not be exaggerated. Many – on career structure, training, administrative specialisation – merely 'set the seal on changes which would have occurred anyway, perhaps at a slower pace' (Brown, 1970, p. 62). Moreover, in concentrating primarily on the higher civil service, the needs of the service at lower levels were largely ignored. Nevertheless, the Fulton Report represented a fundamental rejection of the generalist philosophy. Relevant degrees, training courses, and an open grading structure – while widespread within industry – threatened head-on the generalists' monopoly of senior policy and administrative work. From the outset, therefore, there was powerful potential opposition to Fulton's proposals from the very officials who were to have responsibility for implementing them.

Implementing Fulton

In 1968 Fulton's main recommendations were officially accepted by the government – with one significant exception: the proposal that preference be given to graduate applicants with relevant degrees was rejected. Even for those proposals which were officially accepted, however, civil service attitudes in many cases remained unsympathetic – to a degree which in the event would seriously lessen their impact upon the service.

Implementation focused upon four major areas: *(a)* Creation of a Civil Service Department, *(b)* The abolition of classes. *(c)* The establishment of a Civil Service College, *(d)* Recruitment reforms.

(A)   CREATION OF A CIVIL SERVICE DEPARTMENT (CSD)

This was the first major recommendation to be implemented; necessarily so, for it was to provide the spearhead for implementing the other proposed reforms. Its first Permanent Secretary was designated Head of the Home Civil Service – as Fulton suggested – and ultimate ministerial control vested in the Prime Minister (although day-to-day responsibility was usually delegated to another minister). Its functions encompassed the work of the former Treasury Pay and Management Group, as well as that of the Civil Service Commission. These arrangements gave the CSD responsibility for civil service pay and management, administrative and managerial efficiency, and the recruitment functions of the Civil Service Commission (which formed an independent unit within it).

The CSD, however, never developed the 'central management' capability envisaged by Fulton, and in 1977 Lord Crowther-Hunt described it as 'a very considerable disappointment' (Expenditure Committee (1977), III, p. 1104). Several factors explain this failure:

(i)   Fulton's staffing recommendations were largely ignored by the generalist civil servants appointed to the CSD's upper echelons. Fulton's view (1, para. 255) was that the CSD should not be 'predominantly staffed by officers who have spent most of their careers in the Treasury'; instead, he recommended a mixture of short-and long-term appointments, including staff on secondment from other departments as well as persons from outside with 'experience of managing large organisations'. These recommendations, however, were largely ignored. While some senior officials from other departments were brought in, the CSD, according to Crowther-Hunt (Expenditure Committee (1977), III, pp. 1105–6), was formed largely from the old Pay and Management Group of the Treasury, and the overwhelming majority of its key personnel had generalist backgrounds.

(ii)   The CSD adopted a cautious approach towards other departments. Although Fulton had recommended (1, para. 263, c) that the CSD be empowered 'to call all departments to account for failure to use ... recommended techniques', the CSD in practice tended to interpret its functions 'as a service rather than as mandatory' (Garrett, 1980, p. 63). While this approach – given the strength of departmental independence – is understandable, the fact remains, as Crowther-Hunt observed, that the CSD had 'an unduly limited concept of its role'. He added, 'If the Treasury has the powers, subject to being overridden in Cabinet, to control departmental expenditure, I see no reason why the CSD should not have a similar power over departmental efficiency and manpower' (Expenditure Committee (1977), III, pp. 1105–6).

(iii)   The CSD had an uneasy relationship with the Treasury, which resented its loss of functions to the CSD. As time went on further difficulties arose through separation of the Treasury's public expenditure responsibilities from those of the CSD for manpower costs. Significantly, the Expenditure Committee – which in 1976/7 conducted a major inquiry into the civil service – concluded that 'control of civil service efficiency' should be transferred 'from the CSD to the Treasury' (Expenditure Committee (1977) I, para. 85).

(iv)   Close ministerial involvement in CSD affairs was lacking. Successive prime ministers, although nominally designated Minister for the Civil Service, took little interest in CSD affairs, while 'few of the junior ministers they nominated to take charge of the CSD carried weight in Cabinet or found their political reputations enhanced by promoting the CSD's normal run of business' (Editorial, *Public Administration*, vol. 60, no. 1 (1982), p. 6). There was thus a lack of effective 'political' control over the CSD, which left the generalist officials within its upper echelons considerable freedom to direct its affairs according to their own interests and ideals.

(v)   Successive Permanent Secretaries of the CSD, although designated 'Head of the Home Civil Service', found the CSD somewhat limiting as a base from which to exert influence within Whitehall. Generally, they were little concerned with managerial problems, which they frequently delegated to their deputies within the department.

These factors, coupled with Treasury and departmental resistance, weakened the CSD within Whitehall and in 1981 it was disbanded. The Treasury regained responsibility for manpower, pay, allowances, and pensions, while a new unit within the Cabinet Office, the Management and Personnel Office, absorbed the CSD's other functions (personnel management, recruitment, and training). The latter also initially absorbed the work of Sir Derek Rayner, Mrs Thatcher's 'efficiency' adviser (although this arrangement only lasted until July 1983 – see p. 70). With the CSD's demise the acknowledged instrument for implementing Fulton's reforms finally disappeared. (For discussion, see Chapman, 1983; see also Treasury and Civil Service Committee Report, 1980, HC 54).

(B)   THE ABOLITION OF CLASSES

Fulton's answer to the chaotic class system was to abolish the vertical and horizontal barriers within the service and to replace them with a single unified grading structure similar to that in many large firms and in 'the Civil Service in the United States' (1, para. 218). What Fulton envisaged was 'some twenty grades' containing 'all the jobs from top to bottom in the non-industrial part of the Service' (1, para. 218). While recruitment at different levels, depending on qualifications and experience, would be possible, promotion would be governed not by an official's class but by his or her suitability for the vacant job. This was to apply even at the highest levels – in what Fulton described as the 'Senior Policy and Management Group', embracing the grades from Under Secretary to Permanent Secretary – where the only criterion for appointment was to be 'range of experience, and personal qualities and qualifications' (1, para. 222). Through these arrangements any individual would become eligible for consideration for any job on the sole basis of job suitability.

Single unified grading structures are not unknown in the public sector in Britain: they exist, for example, in the police and the armed forces, in both of which promotion from the lowest to the highest grade (rank) is technically possible. Of course, introducing such arrangements into the civil service would have directly threatened the Administrative Class officials who monopolised major policy and administrative work; and, to a lesser extent, Clerical and Executive officials who, while benefiting from removal of horizontal barriers to upwards promotion, would be exposed to competition from specialists for a whole range of jobs once the vertical barriers were removed. Consequently, widespread opposition to Fulton's proposals developed among generalist civil servants which, coupled with the difficulty of evaluating and grading every job within the service, ultimately proved strong enough to prevent their implementation.

The essence of the post-Fulton structure is that *horizontal* barriers within the service have largely been removed, facilitating upward promotion *within* particular classes (or similar groupings). This has been achieved by merging many former classes into new entities known as 'groups' and 'categories'. Thus in 1971 the Clerical and Executive classes were merged together with the bottom three grades of the Administrative Class (Principal, Senior Principal, Assistant Secretary) to form the new *Administration Group* (see Figure 6.1). This – together with the Economist, Information Officer, Librarian, and Statistician groups – formed part of the General Category, the largest category within the service, employing 235,197 officials in 1982 (*Civil Service Statistics*, 1982, p. 21). Many of the *vertical* barriers within the service, however, have not been removed. These exist not only between the new categories and groups but also between the many remaining departmental (e.g. Inland Revenue grades, Home Office Prison Service grades) and specialist (Medical Officers, Actuaries) classes. Only at the very top of the service, in what is called the *Open Structure*, is

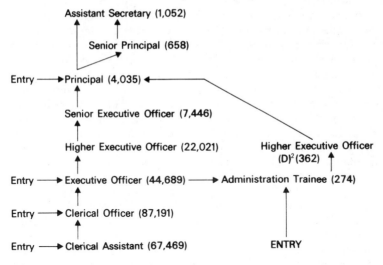

Figure 6.1 *The Administration Group: Grades, Staff Numbers and Career Patterns, 1982*[1]

[1] Full-time equivalents (all staff) in post on 1 January 1982.
[2] Higher Executive Officer (Development) grade replaced former Higher Executive Officer (A) grade in January 1982.
Source: (i) *Civil Service Statistics, 1982*, p. 21; (ii) Civil Service Department (1978), Fig. 3.

there a unified grading structure. Embracing the top three grades (Permanent Secretary, Deputy Secretary, Under Secretary), it included only 736 posts in 1982. Although initially proposed as a 'first stage', subsequent extension to lower levels has not occurred; thus, most of the service is still compartmentalised into vertical units of the kind rejected by Fulton.

While the new structure is undoubtedly tidier than that existing previously, the obstacles to lateral transfer *between* classes (or categories or groups) remain. Only in the Open Structure have vertical barriers totally disappeared, and while promotion into the Open Structure is technically open to staff from any category or group, the small number of posts which it embraces limits its impact upon the service. As a result most specialists are still employed within their own classes (or categories or groups) as also are members of the retained departmental classes.

One corollary of this arrangement is especially significant: the vast bulk of generalists are still organised separately, mostly within the Administration Group, the largest group within the service. Although Assistant Secretaries within this Group seeking promotion to the Open Structure now face competition from personnel at the top of other groups and categories, the 'extra' experience in administration and policy work which employment within the Administration Group provides gives them a marked advantage. In fact the top three grades within the service – those covered since 1972 by the Open Structure – are barely more accessible to specialists than before. A similar proportion, about 40 per cent, are from specialist backgrounds, but most of these are appointed to posts within their own specialism (e.g. an engineer as Chief Water Engineer in the DOE), and very few to Permanent or Deputy Secretary.

To stimulate further movement along the lines suggested by Fulton, the Expenditure Committee in 1977 (I, para. 34) recommended that the Open Structure should be 'speedily' extended 'downwards to Assistant Secretary and equivalent levels', and that the CSD should 'begin work on its extension to the Principal level'. In its reply, however, the government merely promised to 'explore further' the extension of unified grading down to Assistant Secretary and equivalent level (*Government Observations on The Eleventh Report of the Expenditure Committee*, 1978, paras 18–20). There the situation remains. Fulton's concept of a *single* unified grading structure has been abandoned; unified grading exists only in the Open Structure, and the only remaining official commitment is to 'explore' the extension of unified grading to one further grade. The effect inevitably will be to maintain the obstacles for specialists to move into top policy and administrative jobs within the service.

(C) THE ESTABLISHMENT OF A CIVIL SERVICE COLLEGE

The Civil Service College was intended by Fulton to expand central training in three main ways: i) providing post-entry training for administrative recruits in economic, financial or social areas of government; ii) providing courses in administration and management for specialists; iii) to conduct research into administrative problems. In addition the College was to provide 'a wide range of shorter training courses for a much larger body of staff', including staff in local government, industry, and the lower rungs of the civil service.

While these proposals largely built on earlier 1960s developments in training, they nevertheless represented a departure from the traditional 'generalist' view that 'training' was best achieved by practical experience of departmental work. Although the College opened in 1970 – with centres at Sunningdale, London, and (until 1976) in Edinburgh – it nevertheless encountered considerable opposition from within the service and never really functioned as Fulton had intended. Several factors illustrate this:

(i) Fulton proposed an independent governing body drawn from both civil servants and 'a wide range of interests outside the Service' (1, para. 114). This was never implemented; instead, the College was effectively controlled by the CSD and operated as a civil service institution. The bulk of college staff were civil servants, and the minority of academic staff recruited from outside were given only short-term contracts.

(ii) Several College functions recommended by Fulton failed to materialise. For example, the recommendation that generalist administrators should acquire specialised knowledge of either economic/financial administration or social administration (1, para. 100) – a major reason for the College in Fulton's scheme – was never accepted. Again, the research function was barely developed, despite assurances by Wilson in 1968 that the government intended the College to become a major research centre into administrative problems.

(iii) Serious resource constraints 'virtually wiped out' any capacity for 'expansion' after 1970 (Mair, 1977, p. 41). Consequently, the College never provided training on anything like the scale which Fulton had envisaged. In 1980 it provided only 3 per cent of civil service training (Civil Service Department, 1980, p. 49), with most of the remainder being conducted by individual departments. (iv)   Relations between the College and departments were cool. Departments generally did not make promotion dependent upon completing College studies – performance in departmental work usually being the main criterion – and consequently course drop-out rates were high, and morale among College staff and students low.

While many of the College's difficulties stemmed from general-ist-based resistance, the role which Fulton proposed for it was daunting. As an early review (Heaton/Williams Report, 1974, para. 5.3) observed, it was expected 'to combine the roles of All Souls and an adult education centre, with some elements of technical education and teacher training thrown in for good measure'. In practice, the range of courses provided was extremely wide: in 1978/9, for example, it ran 521 courses for 9,300 students, embrac-ing 68,000 student days (Civil Service Department, 1980, p. 49). Most were short courses: the average length was about two weeks. Many covered technical and specialist fields – in subjects such as data processing and managerial services – being attended mainly by junior staff. Courses were also developed for senior staff, although mostly not along lines envisaged by Fulton. In 1976, for example, only 6 per cent of College resources were devoted to graduate specialist courses (Expenditure Committee (1977), III, p. 1,095) to which Fulton attached particular priority. Much of this concen-trated on the *Senior Professional Administrative Training Scheme* (SPATS), designed to provide specialists at Principal level or equivalent with administrative and management skills. It was not a success. Not many 'students' were involved – just 217 between 1972 and 1980 – and most chose to return to their specialisms after 'training' (Garrett, 1980, p. 46).

More disquieting was the *Administration Trainee* (AT) course introduced in 1971 in response to Fulton's criticism of the training of Administrative Class recruits. Comprising about 25 per cent of college days in 1975/6 (15 per cent in 1978/9), the scheme included two ten-week block courses during the first two years. Studies included statistics, economics, public administration, and person-nel management. While an improvement on previous arrange-ments, the programme was widely criticised. 'Many departments', and Administration trainees themselves, frequently complained that courses were insufficiently 'related to the work of departments' (Civil Service Department, 1978, p. 20). 'Reformers', on the other hand, criticised the scheme's superficiality. Two ten-week blocks are inadequate to impart real understanding of the public sector, and fall far short of the equivalent scheme in France (which greatly impressed the Fulton Committee). There, higher civil service recruits – most of which, unlike Britain, have job-relevant degrees – undergo a thirty-month course at the Ecole Nationale D'Administration (ENA). Approximately half the course is college-based, the rest comprises mainly practical work experience in both public and private sectors. Students are stringently assessed and performance has a direct bearing on career prospects (see Stevens, 1978). While the ENA system can be criticised as elitist, it nevertheless produces civil servants of remarkable quality, and illustrates graphically how higher civil service training in Britain could be developed.

To Fulton's supporters the College's record has undoubtedly been disappointing. In a report generally critical of the College the Expenditure Committee (1977, I, paras 16–30) recommended: i) A less 'wide ranging college' concentrating mainly on administrative training, with more specialised training being taken over by departments; ii) 'Additional steps' for the monitoring and assessment of departmental training schemes by the CSD; and iii) the AT scheme to be replaced by a more intensive higher management training course. Admission would be by examination in job-relevant subjects and successful completion would be a prerequisite for promotion beyond Assistant Secretary. These proposals, however, evoked little response from government (see *Government Observations on the Eleventh Report of the Expenditure Committee*, 1978).

Underlying the College's failures it is possible to detect the influence of the generalists to whose continued dominance the Fulton prescription posed a major threat. Perhaps also one can sense a more fundamental problem: whether public administration is an art, to be perfected by practical experience, or a science, to be learned and applied by trained practitioners. The generalist administrator has traditionally accepted the former view; Fulton inclined to the latter. The Civil Service College's halting progress thus probably reflects, partly at least, underlying uncertainty about the nature of public administration itself.

(D)   RECRUITMENT REFORMS

While Fulton dealt with recruitment problems within the whole service (1, paras 59–89), its main focus was upon recruitment at the highest levels. The Report had three main recommendations:

(i)   Preference be given to graduates whose university courses were relevant 'to their future work'. (1, paras 75–7)
(ii) 'Late entry should be considerably expanded' to enable 'people in business, the professions, nationalised industry, local government and the universities' to bring their 'experience' into 'the Service'. (1, para. 124)
(iii) The social and educational base of top civil servants was to be widened, both by recruitment changes, and by the enhanced opportunities for internal promotion throughout the service expected to flow from the introduction of a single unified grading structure.

Some of these proposals, of course, never materialised: preference for relevance was rejected, and single unified grading abandoned. The proposed expansion of late entry also never happened; between 1968 and 1976 an average of only 36 direct-entry Principals per year were recruited. Neither did the AT scheme significantly broaden the social base of post-Fulton administrative recruits. On the contrary, if anything it reinforced the recruitment trends of which Fulton was so critical.

The AT scheme draws recruits from two main sources: i) external applicants with degrees; and ii) serving executive officers (or those of equivalent grades) with a degree or at least two years' service. Initially it was expected that there would be 250–300 ATs per year, 175 from external sources and the remainder from internal candidates. In practice in-service recruits have been fewer than expected – the 1971–80 annual average was thirty-nine and, to compensate, more than 175 external applicants have been recruited in some years. This shortfall of in-service recruits occurred, moreover, despite possible bias against external candidates in AT selection procedures (Chapman, 1982). For various reasons serving executive officers (or equivalents) have been reluctant to apply: only 338 did so, for example, in 1979/80. Consequently, AT recruits have been drawn overwhelmingly from external candidates, with 77.5 per cent of successful applicants between 1971 and 1980 coming from this source.

An additional factor is that internally selected ATs have usually performed less well than external recruits. Within two to four years ATs have normally been 'streamed'. Those with most potential joined the 'fast stream' and were promoted to Higher Executive Officer (A). Originally, it was anticipated that only about one-third of ATs would be fast-streamed: in practice the proportion has been far higher, in some years 80 per cent or more. Based essentially on departmental assessment of performance 'on the job', the Expenditure Committee heard in 1976 that almost all external recruits were fast-streamed compared with only 50 per cent of internal recruits (Expenditure Committee (1977), II.ii, p. 506). Typically, those fast-streamed could expect to reach Assistant Secretary by their late 30s, and thereafter promotion into the Open Structure: those not fast-streamed – as well as other executive officers pursuing their careers by normal upwards progression – would reach Assistant Secretary, if at all, later in their careers, and consequently would be far less likely to secure promotion to grades within the Open Structure. (A further scheme, enabling Higher Executive Officers nominated by departments, whatever their method of entry to the service, to enter a special competition for the fast stream had little effect, with an average of only six candidates per year being re-graded to HEO (A) between 1971 and 1980.) As in the pre-Fulton period, future generations of top civil servants seem likely to be drawn disproportionately from externally recruited graduates.

In other ways, too, pre-Fulton patterns have survived. A pre-ponderance of arts graduates, for example, is still discernible among external recruits, partly because 'preference for relevance' was rejected, but possibly also because of 'bias in favour of Arts and Humanities' within the Civil Service Commission (Expenditure Committee (1977), III, p. 1093). Thus in 1980, 58 per cent of external AT recruits were arts graduates compared with 54 per cent in 1968. Moreover, 60 per cent were Oxbridge graduates (59 per cent in 1968) (Brown and Steel, 1979, p. 77; and Civil Service Commission Annual Report, 1980, pp. 38–9). Commenting on such biases, the Expenditure Committee in 1977 concluded that 'there may be something wrong, with the constitution of the Commission' and with aspects of the selection process (Expenditure Committee (1977), I, para. 13).

The AT scheme, therefore, has failed to widen the background of top administrative recruits. It has also erected an additional barrier to specialists seeking to further their careers within the Open Structure. By providing selected generalists with unique experience in policy and administration, and accelerated promotion to the fringes of the Open Structure, the scheme virtually guaran-tees generalist leadership into the foreseeable future. Specialists, still compartmentalised within their own groups and categories, are not only denied that experience, but are further handicapped by the limited development of courses in administrative studies at the Civil Service College.

The Expenditure Committee, as we have seen, recommended abolition of the AT scheme. It also recommended that:

(i)   Graduates recruited with good degrees should be 'given jobs in the service so that their abilities, other than the solely .academic ones tested by their university, can be assessed. Then they should compete on even terms with others in the service, graduates and non-graduates, for entry' to the proposed new higher management training course.
(ii) The Civil Service Commission (which consisted solely of civil servants) should be enlarged by adding 'a majority of . . . part-time outside Commissioners'.
(iii) Final Selection Boards (which comprised three civil servants and two outsiders) should 'come from a wider variety of organisations' and the proportions 'sometimes be reversed' (Expenditure Committee (1977), I, paras 13, 14, 20).

These recommendations brought little tangible response from the government. Part-time outsiders were subsequently added to the Civil Service Commission, but civil servants remained in a majority. Outsiders were placed, as recommended, in a majority on a proportion of Final Selection Boards, but only on an experimental basis until 1980, after which the practice was abandoned. These changes, of course, had no significant impact on the types of people recruited as ATs; indeed, a subsequent CSC review (Civil Service Commission, 1979) rejected the Expenditure Committee's allegations of bias and praised 'the inherent fairness' of AT selection procedures. Similarly, a CSD review in 1978 'rejected the Expenditure Committee's proposal to put all entrants on an equal footing', arguing that it was unsafe 'to rely on performance in a few early jobs to identify staff of high potential' (Garrett, 1980, p. 35).

In 1982, however, limited changes were introduced. A new scheme (AT/HEOD) was established, whereby trainees, drawn as before from graduate recruits and serving executive officers, after training entered a new Higher Executive Officer (Development) (D) grade. Common standards were applied for both internal and external applicants, and streaming disappeared. By this time, however, the number of vacancies for Administration Trainees had fallen considerably – from 256 in 1974 to a mere forty-four by 1982 – which, coupled with the change to 'fast-stream only' entry, seems likely to increase still further the dominance of Oxbridge candidates. Significantly, in its first year of operation the new scheme managed to fill only twenty-four of the vacant forty-four Administration Trainee posts. Of the twenty-four successful candidates, moreover, no less than twenty-one were external applicants, and about three-quarters were from Oxbridge (compared with 'rather more than half' in two preceding years). (Atkinson Report,

1983, para. 94, and Annex 3.) Subsequently yet another review was instituted which, when it reported in early 1983, proposed only minor reforms designed to attract more graduate applicants from Redbrick universities and polytechnics, as well as more in-service executive officers (Atkinson Report, 1983). While the effect of these proposed changes remains to be seen, Chapman's conclusion (1982, p. 83) that 'the higher civil service in 20–30 years' time is likely to be even more elitist than ... today' seems unlikely to be wide of the mark.

Overview

Fulton's proposals, while producing a more rational structure and a greater awareness of central training needs, had nothing like the impact that their advocates hoped. Major administrative reforms are usually difficult to bring about in any large organisation, and clearly a number of very complex problems and pressures inhibited full implementation of the Fulton recommendations adopted by the government. One important factor, identified by Kellner and Crowther-Hunt (1980, p. 98), is that civil servants were charged with their implementation. As governments changed, and new problems appeared, Fulton's reforms faded from the ministerial agenda, leaving 'the old Administrative Class largely' able to choose 'for itself which recommendation to carry out and which to ignore'. As this suggests, the civil service's actual role went far beyond their theoretical one of impartially implementing ministerial policy. In this context one might question whether radical reform of the bureaucracy could ever be effected given the dominance of civil servants in policy implementation.

7 LOCAL GOVERNMENT: THE ADMINISTRATIVE AND POLITICAL CONTEXT

Administrative Complexity

Superficially British local government appears straightforward with its neat pattern of elected local authorities. In practice, however, government at the local level is particularly confusing because of the variety of agencies which help to shape and administer local services. This complex web includes: a) Local and regional offices of central government departments, e.g. DHSS, DOE (see Young, 1982); b) Non-departmental public bodies usually dealing with a single specialised function, e.g. health and water authorities; c) Decentralised units of public corporations, e.g. gas and electricity boards; d) Innumerable autonomous and semi-autonomous official and quasi-official organisations, each with its part to play in the policy-making process, e.g. Tenants' Liaison Committees, Youth Services Advisory Councils (see Cousins, 1982, 1983); e) Elected local government (see Figure 7.2). Complexity is compounded because of the large number of non-governmental agencies operating locally, e.g. local political parties, local pressure groups, industrial and commercial concerns. All of these can, on occasion, be important elements in local policy-making.

The main focus of this chapter is elected local government, but this in itself is organisationally far from simple – there are several different layers in *every* community in England and Wales. Complex *vertical* relationships (e.g. between county councils and district councils) co-exist alongside *horizontal* relationships (e.g. between different district councils within the same county). Additionally there are invariably complicated networks of relationships between different departments *within* a single local authority. In such circumstances generalising about local administration can be hazardous. As Stanyer (1976, ch. 1) reminds us, it is important to see each locality as a miniature political and administrative system in its own right.

Development and Structure

Elected local government is big business. In England and Wales there are almost 100,000 elected councillors serving on around 8,000 councils and employing 2 million staff. Together, these local authorities are responsible for providing over fifty different services. Its scale is demonstrated by the fact that in 1981/2 some 24 per cent of public expenditure in Britain was accounted for by local authorities. Quite clearly, local government deserves a major place in any study of British public administration.

(A) THE TRADITIONAL PATTERN

The major features of local government in England and Wales prior to 1 April 1974 were laid down by three statutes at the end of the nineteenth century: the Local Government Acts of 1888 and 1894, and the London Government Act, 1899. These Acts created a comprehensive pattern of local authorities throughout England and Wales providing a wide range of services. With some modifications this structure lasted until the 1972 Local Government Act ushered in a new pattern of elected local administration which became operative from 1 April 1974. Figure 7.1 outlines the structure of local government in England and Wales immediately prior to 1 April 1974. There were, however, a number of weaknesses in the traditional structure, notably:

(i) *Outdated structure.*   When the local government map was laid down at the end of the nineteenth century, many of the administrative units – e.g. Anglo Saxon shires and mediaeval boroughs – were already outdated. During the twentieth century, as the residential pattern of communities changed, the local government structure became increasingly irrational.

(ii) *Disparities of size.*   The above factors also produced wide disparities between local authorities of the same type, often producing a mis-match between resources and functions. In particular, many authorities were too small to provide an efficient standard of service (e.g. the smallest housing authority, Tintwistle RDC, had a population of only 1,490).

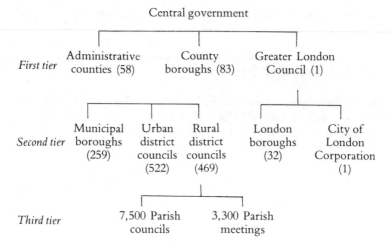

Figure 7.1   *The Pre-April 1974 Structure of Local Government in England and Wales (as at March 1974)*

(iii)   *Administrative confusion*   There were nine different types of elected local authority. In the more built-up areas services were often provided by all-purpose county boroughs; however, in rural areas services were split between the county council and urban/rural district/municipal borough authorities. County councils, moreover, frequently subdivided their territory for administrative purposes. Education and social services, for example, were invariably administered from decentralised 'area' offices as well as from County Hall. From the consumer's standpoint in particular, the 'old' system was, therefore, frequently extremely complex.

(iv)   *Fragmentation of responsibility.*   In many areas local services were provided by numerous different authorities, which often gave rise to acute co-ordination problems. Imagine, for example, the difficulties of community-wide planning on Merseyside where there were twenty-three local authorities (excluding parishes).

(B)   REORGANISATION

Structural change always needs to be seen in its environmental context. As society evolved from the end of the nineteenth century, so pressure for local government reorganisation increased. In

London, population movement from inner London to the suburbs meant that the old London County Council's administrative network had largely outlived its usefulness and in 1957 the Royal Commission on Local Government in Greater London (Herbert Report, 1960) was established to examine the London conurbation, including the Home Counties. This reported in 1960, and in 1963 the London Government Act set a broad boundary to the London area and gave shared responsibility for its local services to the Greater London Council (GLC), and to thirty-two London boroughs and the City of London. Strategic planning and transport functions reside with the top tier (GLC), while more personal services are administered by the boroughs. In addition, some services are shared under special arrangements (e.g. education in inner London is the responsibility of the Inner London Education Authority which consists of members of the GLC from inner London plus a representative from each of the twelve inner London boroughs), while others are the sole responsibility of special agencies (e.g. the Metropolitan Police which answers directly to the Home Secretary).

In 1966 two separate Royal Commissions were established to investigate local government in England (excluding London) and Scotland. When the Redcliffe-Maud Commission (on England) reported in 1969 it recommended the abolition of the old structure and the establishment of a new pattern of local authorities. Its solution, outside the urban conurbations, was unitary multi-purpose authorities (with from 250,000 to 1 million inhabitants). The existing two-tier system, it recommended, should be replaced by fifty-eight unitary authorities which would cover most of the country, but in three metropolitan areas there was to be a two-tier arrangement with responsibilities divided between a metropolitan county council and large district authorities (along lines similar to those operating in Greater London).

While the Labour government basically accepted these proposals (see *Local Government Reform in England,* 1970) the Conservatives, who came to power in 1970, produced alternative ideas which were ultimately incorporated into the 1972 Local Government Act. The concept of unitary authorities was rejected in favour of a rationalised two-tier system.

The Conservatives argued that the size of authority recommended by Redcliffe-Maud (serving populations between 250,000 and 1 million) was too large; hence, the need for a division of responsibilities between county and districts. Interestingly, the Wheatley Commission on Scotland also favoured a two-tier system. Likewise Derek Senior's minority report to the Royal Commission on Local Government in England favoured a two-tier system, although one based on the concept of the city region. The Conservative government's proposals divided the whole of England and Wales into two major tiers (plus parish councils as a third tier). The first tier was to be based largely on existing counties; the major changes were destined to take place in the second tier, the district level. Parish councils (community councils in Wales) made up the third tier which had both minor service and advisory functions at grass-roots level.

(C)   THE NEW SYSTEM IN ENGLAND AND WALES

Outside Greater London, a reorganised local government system was created by a series of Acts of Parliament passed during the period 1972–4.

The 1972 Local Government Act abolished the eighty-three county boroughs in England and Wales and reduced the fifty-eight county councils to forty-seven, ranging from populations of 100,000 (Powys) to 1.5 million (Hampshire). Within these counties, 1,250 municipal boroughs, urban and rural district councils were replaced by 333 district councils with populations ranging from 422,000 (Bristol) to 18,670 (Radnor).

In the major urban conurbations six metropolitan counties (Greater Manchester, Merseyside, West Midlands, Tyne and Wear, South Yorkshire, and West Yorkshire) were created containing thirty-six metropolitan districts with populations ranging from 172,000 (South Tyneside) to almost 1.1 million (Birmingham).

As a third tier, parish councils have been retained in England (known as community councils in Wales). There are some 11,000 parishes (or communities) of which about 8,000 have elected councils. Small parishes (with under 200 electors) may instead hold parish meetings which all local electors can attend. Additionally in some urban areas neighbourhood councils have been formed. These have no statutory functions and merely provide a sounding board for local opinion. Figure 7.2 provides a summary of the reorganised pattern of local government in England and Wales.

(D)   THE NEW SYSTEM IN SCOTLAND

In *Scotland* 'modern' local government was established by Acts of 1889, which created county councils, and 1900, which regularised

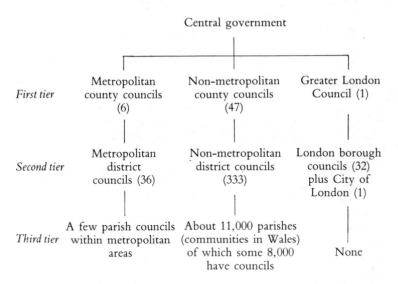

Figure 7.2   *Local Government in England and Wales since April 1974*

town government. At the third tier, parish councils were created in 1894 and charged with administering poor relief. Just as the *development* of Scottish local government closely paralleled that in England so, too, its '*reform*' followed closely on the heels of English and Welsh reorganisation.

The (Wheatley) Royal Commission on Local Government in Scotland (1966–9) saw its proposals (1969) largely adopted by the Conservative government in the *Local Government (Scotland) Act, 1973,* which became effective in May 1975. As in England, the Scottish Commission identified large numbers of small authorities as a major weakness of the old system. The 'new' pattern saw fewer, larger authorities. There are now nine regional councils (ranging from Strathclyde with 2.5 million inhabitants down to the Borders with 100,000), and thrity-six district councils (ranging from 850,000 in Glasgow to 9,000 in Badenoch and Strathspey). In addition, three island authorities were given virtually all-purpose status. At the third-tier level are some 1,350 community councils. Figure 7.3 presents the contemporary Scottish structure in dia-grammatic form.

The new pattern of local government throughout Britain appears substantially different from that which it replaced. But to what extent did the changes constitute 'reform'? A major objective of the

First tier	Regional councils (9)	Island councils (3)
Second tier	District councils (53)	
Third tier	Community councils (1,350)	

Figure 7.3   *Local Government in Scotland since May 1975*

reform movement was the rationalisation of geographical areas with the aim of producing more efficient services, yet some *very small* organisational units still provide crucial services (e.g. housing, education, social services). With reorganisation, moreover, local government lost some important services to other agencies. Under the *Water* Act (1973) the powers hitherto exercised by English and Welsh local authorities in water supply and sewage disposal were transferred to ten new regional water authorities. Likewise, in 1974 local authority *health* powers in England and Wales were transferred to newly created, non-elected Regional and Area Health Authorities (see Chapter 12).

The period 1972–4 thus witnessed important *structural* changes in British local administration. But, as Stanyer (1976, p. 55) has observed: 'It is necessary to understand what a local authority is in legal terms in a particular governmental system only as a prelude to understanding what all local authorities are in behavioural terms'. The structures created between 1963 and 1974 provided a new administrative framework for local government, but such structures in themselves reveal relatively little about the *practice* of local administration.

Further structural change for English local government is imminent. The 1983 Conservative Party Manifesto argued (p. 37) that the six metropolitan county councils and the Greater London Council 'have been shown to be a wasteful and unnecessary tier of government'. The Conservatives pledged to abolish them 'and return most of their functions to the boroughs and districts. Services which need to be administered over a wider area – such as police and fire, and education in inner London – will be run by joint boards of borough or district representatives'. Change, however, was not envisaged immediately since the newly elected Conservative government promised extensive consultation, followed by a white paper, with abolition to take effect from 1 April 1986. This latest proposed reorganisation of local government is arguably the product of political as well as administrative reasoning, as most of the authorities due to disappear are normally Labour controlled.

The Functions of Local Authorities

Local government is both a provider of services to a local community and an instrument of democratic self-government. On pp. 119–23 we examine the 'democratic' dimension of local government; this section delineates local authority services.

Local authorities can only do what the law explicitly allows; all council powers come from Acts of Parliament. Indeed, local government itself exists only by courtesy of Parliament, and Parliament frequently alters its powers and functions. Should any local authority provide a service not specifically permitted by Parliament it would be acting illegally, or *ultra vires* (see pp. 240–1). Nevertheless, local authorities carry out well over fifty functions; indeed, the average British citizen probably has more contact with the state through the services provided by local government than through the outputs of any other level of public administration.

The diversity of services outlined in Figure 7.4 makes any classification somewhat arbitrary. However, Figure 7.5 offers a useful starting point for discussion. As this shows, local authorities provide services in five major fields, although with many of them (e.g. education, housing, social services) other agencies such as government departments, *ad hoc* authorities and voluntary associations may also play some part in implementation.

Services are not, of course, provided uniformly throughout the country. Slum clearance, for example, is only a major problem in some areas. Again, standards of service may vary: between the minimum and maximum standards which are usually laid down by law there is, in practice, often a wide area of discretion (see pp. 144–6). Not all functions, moreover, are mandatory upon local authorities; some, like the provision of leisure centres, art galleries and playing fields are permissive (which means the authority has a choice whether or not to provide them). It is open to any authority, moreover, to promote a Private Bill in order to extend its powers. Although a complex and costly procedure, over the years many authorities have acquired powers by this means to perform particular functions in their localities: for example, to maintain the external decoration of listed buildings (Kensington and Chelsea), and to operate a municipal bank (Birmingham). As this latter

All County Councils	All District Councils
Police (except GLC)	Housing (GLC also has some housing powers)
Fire	Environmental Health
Refuse disposal (districts in Wales)	Refuse collection
Consumer protection (districts in Wales)	Clean air
Major roads and road building	Minor road maintenance
National parks (where appropriate)	Planning (local)
Planning (structure)	

Other Services

Education	Shire counties; met. districts; outer London boroughs; ILEA
Social services:	Shire counties; met. districts; London boroughs
Libraries:	Shire counties; met. districts; London boroughs
Transport:	All counties, but shire districts can run bus services
Parks and recreation	
Museums and galleries	} All county and district authorities have powers
Baths	

Figure 7.4   *Local Government: Who Does What in England and Wales, 1983*

Protective	Environmental	Personal	Social/ Recreational	Trading
Fire	Highways	Education	Sporting facilities	Markets
Police	Environmental health	Housing	Museums	Smallholdings
Consumer protection		Careers	Art galleries	Transport undertakings
Animal disease	Planning	Social services	Theatres, Camp sites	
Licensing (e.g. cinemas)				

Figure 7.5   *Classification of Local Government Services*

example suggests, there is also a wide and varied range of trading activities carried out by local authorities (see p. 182). Additionally, since the Local Government Act, 1972, local authorities have had general power to spend up to the product of a 2p rate on purposes not specifically authorised by statue. Consequently, while local authorities in Britain do not have a 'general competence' to do whatever they wish in their local areas, the variation in functions and standards between one authority and another may be considerable – to an extent which seemingly belies the simplicity of lists of services such as those contained in Figures 7.4 and 7.5.

Inter-Authority Relationships

Further complexity in the pattern of service provision stems from the two-tier nature of local government, especially with services (such as planning) where responsibility is shared between districts and counties. Close liaison between authorities is obviously important in such cases, as well as in those where different authorities provide related services (e.g. social services and housing). This problem is particularly acute in the area of homelessness – a 'social services' condition with a housing 'remedy' (Alexander, 1982b, p. 59). Of course, co-ordination is notoriously more difficult to achieve *between* organisations than *within* a single organisation. At reorganisation the functions of local government were split between four main organisational units – counties, districts, health authorities and water authorities – and relatively sophisticated consultative machinery had to be established in many areas in order to obtain local co-ordinated action. In practice, however, such arrangements have often tended to cause further confusion (particularly for consumers), as well as to create acrimony between the authorities concerned. Such acrimony has often been exacerbated, moreover, because of the tendency since reorganisation for authorities 'to view the relationship between the tiers as an adverary one' (Alexander, 1982a, p. 65); and also because of the problem of 'competing mandates' (Alexander, 1982b, p. 54) where authorities at different levels in an area pursuing different policies (and often controlled by different parties) both claim to be acting in *the* local interest.

One way in which liaison (and confusion) has been institutionalised is by the use of *agency agreements* between authorities. Section 101 of the Local Government Act, 1972, makes it possible for one authority to appoint another as its agent to carry out its statutory duties – this applies to all functions except education, social services and emergency services. In practice the major use of such agreements has been in the sphere of highway maintenance and construction, where old county boroughs and large urban districts have invariably continued to provide the service on behalf of their county council. They have not infrequently been a source of acrimony between the authorities involved, as well as of wider problems. As Alexander (1982a, p. 30) notes, agency agreements, superimposed 'on an already complicated allocation' of local authority functions, have added to the confusion experienced by consumers in service provision and 'ensured that the processes of public accountability and democratic control would be so convoluted as to raise serious doubts about their effectiveness'.

A further source of friction and confusion is found where authorities have *concurrent powers*: i.e. an equal share in providing services. The best example is planning, of which the Reorganisation White Paper (*Local Government in England*, 1971, para. 17) observed: 'All planning applications should be made to district councils ... Responsibility for broad planning policies and for the development of both structure and local plans must, however, rest with the county councils.' In practice these arrangements, like agency agreements, have given rise to confusion and friction, as well as in some cases to delay in determining applications. Ultimately the position was rationalised by the Local Government, Planning and Land Act, 1980, which restricted the definition of a 'county matter' and specified that all planning applications would be initially handled by district councils.

Liaison between authorities is facilitated by the establishment of forums for different authorities to discuss matters of mutual concern. Some of these operate on a regional basis (e.g. East Midlands Forum of County Councils), others on a county basis. Following reorganisation most counties established county liaison committees representing the county council and all the district councils within it, although these have generally proved ineffective and some have been abandoned. Inter-district liaison, however, has proved more successful, being facilitated either by specially formed Joint Consultative Committees or through county branches of the Association of District Councils (Alexander, 1982a, esp. ch. 3). (The latter association, along with the other two major local authority associations – the Association of Metropolitan Associations and the Association of County Councils – also provides opportunities for liaison at national level.) While forums such as these can take a community-wide approach, they rarely have executive power, being largely bodies for debate and comment. These committees are often paralleled at officer level and it is not uncommon to see different outlooks prevail – a further dimension of complexity.

The *formal* relationships outlined above need to be complemented by an appreciation of *informal* linkages, such as the sharing of knowledge and experience through the regional branches of professional associations. *Policy networks* (e.g. local government professionals, 'interested' councillors, local pressure groups, local/specialist journalists, etc.) are also generally of far more practical importance than is often realised. Likewise, Rotary, Round Table, and similar organisations can be important integrative tools. Liaison is often further facilitated by overlapping membership between county and district councils. As Stewart (1974, p. 24) has shown, about half the newly established metropolitan counties initially had one-third or more of their members on district authorities.

Such structures and networks, however, have generally failed to offset the inherent fragmentation of the reorganised local government system or the in-built suspicions which accompanied reorganisation. The goal of co-ordinated local action is difficult to sustain.

Local Politics and Democracy

Some observers, like Sharpe (1970), argue that the strongest justification for elected local government is its claim to be an efficient provider of services. Because different communities have different needs, the system of government needs to be flexible: local government allegedly provides this by enabling local councillors, drawn from and accountable to the local electorate, to determine local priorities. While such claims are today being challenged by the proponents of privatisation, it is as an efficient provider of services that the claims of local government mainly seem to rest.

Local government, however, is also widely regarded as an instrument of democratic self-government. The Redcliffe-Maud Commission, for example, was required to have regard to the need 'to sustain a viable system of local democracy', the assumption being that it was already democratic. What, then, are the grounds upon which local government can be said to promote democracy?

(A) THEORIES OF LOCAL DEMOCRACY

Democratic government does not necessarily entail locally elected councils. Indeed, one strand of continental thinking argues that democracy is essentially concerned with the nation-state and with majority rule, equality and uniformity. From such a perspective local government is seen as parochial, concerned with inequalities and differences between localities. This stance, however, contrasts with the traditional British view that local government enhances democracy, both by providing a vehicle of political education and as a means of increasing the liberty of the citizen by breaking down the power of the centralised state. This view emphasises that democracy is not simply concerned with national majority rule, social and political equality, and uniformity of standards but is, rather, an essential means of enabling individuals and local communities to voice their needs. (For discussion, see Sharpe, 1970; and Smith, 1969.)

(B) PARTICIPATION

Participation, it is often held, can be more widely achieved at the local than the national level. Elected local government enables 'ordinary' people to participate in the work of government without the disruption to their careers and domestic life that national office usually involves. Moving from theory to practice, however, it is clear that public interest in local government is low. Only about 40 per cent of the electorate vote in local elections, but such a figure can be highly misleading. Stanyer (1976, pp. 271–2), for example, points out that in 1967 the turnout in Maidstone Rural District was 14.7 per cent while that in Knighton Rural District was 89.6 per cent. The dangers of generalising about 'apathy' on the basis of aggregate data can be further highlighted by variation in turnout between different wards in the same authority – e.g. in Devon in 1957 town districts ranged from 29.9 per cent to 63.6 per cent, and in Exeter in 1966 the variation was 42.1 per cent to 63.8 per cent. Patterns of participation, even at this minimal level of voting turnout, cannot be divorced from the local social and political environment.

(C) POLITICAL PARTIES

Party politics is now an established part of contemporary local administration. In 1972, before reorganisation, only 53 per cent of English and Welsh local authorities were run on party lines; by 1979 this had risen to over 90 per cent. By 1981, in the counties of England and Wales, only Powys, Dyfed and Gwynedd had a majority of Independent councillors. Partisan local administration has quite clearly arrived. This development is not uncontroversial. The view is still quite widespread that local government is about local issues and that party politics should not intrude. However, this view is somewhat idealistic, particularly with the increased size of local authority units following reorganisation.

According to Dunsire (1956, p. 87), political parties are the 'indispensable element in the conversion of local councils into responsible governments'. Compared with shifting coalitions of Independent councillors, party groupings can make for coherent policy planning and administration. To some extent, of course, local party politics is simply national party politics writ small – the electorate frequently votes on the basis of non-local factors, something well illustrated in 1982 when the local elections were, as Crewe remarked (*The Times*, 8 May 1982, p. 2), 'a referendum' on the central government's 'handling of the Falklands crisis' – a far cry from the *local* population choosing its *local* decision-makers on the basis of *local* political issues.

In his study of Wolverhampton, Jones (1969, pp. 348–9) maintained that 'the parties have enabled individuals to devise a programme of policies and to implement it, and they have presented these programmes to the public in a dramatic and comprehensible way, enabling the public to judge a team of men and measures; thus the accountability of government to the electorate has been strengthened'. This situation is, of course, only one of an infinite number of models, but while it is clearly impossible to generalise about the impact of party politics, any attempt to understand local public administration without reference to the party political dimension is doomed to failure.

While public administration locally is now firmly entrenched within a party political environment, precise management styles vary considerably. Two adjacent Labour-controlled authorities, for example, may operate quite differently. Bulpitt (1967) found that in Manchester Labour group discipline was looser than in Salford. In Rochdale, where the Liberals held the balance of power, there was loose discipline and little formal party organisation in the council chamber. Some Labour groups have very open decision-making structures; others are dominated by the party leader. The Conservative party's belief in hierarchy generally gives their leaderships considerable leverage, but again generalisation is dangerous.

(D)   PRESSURE GROUPS

Pressure group activity at the local level is considerable. Partly because of the diverse interests within local communities, but also because of the ineffectiveness in many areas of more institutionalised channels – bureaucratic officials, unresponsive councillors, decaying parties, etc. – their role in local politics has tended to increase. In Birmingham, Newton (1976, chs 3, 4) identified over 4,000 organised groups, and estimated that there were probably about twice that number in total. Other studies have shown similarly extensive local group activity but, in Birmingham, only about one third were politically active and most of these (63 per cent) were involved only with a single issue. Many groups have very specific and limited demands (e.g. local amenities) and when the particular issue has been resolved they disband.

Dearlove's study (1973, ch. 8) of Kensington and Chelsea showed that the council's response to groups revolved largely around councillor assessment of them. Some groups were not favourably received, partly because they had little to offer the council, but also because they were seen as making 'unreasonable' demands on the local authority – that is, demands which did not square with the councillors' own policy predispositions. Other groups were seen as 'helpful' (e.g. WRVS; housing associations) since they had something to contribute (e.g. cheap welfare provision; extra housing). Likewise, Newton's 'established' groups built up a 'close set' of relationships with public officials in Birmingham (1976, p. 85), while his poorly established groups found it difficult to gain access to decision-makers and thereby had to resort to demonstrations, petitions, etc., which only served to make them even more unacceptable.

The local pressure group universe does not provide equal access to all. Immigrant groupings, squatters and welfare rights workers, for example, usually fare badly in comparison with status quo middle-class groupings. Again, though, generalisation is dangerous since some 'radical' socialist councils may respond favourably to groups challenging the status quo. Equally, of course, as Dearlove (1979, p. 49) emphasises, the inactivity of a particular section of the local population 'may occur precisely *because* that interest is built into the very heart of the council itself' (e.g. National Union of Mineworkers in mining areas). While pressure group influence varies over time and from issue to issue, such groupings must now be seen as an integral part of local public administration.

(E) NON-LOCAL INFLUENCES

Dunleavy argues that too frequently local policy-making is explained purely in terms of factors internal to specific localities. He maintains (1980a, p. 163) that far greater attention should be paid to non-local influences, asserting that 'local political studies have fundamentally failed to explain the observed regularity of urban policy change across many decentralised authorities'. In the educational sphere, for example, he points to the uniformity of local education authorities in adopting a tripartite system of secondary education following the 1944 Education Act. Then, from the late 1960s, most LEAs reorganised on comprehensive lines. In this, and other cited areas (e.g. development of high-rise flats, the commercial redevelopment of numerous town centres since the 1950s), central government did more than simply exhort – it provided financial incentives to help secure compliance.

Local authorities do not generally make policy decisions in isolation. 'In particular, over and above their local roles, councils are located and locate themselves in what may be termed the "national local government system"' (Dunleavy, 1980a, p. 105). Local authority associations, national party organisations, public service trade unions, professional bodies and the innumerable journals, conferences and publications help the nationalising of innovations in local services. Local public administration clearly needs to be seen in the context of the broader political, social and economic system.

Two questions about Dunleavy's framework can usefully be raised:

(a) He tends to *assume* that what applies in the case of high-rise flats or town centre redevelopment applies in other areas of policy-making;

(b) He places a heavy emphasis on the nationalising of urban policy.change, arguing (1980a, p. 98) that within 'broad limits the decentralised authorities implementing policies have moved in step with a precision that cries out for explanation'. Surely this is an exaggeration. It is possible to provide examples of policy patterns varying considerably across the country (e.g. provision for the disabled). Further, the cited examples from education and planning stretch Dunleavy's 'broad limits' to breaking point. Although nationwide policy changes are observable, this should not obscure the fact that there remains considerable variety in the policy and practice of local authorities.

Financing Local Government

Local government finance is important both economically and politically: *economically* because about one quarter of all public expenditure is spent by local authorities (see Table 1.1); *politically* because the finance available to local government largely determines the level of services which it can provide. Whilst it is theoretically true that local authorities, through the rates, have a source of finance independent of central government, finance which can be spent on any object within their statutory jurisdiction, this is not the whole story. In reality the picture is far more complex than that.

To understand local finance it is helpful to make a distinction (although the two do inter-connect) between *current (or revenue)* finance and *capital* finance.

(A)   CURRENT (OR REVENUE) FINANCE

In 1980/1 local authorities in England and Wales incurred a total of £30.3 bn revenue account expenditure. Such expenditure is used to pay for items of a relatively short-term nature (e.g. wages, postage). The *income* to finance that expenditure (£29.95 bn in 1980/1) was raised from three main sources: 1) Rates, 7.8 bn (26.0 per cent; 2) Government grants, £13.9 bn (46.4 per cent; 3) Charges, £8.2 bn (27.4 per cent). (All figures and calculations from *Annual Abstract of Statistics*, 1983 edn, CSO, tables 16.41, 16.43.) While the proportion received from the various sources will obviously vary from authority to authority, virtually all will receive some revenue from all three.

(1)   *Rates.*   Local rates are the most controversial source of local authority income. They are a form of taxation levied on local property, and are calculated on the basis of the rent at which the property might reasonably be let. Each year the rating authority fixes a rate in the pound and the occupier is obliged to pay rates at that poundage. For example, if a property has a rateable value of £100 and the local authority sets its rate at 54.5p the full rates payable would be £54.50p per annum. The crucial elements, therefore, are rateable value and rate poundage. Each year local authorities produce estimates of likely expenditure for the coming year. From this figure they deduct their estimated income from charges and central government grants together with any cash balances available for the purpose. This leaves a balance which then

has to be financed through locally levied rates. In 1966 rate rebates were introduced for those householders unable to pay the full amount and by 1977/8 rebates went to 15 per cent of all households in England and Wales. In addition some properties (e.g. government buildings, agricultural land and buildings, churches) are exempt from rates.

Reform of the rating system has long been on the political agenda. In 1976 the Layfield Report, *Local Government Finance*, suggested that local income tax should supplement the rates, although it listed many difficulties associated with such a venture. However, a government Green Paper issued in response, *Local Government Finance* (1977), rejected this suggestion. In 1981 the Thatcher government issued a further Green Paper, *Alternatives to Domestic Rates*. This did not advocate a particular option but commented on specific alternatives (e.g. local sales tax, local income tax, poll tax, an assigned share of national taxes) while ruling out others (e.g. local duties on petrol, alcohol or tobacco; local vehicle excise duty; charges for licences for sale of alcohol or petrol; and a local payroll tax). Two years later, however, in a further White Paper, *Rates: Proposals for Rate Limitation and Reform of the Rating System* (1983), the government conceded that wide consultation had failed to find any consensus for an alternative local tax. Almost every proposed alternative presents apparently insurmountable difficulties.

What are the major objections to the rates?

(i) They are said to be 'regressive': they bear most heavily on those with low incomes since the key element is the value of the property not the occupier's ability to pay. The availability of rebates has, however, gone a long way to meeting this objection.
(ii) They are said to be unfair. Rate resources are unevenly distributed among local authorities and are not necessarily related to their different needs. Government grants, however, can be used to smooth out this unevenness.
(iii) Their basis (annual rental value) is not adequate. Calculating a notional rental value is fraught with difficulties; hence, the frequently canvassed alternative of capital values for domestic property rating, or site values, as a basis for payment.

Against these objections must be set the *advantages* of the rating system: payment is difficult to avoid, income is predictable, and collection is cheap and easy. The debate about reforming the rating system shows signs of continuing for many years.

(2) *Grants* Government grants take several forms. Some – known as *specific* and *supplementary* grants – are tied to particular services, and in most cases reimburse individual authorities for a fixed percentage of their expenditure on the service concerned. Most important, however, is the *Rate Support Grant* which accounts for around 80 per cent of the total grant paid to local authorities, and is paid over to individual authorities as a block sum. It consists of two elements:

(i) *Domestic Rate Relief*, paid to enable authorities to relieve domestic ratepayers of a certain proportion of their rates (currently 18.5p in the £);
(ii) *Block Grant*, intended to supplement an authority's own finances so that, irrespective of individual local needs and resources, it can provide a similar standard of service for a similar rate poundage to other authorities of the same class.

Each year, following discussions in the Consultative Council on Local Government Finance, central government calculates a) the total amount of revenue spending it will accept for grant purposes (relevant expenditure); and b) the percentage of relevant expenditure to be financed by grant. After climbing steadily over the years, the percentage supported by government reached a peak of 66.5 per cent in 1975/6. Subsequently, however, it was reduced as part of central government public expenditure restraint policies, and by 1982/3 had fallen to 57 per cent (56 per cent for England; and 72.5 per cent for Wales). Following these calculations the government deducts the value of specific and supplementary grants (including domestic rate relief grant) and distributes the remainder as block grant (see Table 7.6).

Table 7.6   *National Rate Support Grant Settlement 1982/3**

		£m	
Relevant Expenditure		20,463	
Grant at 56 per cent	=	11,459	
less Specific grants		1,662	+
Supplementary grants		462	+
Domestic rate relief		678	+
		2,802	
Block Grant	=	8,657	(11,459 − 2,802)

* England only

Government grants to local authorities have now been paid for well over a century. The *justification* for them is well established: many local government services are required by national legislation, local variations in needs and resources can be equalised by grant adjustments, the impact of the regressive rating system can be reduced, and so on. Politically, however, their main effect during the twentieth century has been to make local government financially dependent upon the centre. From the Second World War the percentage of local government income derived from grants increased steadily – from 30.9 per cent in 1943/4 to 49.6 per cent in the mid-1970s – and although the proportion has since fallen (as a result of public expenditure restraint policies) it is still sufficient to provide central government with a powerful instrument for influencing local authorities.

(3) *Charges.* Income from charges is derived from fees, rents, tolls, fares, interest, etc. Obviously, the amounts received by individual authorities vary widely, according to the type and range of chargeable services provided, and the levels at which charges are set. The latter is in some cases subject to statutory regulation, in others it is a matter of local discretion.

(B) CAPITAL FINANCE

Capital account *expenditure* by local authorities (£5.2 bn in England and Wales, 1980/1) is usually spent on longer-term items such as the purchase, construction or improvement of land, property, equipment etc. The *capital receipts* used to finance that income (5.6 bn in 1980/1) can be raised from several sources including 1) *Capital grants* from the government or, occasionally, other bodies (e.g. Sports Council); 2) *Sales* of land, property, equipment etc.; and 3) *Loans*. Both because of the long-term nature of the investments, and the large sums involved, most capital expenditure (up to 70 per cent) has normally been financed by borrowing. There are, however, central government controls on what councils may borrow and loan sanction must usually be obtained from the centre.

Because of tightening central government controls on borrowing during the 1970s, local authorities increasingly financed capital projects out of current revenues (rates, charges, etc.) (for discussion and details see Byrne, 1981, p. 206). While this placed an increased burden upon ratepayers it was the perhaps inevitable response of local authorities seeking to free themselves from centrally-imposed borrowing restrictions (as well as the high cost of borrowing from the mid-1970s).

Total local authority borrowing is, of course, enormous. In 1981 local authorities (England and Wales) had a gross loan debt outstanding of £33.8 bn, and total loan charges for the year amounted to £4.7 bn. Indeed these loan charges, serviced from revenue account, totalled more than the combined revenue expenditure on fire, police and personal social services (£4.6 bn). (All 1980/1 figures and calculations from *Annual Abstract of Statistics,* 1983 edn, CSO, tables 16.31, 16.32, 16.41, 16.43.) The level of such payments, moreover, is largely beyond local government's control, varying according to interest rates. As debt must be serviced to avoid defaulting on creditors, planned 'cuts' in local expenditure – particularly in periods of rising interest rates – invariably have to fall on other revenue items, namely salaries, running costs and services. By the early 1980s the effect of several years of high interest rates, coupled with inflation and tight centrally-imposed borrowing limits, were placing larger than ever burdens upon ratepayers. In some areas rate levels were already beyond the limits which were regarded as socially and politically acceptable. It is in this context that the continuing debate about rating reform, and the controversy surrounding increased central control over local expenditure, should be seen.

8 INSIDE LOCAL GOVERNMENT

The apparently straightforward pattern depicted on formal committee and management charts massively over-simplifies the internal working of local authorities. At a basic level *informal* as well as *formal* relationships must be considered, as must *political* as well as *administrative* dimensions. Indeed, with some 90 per cent of councils now organised on party lines in 'many, perhaps most ... new councils the party group' – which rarely figures on organisation charts – 'has become the *locus* of political decision' (Alexander, 1982a, p. 97). This chapter looks inside local government at internal authority organisation and officer–councillor relationships.

Formal Structures

While the administrative style of local authorities varies enormously, all conduct their work through: a) meetings of the *Council*, consisting of all elected members; and b) *Committees* and *Sub-committees* consisting of small groups of members whose numbers and designations differ from authority to authority. Some committees focus on single services (e.g. housing or education) and are frequently called *vertical* committees; others, usually known as *horizontal* committees, deal with a single aspect of all services (e.g. personnel, finance). The trend in recent years has been towards establishing more horizontal committees in the interests of greater internal co-ordination. Even so, the committee system – where political control of policy and administration for each service is vested collectively in a group of councillors – offers a sharp contrast with the ministerial system in central administration. As Alexander (1982a, p. 121) puts it, 'the committee system of decision-making which predominates in British local government makes no provision for a political executive, either individual or collective'.

The committee system generally ensures detailed coverage of council business. Different items can be dealt with concurrently in different committees, and the relative informality of proceedings encourages frank discussion by councillors and officers alike.

Indeed, by enabling them to work together in committee – often over many years – the system facilitates contact between officers and councillors. Likewise, because committees usually contain members of different parties with different degrees of seniority and influence, contact is also facilitated between councillors of different political standing and party affiliation. One danger, however, is that committee loyalties might become too strong, causing members to become isolationist or even antagonistic to other service areas, thereby making an integrated authority-wide approach more difficult to obtain.

Just as committee systems vary between authorities, so too do departmental patterns. As in central government, the functional principle of allocation (pp. 26–8) is widely used, with departments having responsibility for particular services (education, housing, social services, etc.); however, in local government allocation by process is also quite widespread, with departments of engineers, architects, etc. providing specialist services throughout their authority. Although invariably fewer, smaller, and less multi-functional than central governmental departments, the differences are relative and problems of co-ordination both *within* and *between* departments are nevertheless frequently found within local authorities.

While formal management and committee structures require study, *informal* relationships are also crucially important. At the local level, where departments are often housed in the same building, and where officers and councillors – as well as prominent local interest group officials, journalists, council 'clients' (headmasters, businessmen, builders, etc.) – live in the same locality, the informal dimension is especially important and should not be obscured by undue emphasis on formal hierarchies.

Corporate Planning

The fragmentation of council functions between different departments and committees produced in many authorities prior to the 1970s 'a loose confederation of disparate activities' which, in the view of the Maud Committee on the Management of Local Government (Maud Report, 1967, vol. 1), dispersed 'responsibilities and scatter[ed] the taking of decisions'. In some of the larger authorities, the Committee (Vol. 5) found that there were thirty or more committees and forty or more sub-committees, while in local government generally 'there [was] hardly any systematic attempt at committee level to . . . co-ordinate policy as a whole'. Sometimes finance committees exerted some degree of co-ordination but they were usually ill-equipped for the task, being primarily concerned with financial implications. Consequently, Maud recommended each authority to establish 'a management board' of between five and nine members to co-ordinate council work. Committees would only be *deliberative*, making recommendations to the management board, which would perform functions similar to those of the Cabinet in central government.

The Maud Report provoked considerable hostility, particularly on the grounds of dividing councillors into first class members (sitting on the management board) and second class (backbench) members. Not a single authority implemented Maud's 'cabinet style' solution in its entirety; nevertheless, many streamlined their committee structures and some even established policy co-ordinating committees. More generally, Maud generated a climate for greater integration, something which became particularly appropriate during the preparations for reorganisation when two major committees (Bains for England and Wales, and Paterson for Scotland) were established to advise on management structures for the new local authorities.

The Bains Report (1972) and its Scottish equivalent, the Paterson Report (1973), both recommended a corporate approach to internal council management and policy-making. *At councillor level* a policy and resources committee was proposed to prioritise resources, co-ordinate policy, and control programme implementation throughout the authority. To assist with these tasks each policy and resources committee was recommended to have four sub-committees: finance, land, personnel, and performance review. *At officer level* there was to be a chief executive (in place of the former town clerk) whose role was to advise the policy and resources committee and head a small management team (consisting mainly of chief departmental officers) which would prepare plans and programmes as well as co-ordinate policy implementation. Bains also favoured committees based on broad programme areas and 'serviced by several different departments and disciplines', in place of the 'traditional separatist structures' (Haynes, 1980, p. 54) whereby each service committee had tended to be associated with the appropriate functional department and its principal officer.

In the post-Bains era corporate *structures* have been widely adopted. According to Greenwood *et al.* (1980, p. 50), 95 per cent of authorities established policy committees and 98 per cent appointed chief executive and management teams. Nevertheless, whether corporate *planning* has become a reality is a separate issue.

Powerful programme committees, and influential members serving on them, have sometimes been reluctant to defer to policy commit-tees (particularly as many councillors still cling to the traditional view that co-ordination is the role of the full council).

Similarly, there has often been a reluctance by specialist depart-mental officers to accept the decisions of non-specialist chief executives and management teams. Consequently it has sometimes been difficult for the new patterns to establish themselves in the face of combined resistance from programme committees, estab-lished departments, and professional senior officers. It also needs to be recognised that in some authorities – particularly small district councils where there are fewer personnel, resources and program-mes – much co-ordinating work occurs informally, and the elabo-rate corporate structures advocated by Bains are perhaps less appropriate.

Changes in attitude conducive to the development of a corporate approach would have been difficult to effect at any time. During the post-reorganisation climate of economic and financial strin-gency, however, where departmental and committee defences rise easily, it has been especially difficult. Consequently, while corporate *structures* have developed apace since reorganisation, it is questionable whether the corporate *ethos* has become deeply rooted. Indeed, a few authorities have retreated from corporate structures – management teams have been disbanded and some chief executives dismissed. The reason normally given is economy, but the real cause is frequently a re-assertion of anti-corporate attitudes.

Other factors, of course, contribute to the difficulty of effecting a corporate approach. Statutory obligations inhibit what is structur-ally possible; for example, non-metropolitan county councils must have education and social services committees. There is also a fragmentary approach by central government to local authorities. As the Central Policy Review Staff (1977, p. 22) noted, most circulars 'relate to a single service and are drafted and circulated by the single department responsible'. Corporate planning must also be seen in the context of party politics. Sometimes policy and resources committees consist entirely of members from the con-trolling party group. More likely, however, they are politically and geographically representative which – coupled with access by the press and public – often prevents frank discussion by controlling group members of planning, prioritisation, and co-ordination in politically sensitive fields (along the lines of the Cabinet in central government whose proceedings are, of course, confidential). As a result, policy and resources committee proceedings have in many authorities 'become either duplicates of, or substitutes for, the work of the full council and the function of policy co-ordination has shifted to the party political groups, or to the chief executive and management team, or ... both' (Alexander, 1982a, p. 91).

It should also be stressed that a local authority's corporate planning is only one variable in securing efficient management within a local community. There are a range of bodies other than local councils responsible for the provision of local services (see Chapter 12) which, coupled with the tiered nature of local government, makes a community-wide approach to management almost impossible. Developing inter-governmental as well as inter-authority networks is crucial if *real* co-ordination of local services is to be effected.

While an authority's management style is usually affected by environmental factors there always remains an element of *choice*. There can never be a purely mechanistic relationship between an organisation and its environment. Party political factors, professionalism and the dispositions of key personalities all usually have some bearing on internal management structures. The advocates of 'rational administration' remain just one voice amongst many.

Councillors

(A) SOCIAL CHARACTERISTICS

While councillors are *representatives* of their local communities they are certainly not *socially representative* of the population. In 1976 only 17 per cent were female, and 50 per cent were aged 54 or over. In addition, 76 per cent were home-owners (compared with 53 per cent of the population); 50 per cent had been through higher education (compared with 8 per cent); and only 27 per cent were manual workers (compared with 60 per cent) (Robinson Report, 1977, Vol. 2, tables 1 and 2). As these figures suggest, councillors are predominantly male, middle-aged, and middle-class, to a far greater extent than the population as a whole. This pattern, of course, largely reflects the demands of council work. Its essentially unpaid nature, and the heavy workload involved, make council service less attractive for young people with young families, building careers. (The Robinson Report, 1977, Vol. 2, found that councillors spend on average seventy-nine hours per month on council duties, and committee chairmen and majority party leaders

ninety-five and 112 hours respectively.) The middle-class skills –
public speaking, etc. – required to be an effective councillor may
also discourage many manual workers. It must, nevertheless, be
stressed that the figures quoted are averages; individual localities
often have distinctive patterns, and Labour-dominated areas may
often have a high proportion of working-class councillors.

Do the trends revealed above have any significance for the
outputs and conduct of local government? In one sense it can be
argued that generalisations are of little use. Councillors are not a
homogeneous, undifferentiated grouping; their interests, outlooks
and backgrounds vary enormously. There are disagreements between councillors of the same party just as there are disagreements
between those of opposing parties. Such disagreements may stem
from a variety of causes: ideological perspectives, ward and area
considerations, seniority (old v. young), status (chairman/spokes-
men v. backbenchers), committee and pressure group loyalties, or
simply politicking or 'bloody mindedness'. As Newton (1979,
p. 112) observes, there are also varying ability levels. While some
of the 'ordinary members' may accurately be depicted as ignorant
and unintelligent, 'council leaders are more usually of a much
higher calibre'. Increasingly, moreover, in the larger authorities
council leaders and key committee chairmen work effectively full
time – a development given some impetus by the introduction of
Special Responsibility Allowances (SRAs) for senior councillors in
1980 (Skelcher, 1983).

Compositional trends, however, should not be dismissed too
easily. As Byrne (1981, p. 127) asks, 'does the lack of women
councillors explain the apparent inadequacy of nursery provision,
while there is an arguably ample supply of municipal golfing
facilities?' Social elitism, it is frequently asserted, effectively
squeezes out working-class interests. Indeed Dearlove (1979,
p. 245) maintains that part of the case for reorganising local
government in 1972 and creating larger units was 'to make local
government more functional for dominant interests' (i.e. less
accessible to working-class representation).

Social elitism, however, needs to be distinguished from political
elitism – Labour and Conservative councillors on a local authority
could easily have relatively similar (and relatively elitist) social
backgrounds but very different political priorities. The political/
ideological dimension is perhaps a more crucial factor than social
background in determining policy priorities, although the two can
never be entirely disentangled. Perhaps, ultimately, the issue is this:

there is nothing amiss with manual workers (or any other grouping) being councillors, provided they can control their officers. If they cannot, councillors develop policy only in so far as the bureaucracy permits.

Training for new councillors might, in this context, be a useful resource but, as Greenwood and Wilson (1980) show, most training is lamentably inadequate not least because chief officers are usually unenthusiastic about new councillors being too well briefed. Payment for councillors might also persuade more working-class representatives to come forward. Indeed the attendance allowance system has made it possible for councillors from a broader social range to serve on local authorities, but this is far removed from receiving a salary.

(B)   REPRESENTATIONAL ROLES

The literature often focuses excessively upon officer/councillor relationships thereby overlooking the very different roles which councillors themselves adopt. As Jennings (1982, p. 67) has observed, most councillors are backbenchers, not policy-makers, and about the only vital service they see themselves doing is casework for their constituents. This generalisation, however, needs refining. Jones (1973, pp. 135–46) provides a useful *quantification* of roles, arguing that three broad categories are identifiable: (i) 75 per cent mainly concerned with representing ward and constituents' interests; (ii) 5 per cent serving as general policy-makers; (iii) 20 per cent serving as policy-makers in specific service areas. Newton (1976, ch. 6) offers an even more detailed classification of councillors, based on his study of Birmingham:

(i)   *Parochials* – whose world is largely bounded by the ward, individual constituents and their problems (15 per cent of sample were in this group).

(ii)   *People's agents* – similar to the above, but for this group ideology is more important. They see themselves as protecting citizens' interests rather than as delegates (18 per cent).

(iii)   *Policy advocates* – a preference for policy matters on a city-wide not a ward perspective. Strong ideological orientations (24 per cent).

(iv)   *Policy brokers* – similar to policy advocates but essentially moderates, compromisers and bargainers (20 per cent).

(v)　*Policy spokesmen* – concerned with broad policy matters but also see themselves as delegates. By speaking on behalf of their constituents they occasionally thereby disagree with aspects of party policy (8 per cent).

Such classifications inevitably simplify reality, but it is clear that different members may hold very different views about the role of local councillors.

(C)　PARTY GROUPS

Party groups are now an integral part of most local authorities, although operational styles vary enormously. The vast majority of councillors are members of a major political party, and although 'group politics' is not new to urban areas it has helped to transform the operating style of many county authorities. Very many decisions are now taken in private party meetings (in some cases with officers in attendance to give advice). However, as Alexander (1982a, p. 98) argues, the contribution of party groups to the policy-making process 'is more often than not reactive rather than initiative. Except when the controlling group comes to power with a programme worked out in detail, the relationship between professional expertise and political organisation will ensure that much of the business of the authority will be generated by officers'.

Green's study of Newcastle-upon-Tyne (1981, p. 62) suggests that the Labour group 'did not play an important part' in initiating and developing policy. 'Nor did it effectively evaluate proposals which had been initiated elsewhere.' Partly this was because the group was not united and in practice a small group of individuals, centred on the leader, was dominant. Jones's study of Wolverhampton (1969, pp. 175–6) showed, likewise, that the majority Labour group lived 'hand to mouth ... from agenda to agenda'; Hill's study of Leeds, however, saw policy development given much greater priority (Hill, 1967, p. 146).

Generalising from the few case studies available is obviously dangerous. Perhaps the most that can be said is that group decisions can, in some authorities and on some issues, be crucially important in policy direction. However, there is little evidence on 'the interactions of the leadership and the rank and file in reaching these decisions' (Jennings, 1982, p. 83). Moreover, although invariably held in private, party groups are nevertheless open to a variety of influences, not least that of the professional officer.

Officers

Unlike civil servants local authority employees are not part of a single unified service: each council employs its own staff. Altogether, in 1983, over 2 million people were employed by English, Welsh and Scottish local authorities, engaged in a range of occupations from architects, engineers and accountants to labourers, dustmen and park attendants. Although local authorities have considerable discretion in staffing matters, some officers must statutorily be appointed. For example, non-metropolitan counties and metropolitan districts are required to appoint chief education officers and directors of social services. Traditionally, local authority employees are categorised into *officers* (20 per cent of all employees: professional, technical and clerical staff) and *servants* (50 per cent, incorporating manual workers, e.g. cleaners, road labourers). Additionally, some 30 per cent of local authority employees (teachers, firemen and police) form a third category. It is, however, the first category, officers, who form what is known as the local government service: it is these who have most contact with councillors and who perform primary policy advisory and managerial roles.

Unlike central government, where top civil servants are usually generalists, chief officers in local government are normally specialists. Generally at the head of each department is a chief officer with appropriate technical qualifications who advises councillors and implements policy in fields relating to his specialism. In local government it is extremely difficult for a non-specialist to reach chief officer status. As Poole (1978, p. 43) observes, the local government administrator typically works 'as the subordinate of the specialist, relieving him of those tasks which have not called for specialist experience and qualifications'. In one other respect, too, local government officers offer a contrast with central government. While they are politically neutral they are not anonymous; they may speak in public at committee and other meetings, and often acquire public prominence within their locality.

The distinctiveness of localities and the relative freedom which authorities now enjoy in staffing mean that generalisations are dangerous. Nevertheless, specialist officers invariably have loyalties to their profession as well as to their employing authority and this further weakens the concept of a unified service. It can also lead to narrowness, in that staff may have technical and specialist information in a single field but little concern or understanding about the work of other departments. Narrowness not only increases co-ordination difficulties between departments, but is not conducive to corporate planning. Specialists, moreover, often build their career by moving from one authority to another rather than by climbing within one authority. This, at times, can cause instability within an authority, although, equally, mobility can bring new ideas. The mobility of specialists, moreover, needs to be seen against the 'localist' orientations of councillors and administrators.

Since Bains an increasing amount of chief officers' time has been devoted to liaison with other departmental heads to formulate corporate strategies. In this context working relationships are extremely important. Whatever management *structures* are created in the interest of co-ordination, 'personality' remains an important variable. While academic literature is full of material on officer-councillor relationships, relatively little is known about relationships between departmental chiefs within the same authority, but these, obviously, can be of crucial significance.

Chief officers also liaise with other administrative units operating in the locality (e.g. field offices of government departments notably the regional offices of the DOE, health and water authorities) and there are also important linkages with other councils, members of the public, and local pressure groups (e.g. ratepayers' action groups, local trade union branches, tenants' associations). The work of a senior local government officer is, therefore, far broader than the confines of his own department or even his own authority.

Officer–Councillor Relationships

(A)   VARYING PERSPECTIVES

One particularly crucial relationship at local authority level is that between officers and councillors, but there is no uniform pattern. Relationships vary *between* as well as *within* local authorities. Relationships in a single policy area also *vary over time* according to the issues and personalities involved. One must, therefore, beware of generalisations. As Newton (1976, p. 147) notes, the literature 'includes case studies of powerful officers, and powerless ones, as well as the conclusion that it all depends on the department'.

Two distinctive themes have, however, been dominant in recent years: (i) The 'formal' stance, that councillors make policy and officers simply implement it; (ii) The 'dictatorship of the official' thesis which holds officials, with their technical expertise, as dominant in policy formulation. Such dichotomous standpoints are, however, somewhat misleading since *both* groups are involved in policy formulation. As Collins *et al.* note (1978, p. 34), 'The evidence of the various case studies in local government leads not to the question of whether officers or members control but rather *in what ways both are involved in the process of developing and administering policy?*'

(B) FORMAL AND INFORMAL RELATIONSHIPS

Recent studies have made it clear that the 'formal' stance outlined above is totally redundant. Given the technical, specialist nature of much contemporary local government activity, officers are clearly important. Yet, as Newton (1976, p. 148) reminds us, while the 'dictatorship of the official' thesis has 'a certain commonsense plausibility . . . it has very little empirical evidence to support it . . . because little research has been done on the subject'. At a *formal* level the council and its committees meet, with officers in attendance, to consider reports prepared by officers, usually incorporating recommendations for action, but precise working relationships vary enormously. In some authorities officers intervene in discussions at will whereas in others more formal rules apply. At an informal level officers and councillors meet frequently at civic functions, receptions and so forth as well as before and after official meetings, and this too serves to blur the formal relationship between them.

(C) OFFICER-COUNCILLOR RESOURCES

(i) *The professionalism* of officers provides a level of technical expertise which councillors frequently lack. Nevertheless, councillors, through lengthy service on committees, may acquire considerable knowledge of certain subject areas. Many councillors, moreover, are builders, businessmen, transport workers, accountants, and so forth who may have appropriate specialist knowledge. Councillors can also be advantaged by their knowledge of local circumstances and because the mobility of senior officers often exceeds that of senior councillors. Indeed in many authorities permanence may be characteristic more of councillors and committee chairmen than the nominally 'permanent' officials who advise them.

(ii) The officers' *control of information* is particularly important. Officers collect and present material both to committees and to the whole council. There are obvious dangers of distortion, omission or misrepresentation, not necessarily for sinister reasons but, more likely, because of subconscious or professional bias. Moreover, as Gyford notes (1976, p. 45), 'officers may also be able to participate in ... decision taking by suggesting the appropriate wording of resolutions or amendments and ... by ... drafting' minutes of meetings. Nevertheless, councillors do have access (via pressure groups, the media, and party research departments etc.) to alternative sources of information which can, in certain circumstances, enable them to challenge officers successfully. Likewise, the accumulated experience of councillors in specific functional areas, coupled with their local knowledge, means that, on occasions, they are a force to be reckoned with.

(iii) Considerable influence accrues to officers in *implementing council policy*. Typically, councillors are part-time and serve on only a few committees. They therefore rarely see 'the complete picture' and tend to lose track of an issue once discussion of it has been concluded. Usually they have few opportunities to check that their instructions are being pursued, and almost none to supervise their execution at first hand. On key issues, or those with important constituency 'angles', assiduous councillors will take every opportunity to ascertain progress. On less important issues, however, not only councillors but sometimes whole committees may 'lose track' of implementation, particularly in larger authorities where there are frequently many pressing problems. Consequently, not only may inadvertent delay or failure to implement decisions go undetected, but officers may attempt to 'amend' or 'shelve' decisions which they dislike (see Greenwood and Wilson, 1982).

(D) CHIEF OFFICER – CHAIRMAN RELATIONSHIPS

The most crucial relationship is that between committee chairman and chief officer. This in many ways resembles the minister–civil service relationship (see pp. 77–82) with the chairman performing a quasi-ministerial role. The specialism of chief officers and the part-time nature of council service, however, makes the chairman's role arguably more difficult than that of ministers. On the other hand, policy-making is *relatively* less complex at the local level, and in many authorities a committee chairman may have acquired considerable specialist knowledge by holding the chairmanship – or serving on the committee concerned – for many years. Frequently, at pre-committee 'agenda meetings' the chief officer goes through recommendations pointing out difficulties and likely contentious items. A close, respectful relationship is crucial if policy is to develop smoothly and clearly. Informal linkages often develop because of the frequency of their meetings and the closeness of their working relationship, something fraught both with dangers and opportunities.

In Birmingham, Lambeth and Croydon the relationship between officers and councillors certainly appears to have been more equal than the 'dictatorship of the official' thesis would suggest. As we have seen, councillors sometimes do have resources to call upon when they confront experts. These resources are not, by any means, negligible and 'they are least negligible for the members who generally fill the most important positions' (Newton, 1976, p. 164).

One change which might increase the influence of councillors would be the payment of councillors. As already observed, many councils have members who are effectively full time (pensioners, housewives etc.). Since reorganisation councillors have been entitled to claim an attendance allowance for approved duties up to a maximum (£15.07 a day in 1983). Subsequently a small minority of (mainly Labour-controlled) councils required key committee chairmen to serve on a full-time basis. As Alexander (1982a, pp. 121–3) notes, the 'motivation for becoming full-time is clear enough: it is to assume control of the authority's policy-making and policy implementation'. Its effect is to make 'the relationship between the political and administrative heads' of the council 'closely akin to that between the minister and the permanent secretary' at national level.

The 1980 Local Government, Planning and Land Act gave local authorities the power to pay Special Responsibility Allowances (SRAs) to their leading members. This, however, is only a discretionary power but, as Skelcher (1983, p. 11) notes, 'Almost 20 per cent of local authorities in Great Britain are known to have adopted SRAs' and others are still considering the matter. In about half of the councils concerned payment was made to the opposition as well as to the majority party. The main recipients are the chairmen of service committees, the leader of the council and the chairman of the Policy and Resources Committee. Skelcher argues (p. 15) that SRAs probably do not mark the way towards full-time salaried councillors, but what they could well have done is to 'revitalise the debate within local authorities about services and facilities for elected members. This is as important as the financial issue, for both are about aiding the councillor in the effective performance of his job'.

(E) A FALSE DICHOTOMY?

To what extent is it realistic to see local political relationships in officer–councillor terms? One of the underlying themes of corporate planning is the notion of *partnership* between officers and councillors. Elected members and officers are now increasingly *working together* on council activities. As Collins *et al.* (1978, p. 42) observe, what frequently happens is that 'a joint councillor–officer elite arises, often in a very visible form, as the major power centre of the local authority'. There is neither the domination of an officer nor a member elite, but rather the domination of an officer–member elite. Saunders (1980, p. 224), for example, paints a picture of leading councillors and leading officers as allies rather than adversaries.

Perhaps local politics needs to be seen as a series of shifting alliances, varying over time and from issue to issue. To distinguish too sharply between officers and councillors is frequently to distort reality. Senior elected and non-elected personnel might be dominant in some authorities on some issues, but this is only one possible alliance; second-tier officers and party activists might combine effectively in other policy areas – the permutations are infinite. In Croydon, for example, Saunders (1980, p. 313) identified 'a relatively dense and cohesive network of business and political activists, interacting regularly and relatively informally in a variety of institutional contexts'. Networks and alliances vary enormously, but one conclusion is clear: there is far more to local authority decision-making than simply the officer–councillor dimension.

9 CENTRAL–LOCAL GOVERNMENT RELATIONSHIPS

Although local authorities are accountable to the local electorate, their powers and much of their finance are derived ultimately from Parliament (which in practice is invariably dominated by government). For local councillors this sometimes presents a stark dilemma: whether to put first the perceived interests of local people, or the directives and requests of central government. Central–local relations, in fact, are crucial to understanding the way local government works and to recognising its role within the wider administrative system. Unfortunately the relationship is far from simple, being characterised, according to Rhodes (1981, p. 28), by 'ambiguity, confusion and complexity'. Relationships vary over time, from authority to authority and from service to service. This chapter begins by examining three analytical models and discusses their usefulness as tools for analysis. Formal relationships are then examined, followed by a discussion of what happens in practice. There is an account of the changing nature of central–local relations in the early 1980s and, finally, the new radical literature is examined and alternative analytical perspectives presented.

Analytical Models

Until relatively recently the central–local relationship was viewed rather simplistically in legal, institutional and financial terms. This approach not only ignored wider political and administrative factors but, as Regan (1983, p. 45) observes, was too limiting: it was unable to encompass the 'variability, ambiguity, complexity and reciprocity' that subsequent studies have suggested obtain in central–local relations.

Broadly speaking three major models which attempt to offer insights into central–local relations can be identified, and these are discussed below.

(A) THE AGENCY MODEL

This model sees local authorities as having a subordinate relationship to central government with little or no discretion in the task of implementing national policies. This was the traditional view which held sway for many years. Local authorities were subject not only to central government initiated legislative changes, but financially were seen as increasingly dependent on central government grants. As late as 1966 W. A. Robson wrote: 'Local authorities have become subservient to the central government, mainly but not entirely because of their excessive dependence on central grants' (p. 149). While Robson's view is, today, largely rejected by academic observers, the agency model is still widely adhered to by many practitioners at local level – both councillors and officers – who see central controls inhibiting their freedom to act in what they regard as the local interest.

The difficulty with the agency model is that it produces a somewhat 'blinkered' analysis of what is a highly complex relationship. While local government, like all public authorities, is subject to Parliament, its relationship with government is not purely legalistic; political and administrative factors are also involved. Likewise, while the proportion of local government revenue income derived from central government grants increased from 30.9 per cent in 1943/4 to nearer 50 per cent by the 1970s, increased central financing of local services did not automatically mean central control. There is, furthermore, substantial empirical evidence of variations in local policy outputs. In some areas the agency model holds good (e.g. county councils serve as agents of the Department of Transport in constructing motorways and trunk roads) but in general it conveys an over-exaggerated picture of central domination, particularly as there is a great deal of evidence of continued local discretion in service provision. Several studies, for example, show that policy outputs vary from authority to authority in a manner which is not simply related to differing resources or needs. According to Boaden (1971), party control clearly affects expenditure patterns. He found that Labour councils spent more on education and built more council houses than Conservative councils. Labour councils also paid higher subsidies in the housing field than other councils, irrespective of needs or resource availability. Conservative councils, by contrast, spent more on police than Labour. Alt (1971, p. 60) has likewise shown that before Health Service reorganisation in 1974 there was a 'consistent, positive and generally significant correlation between

Labour representation and spending on local health services'. Davies (1968 and 1972) develops similar themes in the context of social services. Likewise, Duke and Edgell (1981), in a study of two northern cities, demonstrate the importance of local political control with reference to spending cuts.

Distinguishing between a multiplicity of variables in accounting for policy variations is, of course, a hazardous exercise, but despite the methodological difficulties it seems clear that a simple agency model, with local authorities implementing national policies with little or no discretion, is far from accurate. Table 9.1 illustrates this with reference to revenue expenditure on basic services by the ten district councils in Greater Manchester in 1982/3. Similar variations are evident on a national scale. For example, in 1982/3 Barking and Dagenham planned to spend £323.04 per head on education compared with £143.45 per head budgeted by West Sussex. Likewise, spending on social services was £76.71 per head in London compared with £28.36 in East Anglia. (Source: *Financial and General Statistics 1982/83*, CIPFA, 1982.)

Table 9.1   *Variations in Revenue Expenditure in Greater Manchester 1982/3 (£ per head)*

	Education	Housing	Social services	Recreation and culture
Bolton	275	112	48	27
Bury	250	62	47	22
Manchester	371	311	99	46
Oldham	228	164	52	26
Rochdale	274	140	63	22
Salford	268	207	65	32
Stockport	236	60	42	26
Tameside	245	126	57	32
Trafford	190	55	41	25
Wigan	256	117	48	27
Range	190–371	55–311	41–99	22–46

Source: Greater Manchester Council (1982).
Note: These figures were *estimates* provided at the start of the 1982/3 financial year. *Actual* expenditure may be different.

Case studies also reveal evidence of local discretion in other respects. In numerous policy areas (e.g. smoke control, comprehensive education, selling council houses) central government has often been frustrated by local authorities. Dearlove (1973, p. 20), for example, observed that the Royal Borough of Kensington and Chelsea frequently ignored or resisted central government 'advice and direction'. He concluded: 'The impact of central government upon day-to-day decisions of local authorities often depends on local responsiveness, and the preparedness of local authorities to accept advice or guidance'. Distinctiveness, albeit within a framework established by the centre, appears to be an unmistakable feature of local policy-making.

(B) THE PARTNERSHIP MODEL

A second model, often regarded as the 'ideal' at the local level, sees local authorities as more or less co-equal partners of central government in providing services. Traditional writers – noting the increased central constraints upon local government which have undoubtedly occurred during the twentieth century – often depicted a move from an earlier period of partnership to one of agent. In fact, the partnership model, as Regan (1983, p. 46) puts it, 'is so loose as to be almost vacuous'. He continues:

> Only in a formal constitutional sense are the government departments and the local authorities equal. In the sense of working together on common tasks partnership is a banal truism – of course both central and local government are involved in education, housing, transport, social services etc. but having said that there is little else one can say under the umbrella of partnership.

For Regan, then, the partnership model is too imprecise to be a useful analytical tool; hence the need for an alternative insight.

(C) THE POWER-DEPENDENCE MODEL

This model postulates that both central departments and local authorities have resources which each can use against the other and against other organisations. In a sense this is a sophisticated variant of the partnership model, in that dependence is reciprocal. However, the relationship is far more complex and varied than that postulated by the partnership model. Resources other than the legal/constitutional and financial are built into the model: for example, political, informational and implementational resources. While there are likely to be inequalities in the distribution of resources, these are not necessarily cumulative. Rhodes (1979, pp. 29–1) observes:

The fact that a local authority or a central department lacks one resource does not mean that it lacks others. One resource could be substituted for another. For example, a central department lacking the constitutional/legal resources to prevent (or encourage) a specific local initiative can attempt to get its way by withholding (or supplying) financial resources. Conversely, a local authority which has been refused financial resources can attempt to reverse this state of affairs by embarrassing the central department. Press and television reports on the adverse consequences of the centre's decision may lead to the decision being reconsidered.

In this model power is seen in relative terms, hinging upon a process of bargaining and exchange.

The power-dependence model undoubtedly offers a useful analytical tool for exploring central–local relationships. It reveals clearly that neither central nor local government should be seen as monolithic blocs, and that the relationship varies according to the agencies, personnel, policy areas and goals involved. For all its sophistication, however, it fails to place central–local relationships in the wider political and economic setting. The focus is upon inter-organisational relationships, and changing political and economic circumstances receive insufficient emphasis. As Dunsire (1982, p. 21) has written, 'the bargaining network model has been made to look a little shop-soiled ... See how fiscal crisis and a streak of Thatcherite obduracy fills one's mind again with the "reality" of the power of the state, when a government chooses to use it.' The central–local relationship is dynamic and multi-dimensional, and no one model seems capable of portraying it in its entirety.

Of course, analysing any relationship depends upon the angle from which it is viewed. Saunders (1982, p. 55) illustrates this with reference to a Conservative government committed to a monetarist economic strategy. For the government, he writes,

the problem is how to develop and enforce policies involving cuts in services and reductions in the public sector workforce in the face of local resistance and antagonism on the part of Labour local authorities, public sector unions, organised groups of consumers of state services, and so on. From the point of view of local Labour-controlled councils, on the other hand, the problem is how best to counter central government policies and directives in order to fulfil election pledges and principled commitments to a 'no cuts/no redundancies' platform.

The 'top-down' view of central–local relations can be very different from the 'bottom-up' view; both perspectives require recognition.

The Formal Framework

This section examines *formal* relationships between central government and local authorities, an essential prerequisite to the analysis of *actual* working relationships on pp. 152–60.

LEGISLATION

The sovereignty of Parliament means that it can create, abolish or amend the powers of local authorities as it determines. While legislation is, therefore, an obvious means of central control of local authorities, statute also serves to restrict the role of central government, as the Tameside dispute (1976) demonstrated.

Following reorganisation the Labour-controlled *Tameside* Metropolitan District made arrangements for the introduction of comprehensive education, but in May 1976, shortly before the changeover was scheduled, the Conservatives won control of the local authority and they were pledged to retain some grammar schools. In June 1976 the Labour Secretary of State for Education and Science issued Tameside a directive to proceed with comprehensive reorganisation on the grounds that to do otherwise at such a late stage would be unreasonable. This intervention was on Section 68 of the Education Act, 1944, which states that when a local authority is deemed by the minister to be acting unreasonably, intervention by the minister is appropriate. Tameside resisted, and when the matter came before the courts the House of Lords determined that the minister's decision was invalid, holding that there was no basis upon which the Secretary of State could say that Tameside was acting unreasonably. Legislation, as this case suggests, is not simply an instrument of central control; it can also protect local authorities against central direction which is not backed by statutory powers. Interestingly, however, the Secretary of State subsequently acquired stronger powers to require education authorities to embrace comprehensive reorganisation, by securing a change in the law. So, perhaps, the minister had the upper hand in the end.

CIRCULARS

Circulars, issued by government departments to appropriate local authorities, are a major instrument of central–local communications. (In the year ending April 1981, according to the DOE, 1,873 circulars and similar communications were issued to local authorities; however, in the following year the figure was only 592.) Although they are often cited as an instrument of central control, their effectiveness is difficult to determine because individual local authorities – and sometimes, even, different departments within the same authority – react differently to them. Indeed, many circulars do not contain central directives, and do not have statutory force, being issued simply for guidance and advice. Moreover, as Richardson and Jordan (1979, p. 107) observe, circulars often follow exhaustive discussion 'in the labyrinth of central/local consultative machinery'. Consequently, it can be misleading to see circulars as evidence of central departments attempting to regulate local authorities.

JUDICIAL CONTROL

Local authorities have no powers except those conferred upon them by statute, and when they take action which is not sanctioned by the law they are said to be acting *ultra vires* (beyond the powers). Any councillors (or others) who support expenditure on *ultra vires* acts resulting in loss may be made financially responsible. They might also be banned from holding public office for a period determined by the courts.

Ultra vires is obviously a restrictive doctrine (although local authorities are now permitted to raise a two-penny rate to finance functions not specifically authorised by statute). Its effect is to expose to restraining action in the courts any local authority activity not backed by statutory authority. One controversial instance of this occurred in 1981 when the Greater London Council's 'Fare's Fair' policy – which introduced heavy subsidisation of London Transport fares from the rates – was declared illegal by the House of Lords. In January 1983, however, the High Court ruled that the GLC had power to launch a similar plan designed to reduce London Transport fares by 25 per cent. In central–local relations, as this example suggests, the courts are something of a two-edged sword. Their role, however, is highly controversial: the 1981 decision led to accusations that an 'undemocratic' court ruling had substituted the views of judges for those of councillors whose policies had been endorsed by the local electorate.

DEFAULT POWERS

These powers, granting a minister default powers over local authorities which, in his view, fail to provide a satisfactory service, are *very* rarely used. A minister may temporarily remove a particular service from a local authority and administer it himself (or authorise someone else to act) if he is dissatisfied with a local authority's performance. Two cases, Clay Cross (1972) and Norwich (1981–2), are particularly interesting: here, as with the GLC 'Fare's Fair' issue, the party political dimension was very much in evidence.

(i)   *Clay Cross (1972)*.   This dispute arose when the Labour-controlled Clay Cross Urban District Council refused to operate provisions in the Housing Finance Act, 1972, requiring council house rents to be raised to the 'fair rent' level defined by the Act. The Conservative government ultimately appointed a Housing Commissioner to take over responsibility for the housing function, but in 1974 the local authority ceased to exist as a result of local government reorganisation. Eleven Clay Cross councillors were surcharged for the money which would have been obtained had the Act been implemented and they were also disqualified from holding public office for a period. In practice, however, the Commissioner found it difficult to operate because of non-co-operation by the council: the use of default powers may be clear in statute but implementation can be more problematical. Rhodes (1981, p. 17) observes that 'although central government has an impressive list of controls at its disposal they constitute only a *potential* for control'.

(ii)   *Norwich (1981–2)*.   Perhaps the most notorious default power is that contained in the Housing Act, 1980, which can be brought into effect whenever the minister considers that tenants are having difficulty in exercising their right to buy a council property 'effectively and expeditiously'. In December 1981 the Secretary of State for the Environment threatened to activate these default powers in Norwich, where the Labour-controlled City Council had sold only 250 properties in the first year of the Act. The minister's position was ultimately upheld by the Court of Appeal in February 1982. In his judgment Lord Denning suggested that if Norwich would 'get a move on' in processing applications to buy there might be no need for the minister to act. This in fact happened. Norwich agreed to take on an extra twelve staff and to clear the backlog of applications.

DEPARTMENTAL INSPECTORS

The use of inspectors as a form of central supervision goes back to the Poor Law reform of 1834. Basically only four local authority services are subject to oversight by inspectors: education, child care, police and fire. While such inspectors are usually required to satisfy their departments that local services are provided efficiently and that minimum standards are being met, their role has increasingly been educative rather than coercive. As Stanyer (1976, p. 223) observes, they 'both educate and learn ... and ... can carry knowledge of best practice directly from one authority to another'.

APPELLATE FUNCTIONS OF MINISTERS

Some statutes require local authorities to submit schemes or orders to the relevant minister for approval (e.g. structure plans) or confirmation (e.g. compulsory purchase orders). Likewise, ministers exercise various appellate functions in adjudicating between citizens and local authorities (e.g. appeals against a local authority's refusal of planning permission – see pp. 241–2). Despite the quasi-judicial character of the process it is likely that his appellate functions serve to 'heighten a minister's perception of his supervisory role' (Boynton, 1982, p. 205).

FINANCE

Central government attempts to control local authorities by: a) carefully regulating the amount of money which they can spend locally, and b) scrutinising the way in which money is actually spent. The increasing dependence of local government on financial support from the centre has already been noted, and through a variety of devices central government now restricts local authority revenue and capital expenditure (see pp. 124–8; 155–60). Although empirical research (e.g. Boaden, 1971) suggests 'that the financial relationship has [not] decreased the decision-making autonomy of *individual* authorities, it is generally believed in local government that it has led to increased, and increasing, control over local government *as a whole*' (Alexander 1982a, p. 148). This section, however, only examines the *scrutiny* of local authority expenditure.

Traditionally, government appointed *district auditors* have been responsible for examining most local authority accounts. The Local Government Act, 1972, allowed local authorities to choose between district auditors and private auditors, who needed to be approved by the Secretary of State, but the Local Government Finance Act, 1982, removed an authority's right to choose its own auditor. The Act also established an *Audit Commission* for Local Authorities in England and Wales which became operational in 1983. Auditors are no longer employed by the Secretary of State,

although the Commission itself is appointed by the Secretary of
State after consultation with local authority associations and professional accountancy bodies, and he is empowered to issue directions
which the Commission must observe. Widely seen as part of the
Thatcher government's policy of 'privatisation', the 1982 Act
effectively allows the government to impose specific private auditors on local authorities. It also requires auditors to satisfy
themselves that the local authority concerned 'has made proper
arrangements for securing economy, efficiency and effectiveness in
its use of resources'.

Working Relationships

The formal legal framework of central–local relations needs to be set
against actual working relationships. These relationships are extremely complex and varied. Griffith (1966), for example, showed
that government departments varied enormously in the extent to
which they sought to exercise control over local authorities.
However, three major types of relationship could be identified:

1 *laissez-faire* – in 1966 Griffith cited the Ministry of Health as a
  department which exercised minimum intervention. The
  DHSS today would certainly not qualify.
2 *regulatory* – ensuring that minimum standards of service provision are maintained and occasionally enforcing national policies
  on local authorities (e.g. Home Office).
3 *promotional* – here the central department either persuades or
  forces local authorities to adopt and implement national policies
  (e.g. DES).

Developing this theme further, Regan (1977, p. 34) shows that
there can also be markedly different outlooks in different parts of
the same government department – for example, the 'DES is not as
promotional in the youth service as in primary education'. This
further reinforces the view that central government is not a
monolith in its dealings with local authorities. As Rhodes (1981,
p. 18) observes, 'it is misleading to talk of central control. Rather
there are different types and degrees of control exerted by the
various constituent units of central government.'
   In 1977, in similar vein, a report by the Central Policy Review
Staff (1977) highlighted the great *complexity* which existed in
channels of communication between central government depart-

ments and local authorities. It showed that central government departments, in making and implementing policies, acted largely in isolation from each other and conducted their relationships with local authorities accordingly. The CPRS recommended that central government should deal with local authorities more on an inter-departmental programme basis than on a separate service-by-service basis.

Regan has argued that there is an even more fundamental quality to be added to the variability, ambiguity, confusion and complexity outlined above, namely *reciprocity*. He remarks (1983, p. 45) that Friend *et al.* (1974) in their study on the expansion of Droitwich 'revealed government departments and local authorities closely involved on a common task. The process was marked by negotiation and bargaining and in these circumstances the hierarchical central–local relationship broke down and constraints were imposed mutually on all sides'. It is clearly naive to talk in general terms about 'central government control' over local authorities, or indeed to generalise about the relationship at all. As Rhodes (1981, p. 27) observes, in future 'the starting point must be the complexity of interactions and the constraints imposed thereby on *both* levels of government'.

LOCAL AUTHORITY ASSOCIATIONS AND PROFESSIONAL BODIES

Griffith (1966, p. 23) suggests that

Any description of central and local public authorities in Britain would be incomplete without some mention of the role of the local authority associations. It is difficult to exaggerate their importance in influencing legislation, government policies and administration and in acting as coordinators and channels of local authority opinion.

In 1973 three major local authority associations were established: the Association of County Councils (ACC), the Association of Metropolitan Authorities (AMA) and the Association of District Councils (ADC). The extensive consultation which takes place between central government and these associations should not be seen as a generous concession by government but as 'the inevitable response in a situation where the centre lacks detailed control. The associations act as filters, ranking matters according to importance, aggregating individual cases so that wider implications can be recognised' (Richardson and Jordan, 1979, pp. 105–6).

There is also a range of specialist bodies which similarly represent aspects of local government at national level, e.g. the Society of Local Authority Chief Executives (SOLACE). Others, like the Chartered Institute of Public Finance and Accounting (CIPFA), are professional associations with large numbers of members at officer level within local government (and sometimes also within central government as well). According to Rhodes *et al.* (1981, pp. 31–2), policy statements which emanate from government departments are often, in practice, the product of prior consultation and negotiation between the centre and one or more of the many associations and committees – not least the professional bodies which on occasions 'unite' civil servants and local authority employees.

THE CONSULTATIVE COUNCIL ON LOCAL GOVERNMENT FINANCE (CCLGF)

In 1976 the Layfield Report argued that ambiguity and complexity characterised the financial relationship between central and local government. In the previous year, 1975, some attempt to rationalise communications in this sphere was made with the creation of the Consultative Council on Local Government Finance (CCLGF). As Alexander (1982a, p. 158) observes, 'The creation of this body was announced' in a way which 'suggested that the council was intended more to facilitate central control of the economy than to increase local government's capacity to protect its position and to maximise its influence on the government and on individual departments'.

The CCLGF meets six or seven times a year and is chaired by the Secretary of State for the Environment. Meetings are attended by ministers and senior officials from the DOE, Treasury and other interested departments, along with elected members and officers of the local authority associations. Although it has no formal terms of reference, its discussions principally concern grants and expenditure levels. According to Binder (1982, p. 36) 'the great significance of financial issues in the central/local relationship has led to the CCLGF attaining a predominant status in the hierarchy of Central Government/Local Authority consultation bodies'.

CCLGF business is first discussed in a body known as the Official Steering Group (OSG) which consists of senior officials of the associations and their advisers on the one side, and of senior government officials on the other. 'Ostensibly the main purpose of the OSG is to filter out and deal with items of lesser importance and to clarify issues for the "political" side. Of course, in practice, matters of substance can be dealt with in the technical setting. A second tier of officers' groups have specialised remits and report to the Consultative Council through the OSG' (Richardson and Jordan, 1979, p. 108). Furthermore, as Binder (1982, p. 38) notes, discussions of CCLGF issues between leading association members and ministers often take place on a party political level outside the formal council. On some issues such discussions 'have had a very substantial influence on government policy – indeed an influence far in excess of that of the CCLGF'. Of course, partisan divisions within and between the various associations are a 'two-edged sword': on many issues they prevent local authorities from speaking with any sort of united voice.

The development of the CCLGF has been mirrored in other policy fields (e.g. housing) by the creation of similar consultative bodies together with various working parties, specialist groups and so forth. Such channels provide important mechanisms for the exchange of information and influence and, together with the predominance of the associations in the central–local consultative process, have possibly resulted in a reduction of direct discussions on policy between individual local authorities and individual central departments. While bodies like the CCLGF may 'not greatly' have 'increased the power of local government' (Alexander, 1982a, p. 163) they enable local authorities (increasingly through their association representatives) to obtain access to, and collaborate with, departmental ministers and officials. Whatever the centre's theoretical potential for power might be, in practice the realities of policy formulation *demand* collaboration between both levels of government.

Changing Relationships: the Early 1980s

During the 1970s and early 1980s overt tensions in central–local relationships became increasingly evident. One of the roots of the problem was the sharp cutback, at a time of high inflation, of financial resources provided by the centre, but this needs to be seen alongside the emergence of strongly ideological politics at both central and local levels.

The Thatcher government came to power in 1979 deeply suspicious of the size of the public sector and the levels of public expenditure. Local authorities (especially 'high-spending' Labour-controlled councils) were prime targets, particularly since local government accounted for a quarter of public expenditure in 1979/80. This section focuses on three major developments with important repercussions for central–local relations: a) The Local Government, Planning and Land Act, 1980; b) The Local Government Finance Act, 1982; c) Rate limitation proposals, 1983.

(A) THE LOCAL GOVERNMENT, PLANNING AND LAND ACT, 1980

Prior to this Act the traditional approach of central government had been to view local expenditure in global terms; hence, as long as local spending as a whole remained on target, individual authorities spending above the norm were not penalised. The 1980 Act, however, 'allowed the government to fix expenditure targets for each authority and allocate grant in terms of how far those targets were breached' (Greenwood, 1982, p. 259). As the same author notes, 'The Conservative Government's attempts to extract deeper cuts from higher rather than the lower-spending authorities represents a movement away' from the former 'philosophy'.

Under the former Rate Support Grant (RSG) arrangement, as a local authority increased its expenditure, government grant met a constant percentage of the additional expenditure. Since 1981, however, as an authority's total spending rises above a standard level, set by central government for each individual authority, the proportion of additional expenditure met by the centre drops, thereby placing a heavier burden on local rates and deterring increased expenditure. Each authority is set a *Grant Related Expenditure Assessment* (GREA) based on computation by the Department of the Environment of how much each authority needs to spend to achieve a common level of services with other authorities of the same type. Expenditure above the GREA level results in a reduction of block grant, with a 'steepening' effect built in above a certain *threshold* to penalise the high spenders.

Soon after the introduction of GREAs the government recognised a danger that some authorities might use them as targets, with the consequence that some authorities spending below their GREAs might be encouraged to spend more, while those spending far above them might find the task of cutting back to GREA level too difficult. Fearing that this might produce an aggregate *increase* in local government spending the government responded by introducing a second expenditure control mechanism known as *targets*. Based on inflation increases and previous authority expenditure patterns, each authority is set a volume expenditure target by the Department of the Environment. Authorities exceeding their target incur a *penalty* which involves loss of grant for each additional pound of expenditure per head of population above target.

Essentially the GREA and target mechanisms are two separate systems. The former assesses need to spend by an authority as a basis for calculating entitlement to block grant; the latter is a system of expenditure controls based around the progressive removal of grant above the 'target' expenditure level set for each authority. The effect, however, is that authorities have to live with both a GREA and a target and authorities spending above their target suffer a penalty even if their expenditure is within the GREA figure. In 1983/4 these penalties were made 'open-ended', with no limit until an authority has no grant left.

These provisions have inevitably aroused much controversy. The Thatcher government had a major policy aim of cutting public expenditure, and saw the GREA and target system as a means to that end. The local authority associations, however, have generally deplored the imposition of targets for individual authorities as an unwarrantable increase in central control. Centrally imposed expenditure targets not only infringe the rights of elected councillors to determine local spending needs and priorities, but also undermine their accountability to local ratepayers. What from the central perspective might be seen as an essential instrument of public expenditure control, from the local level might be seen instead as a threat to the fabric of local government itself.

The 1980 Act also considerably tightened central controls upon *capital expenditure*. Government approvals now mainly apply to *programmes* rather than individual projects and relate to only one year at a time. Local authorities now receive allocations for capital expenditure under five blocks: housing, education, transport, personal social services and other services. Allocations can be transferred between authorities and, to a limited extent (currently 10 per cent) between years. They can also be supplemented by capital receipts and trading profits. Authorities can also switch expenditure between services to a greater extent than hitherto, as virement (transfer) between blocks is permitted. These new found freedoms, however, are somewhat illusory. Allocations relate not only to borrowing but also to expenditure (i.e. loan sanction is given in line with expenditure allocations), and are determined nationally to meet government public expenditure targets. Individual authorities overspending their allocation are likely to suffer compensating reductions in subsequent years; indeed, those deliberately overspending supplemented allocations can be prevented from letting new contracts by ministerial order. The effect, therefore, has been to impose firm statutory controls on the level of capital expenditure that any authority can incur in any year.

(B)　THE LOCAL GOVERNMENT FINANCE ACT, 1982

This measure strengthened still further the expenditure controls over local authorities imposed by the 1980 Local Government, Planning and Land Act. It contained two main provisions. First, it legitimised retrospectively the grant penalties associated with targets set in 1981/2 and 1982/3, and set out the context in which expenditure guidance or targets could be issued in future years. Secondly, it prohibited local authorities from levying supplementary rates. This latter provision effectively requires rate precepts to be made or issued for complete financial years. Although intended to further curtail local government expenditure – by requiring authorities to meet any unforeseen expenditure from existing budgets – the effect may well be to persuade local authorities to set high initial rates (to provide adequate balances to meet unexpected contingencies or loss of income). However, as Greenwood (1982, p. 263) emphasises, the Act also enables the Secretary of State to withdraw 'grant *during the middle of the financial year* from any authority which in his view is overspending'. He adds, 'it is difficult to escape the conclusion that the government has taken power: (a) to set for each authority what is to be regarded as the "needed" level of spending, (b) to enforce that level of spending by manipulation of grant'. To avoid the prospect of local authorities, whose rate fund becomes overdrawn *within* a year, from 'going bankrupt', the Act provides that authorities concerned may be given permission to borrow temporarily on revenue account, but only on such terms as the Secretary of State may impose.

(C)　RATE LIMITATION PROPOSALS, 1983

Despite the provision of the 1980 and 1982 Acts, a small number of local authorities continued to spend well above target levels. In a White Paper (*Rates: Proposals for Rate Limitation and Reform of the Rating System*) published jointly by the DOE and the Welsh Office in August 1983 the government proposed that it should have the power to cap the rates of the small number of councils – between a dozen and twenty – which, it maintained, were responsible for the bulk of the 'excessive' spending. Furthermore, if total council spending continued at levels deemed too high, the government proposed taking a reserve general power to introduce a cap on the rates of *all* local authorities.

The initial major targets were a small number of Labour-controlled authorities. According to the White Paper, the government will select a small number of councils in 1984 to have their rates capped in 1985/6. The criteria for selecting these councils include spending performance against government targets and spending according to grant-related expenditure figures (GREAs). Smaller district councils are excluded and of the 296 shire districts in England some 275 are to be removed from consideration because their budgets are less than £10m. Thirty-four out of the thirty-seven Welsh districts are similarly exempted.

Council budgets being prepared in Autumn 1984 will be assessed by civil servants in the DOE. Subsequently a small number will be given figures for their permitted rate rise and if they refuse to comply a maximum rate will be determined by Parliamentary Order. This, of course, cuts further across the traditional right of local authorities to determine their own spending levels, and the proposals were immediately widely attacked. However, according to the White Paper, 'the government have had no alternative but to develop the selective rate limitation scheme. The behaviour of a few authorities has made action inevitable.' Labour-controlled councils such as the GLC, South Yorkshire and Camden seemed likely to be included among the initial candidates for rate capping. As something of a foretaste, in July 1983 the Secretary of State for Scotland limited the rates of four Scottish local authorities (Lothian Regional Council, City of Glasgow District Council, Kirkcaldy District Council and Stirling District Council). This action is possible because of the Local Government (Miscellaneous Provisions) (Scotland) Act, 1981 which gives the Secretary of State for Scotland virtually direct control over the level of a local authority's expenditure – similar (although not identical) powers seem set to apply to England and Wales from 1984 onwards.

The independence of local government has gradually been eroded by the developments outlined above. In the past individual authorities could always escape centrally-imposed financial constraints by raising extra income from the rates without penalty (so long as it was prepared to risk the 'political' reaction from local ratepayers). That option, however, has now largely been closed. The switch in emphasis from concern with local *government* spending towards concern with local *authority* spending has been marked. As Greenwood (1982, p. 254) observes, 'strident tension' and 'bitter rancour' characterised central-local relations in the early 1980s.

The Local State?

On pp. 143–8 three 'models' of central–local relations were discussed. There are, however, alternative approaches. One such is provided in recent Marxist literature. Cockburn (1977) in her study of Lambeth provides the best known example of this perspective which assumes that local government is simply one arm of the capitalist state, providing the conditions for continued capital accumulation and the maintenance of social order. In other words, a general theory of the capitalist state is applied with little modification to what has become known as the 'local state'.

Saunders (1981), however, suggests that this approach is inadequate. He argues that the 'local state' is not simply the national state writ small, and that a general theory of the state cannot be applied to the local level. He criticises Cockburn's as 'a surprisingly crass agency model' which reduces local government to a mere agent of central government. In Saunders's view, the 'local state' cannot simply be reduced to a functioning part of a national capitalist state, for within certain constraints 'non-capitalist interests can win at the local level in a way that is becoming increasingly difficult at national level' (pp. 4, 11). In 1983, for example, there were 'radical' authorities of the 'left' (e.g. GLC), as well as of the 'right' (e.g. Wandsworth), which operated with particular local distinctiveness.

As a basis for understanding 'the current crisis of central–local relations in Britain' (p. 10) Saunders offers an alternative analytical framework encompassing four main dimensions: organisational, economic, political, and ideological. Each dimension can be observed from both the central and local perspective.

From the perspective of a right-wing central government these four dimensions can be seen thus:

1 The *organisational* problem of how to impose central controls against the demand for local self-determination, especially on the part of radical Labour councils claiming a mandate for opposing government policies;
2 The *economic* problem of how to enforce reductions in local social consumption expenditure;

3 The *political* problem of how to reconcile local democratic accountability with the pursuit of a long-term economic strategy;
4 The *ideological* problem of how to break down popular expectations regarding social provisions which became established during the postwar years of Keynesian consensus politics.

From the perspective of radical Labour councils (seeking to oppose Conservative central government cuts) Saunders puts forward the same four dimensions:

1 The *organisational* problem of how to fight central government policies through local authorities which are subordinate to central departments;
2 The *economic* problem of how to finance and defend services while at the same time transforming their character in a socialist direction;
3 The *political* problem of how to mobilise alliances among different consumption sectors and between these and class-based producer movements;
4 The *ideological* problem of how to assert the principle of need in the face of central government's desire to trim welfare services.

Saunders's analysis of central–local relations goes beyond the inter-organisational focus of the power-dependence model. Rightly, he stresses economic, political and ideological dimensions as well as 'top down' and 'bottom up' perspectives. His approach is particularly helpful in understanding the relationship between central governments and local authorities which are opposed on political and ideological grounds. It is less helpful, however, where there is little or no political or ideological distinctiveness – in technical fields, for example, or where there is sustained political consensus between individual authorities and the centre. Perhaps, as Dunleavy (1980b, p. 131) suggests, future research into central–local relations needs to adopt a variety of analytical perspectives. Organisational issues are only one dimension of inter-governmental relations.

Overview

Central–local relationships are in a continuous state of flux. The absence of a written constitution means that the relationship lacks any precise definition. As Shell (1982, p. 129) has observed, 'precisely because this relationship in its full sense is not part of a written constitutional settlement, it is possible for it to alter gradually [or] for it to be changed bit by bit'. While in a formal sense local authorities are entirely subordinate to Parliament, in practice working relationships are tremendously diverse.

Sharpe (1981, p. 5) points to an 'unresolved tension' in central–local relationships arising from the ambiguous status of local government, which is subordinate to Parliament, but at the same time 'has the potential for independent power' through being elected and by having the capacity to raise at least some of its revenue by local taxation. Political, economic and social priorities can vary enormously between central government and local authorities, as well as between local authorities themselves, and over time. Interestingly, in the light of increasing central 'controls' during the 1970s and early 1980s, Alexander (1982b, p. ix), in what could be interpreted as a swing back towards an agency model approach, argues that there has been a 'decline in the autonomy and independence of local government [which] . . . constitutes a threat to the nature of our democracy and to the sensitivity and effectiveness of our public services'. Clearly, however, the infinite number of variables prohibits the formulation of any 'rule of thumb'; complexity remains the order of the day, hence the inappropriateness of generalisations.

10 QUASI-GOVERNMENT

Introduction

The term 'quasi-government' refers to both the government-created and semi-private organisations which are both distinct from, but usually relate to, either central departments or local authorities. As a field of study quasi-government is both complex and confusing, being partly public and partly private, voluntary or commercial. So great is the number and variety of organisations included within it that generalisations, definitions and classifications are fraught with difficulties. Even terminology is a problem. The organisations comprising quasi-government are referred to by a variety of terms: 'fringe bodies', 'non-departmental public bodies', 'semi-autonomous authorities' and 'quangos', to name but a few. The latter term, usually an acronym for 'quasi-autonomous non-governmental organisation', has now entered popular usage, indicating the interest which quasi-government has recently begun to attract.

The word 'quango', however, is essentially an umbrella beneath which a tremendous variety of organisations shelter. Compare, for example, a local association for the disabled, the Apple and Pear Development Council, the Atomic Energy Authority, and the Arts Council – all are 'quangos' but their diversity in terms of finance, organisation, objectives and accountability is enormous. Generalising about 'quangos' can be hazardous – even their origins are remarkably diverse as Barker (1982, pp. 7–8) observes:

> Many are statutory, under an Act itself (for example, Manpower Services Commission or Health and Safety Commission) ... The founding instrument may be a royal charter (BBC or the research councils); a Treasury Minute (University Grants Committee); the articles of a non-profit company (National Consumer Council); or, more humbly, but apparently almost as effectively, a mere Answer in the House, a memorandum from the Minister to himself, a wave of the hand, or whatever else may signify a decision to establish a new body (Schools Council,

Technician and Business Education Councils and that unusual 'central–local government voluntary' body, the Women's Royal Voluntary Service).

The problem of discussing quasi-government is further complicated, as Doig (1979, p. 311) notes, 'by the fact that there is no one characteristic, or lack of characteristic, that distinguishes quangos or non-departmental public bodies from other organizations in the structure of government'. Nevertheless, most, if not all, of the organisations concerned carry out their work at arm's length from central government departments and/or local authorities. Indeed, quasi-government is sometimes presented as part of a public/ private continuum: from Government (G) e.g. central departments; through Quasi-Governmental Organisations (QG) e.g. nationalised industries; to Quasi-Non-Governmental Organisations (QNG) e.g. National Research Development Organisation; to Non-Government (NG) e.g. private companies (see Hague, Mackenzie and Barker, 1975). This is obviously a simplified and inevitably imprecise scheme but it is helpful in placing quasi-government within the broader administrative and political context.

While the rationale for the arm's length approach, as well as the length of the arm, varies widely from organisation to organisation, the desire to distance important areas of public administration from direct political control has been a major factor in the twentieth-century growth of quasi-government. Of course, where politicians are denied control, they cannot normally be expected to assume accountability, thus undermining the principle that public administration should be publicly accountable. As Sir Norman Chester (1979, p. 54) has observed:

> The growth of fringe bodies is a retreat from the simple democratic principle evolved in the nineteenth century that those who perform a public duty should be fully responsible to an electorate – by way either of a minister responsible to Parliament or of a locally elected council. The essence of the fringe body is that it is not so responsible for some or all of its actions.

Numbers and Types of Quangos

There is much disagreement about precisely (or even roughly) how many organisations exist within the field of quasi-government.

This is partly because of the difficulty in deciding where boundaries should be drawn, a difficulty which has increased in recent years with the development of new organisational forms (such as 'hived-off' agencies) and with the increasing interpenetration of the public and private sectors. As Hood (1979, p. 9) asks, 'Does one include advisory committees as "government bodies"? Contracting firms? Grant-aided bodies? Firms in which public money is invested?' Quasi-government is a grey area between not only government departments and local authorities, but also frequently between the public and the private sectors.

Another analytical difficulty is that organisational units are often not clear-cut. For example, it is always problematic whether or not to count Scottish and Welsh divisions of an agency as separate units or as part of a single organisation. Because of these various difficulties a count of quangos is beset with problems. In 1978 the Civil Service Department reported that there were 252 non-departmental public bodies, compared with 196 in 1971, 103 in 1959 and only ten before 1900 (Bowen, 1978). The definition the CSD used for its survey was: 'organizations which have been set up or adopted by Departments and provided with funds to perform some function which the Government wish to have performed but which it did not wish to be the direct responsibility of a Minister or Department'. The CSD survey excluded non-permanent bodies, advisory committees and working parties. Other sources, using broader definitions, produce far higher figures. For example, Anderson lists almost 1,000 official organisations, many of them advisory and consultative (cited in Hood, 1979, p. 8). Philip Holland (1979) produced a list of 3,068 quangos but this was because he defined a quango as an official body to which ministers appoint directly members other than civil servants. He thereby included hundreds of advisory committees and hundreds of judicial tribunals and many more bodies with no governmental function at all (e.g. several public schools). The Outer Circle Policy Unit (1979) included 603 bodies in its list, having excluded departmental advisory committees and organisations whose function was primarily judicial.

'Head counts' of quangos are the more difficult because, as Hood (1979, pp. 9–10) observes, 'the "heads" involved are of enormously differing size and importance – on a scale more like the difference between the head of an ant and an elephant than the difference between one human head and another'. Quangos, in fact, are analogous to pressure groups; both involve tiny, relatively insignificant groupings, as well as massive and extremely powerful organisations. Indeed quangos are frequently the target of pressure group activity, and may at times themselves behave like pressure groups exerting pressure on other parts of the government machine.

The volume and variety of quangos also makes any attempt at meaningful classification difficult. However, the Pliatzky Report (1980, pp. 1–2) delineated three distinctive types – executive bodies, advisory bodies, and tribunals – which offers a useful basis for categorisation:

1   *Executive bodies:* 489 in total, spending (in 1979) £5,800m. and employing 217,000 staff;
2   *Advisory bodies*: 1,561, involving expenditure of £13m. by sponsoring departments;
3   *Tribunals*: 67 'tribunal systems' with administrative costs in 1978/9 totalling £30m.

The number of quangos identified by Pliatzky, large though it is, nevertheless *excludes* important areas of quasi-government. It ignores, for example, the 'innumerable autonomous and semi-autonomous, official and quasi-official organisations, each with its own part to play in the policy-making process' of local government (Cousins, 1982, p. 152). It also *excludes* various administrative agencies connected with the National Health Service and the nationalised industries – the latter including both public corporations as well as, arguably, companies in which the government has a major shareholding (e.g. Rolls Royce (1971) Ltd). The size, diversity, and importance of quasi-government is vast; one is dealing with a genus rather than a species. All that can really be said with certainty is that quasi-governmental bodies generally operate in narrower, more specific areas than government departments or local authorities.

Inevitably, any classification of such bodies must be arbitrary; clear boundaries between quasi-government and more orthodox areas of public administration cannot always be drawn. For presentational purposes, however, this chapter will follow Pliatzky and focus upon the major forms of quasi-government at national level, namely, *executive and advisory non-departmental public bodies*. The other major form of non-departmental body, *the public corporation*, will be discussed in Chapter 11, within the wider context of the nationalised industries. *Health and water authorities*, while part of quasi-government, have a strong regional network, and are discussed in Chapter 12 along with other forms of regional administration. *Administrative tribunals*, although included within Pliatzky's survey, are most appropriately considered alongside other channels of redress, and are therefore dealt with in detail in Chapter 14. Space does not allow consideration of quasi-government at the local level (for details of which see Cousins, 1982, and 1983).

Non-Departmental Public Bodies: Rationale

Quasi-government is not new although its scale is new. The Crown Agents, for example, date from the mid-nineteenth century, the Development Commission was set up in 1909 and the Horserace Totalisator Board (the Tote) goes back to 1928. As Hood notes, however, they came into 'high fashion in the 1940s and again in the 1960s when the Fulton Committee endorsed the idea of government growth outside Whitehall by "hiving-off" units from civil service departments to non-departmental bodies' (1981, p. 100). Pliatzky (1980, pp. 2–3) presents the rationale for non-departmental bodies in the following terms:

(A)   EXECUTIVE BODIES (e.g. Hops Marketing Board; Design Council)

Certain functions, it is argued, can best be carried out at arm's length from central government:

(i)   because the work is of an executive nature which does not require ministers to be involved in day-to-day management;

(ii)   because the work is more effectively carried out by a single-purpose organisation rather than by a government department with a wide range of functions;

(iii)   to involve people from outside government in the direction of the organisation;

(iv)   to put the performance of particular functions outside direct party political control.

(B)   ADVISORY BODIES (e.g. China Clay Council; Advisory Committee on Pesticides)

The major reasons for advisory committees (incorporating outside representation) are:

(i)   that the department's own staff are unable to provide the necessary advice by themselves; and

(ii) that it may be desirable to enlist participation by outside interests in order to develop publicly acceptable proposals.

Control and Accountability

These two concepts (see pp. 8–9) are central to any discussion of quasi-government:

(A) CONTROL

The arm's length approach usually associated with quangos means that normal departmental patterns of ministerial control do not apply. Indeed, a minister may even 'expressly desire to keep out of the affairs of quangos within the ambit of his department, arguing that to behave otherwise is merely to frustrate the whole purpose of this way of organizing public services' (Johnson, 1979, p. 389). On day-to-day matters most ministers and departments 'maintain an arm's-length relationship' from the organisation which they sponsor, although considerable pressure may be brought to bear upon them on 'broader policy and resources' matters (Johnson, 1982, p. 213).

The precise way in which many quangos are controlled is difficult to determine. Obtaining even basic information can be problematical. For example, while annual reports usually name the chairman and board members they do not always reveal their salaries. Likewise the breakdown of expenses between board members and staff, and between different types of expenses, is relatively detailed in some cases but not in others. A further problem is that the governing authority of quangos often consists of a board or council. Often the only paid member is the chairman, suggesting that he may really be in charge. However, generalisations are dangerous: some chairmen are only part time and some councils are large while others are small and highly specialised. While the staff running some are technical specialists, this is far from universal. Sometimes the relationship with the parent department is close; sometimes it is not. The permutations are infinite.

(B) ACCOUNTABILITY

Three aspects of the accountability of non-departmental bodies require consideration:

(i) *Relations with ministers.* With non-departmental bodies, as Johnson (1982, p. 213) observes, 'accountability of Ministers' must remain 'attenuated', for 'otherwise there would be little point in having this form of administrative organisation'. Usually ministers are formally answerable to Parliament only for discharging their own responsibilities relating to sponsored bodies (e.g. for broad policy and general oversight), while responsibility for efficiency and day-to-day matters normally rests with the organisations' own management. In practice, however, the precise boundaries of ministerial responsibility are often difficult to define. Not only is there considerable variation in relationships between ministers and managerial boards, but the borderline between ministers' policy and oversight responsibilities, and those of boards for efficiency and day-to-day administration is often blurred (see pp. 2–3). In any event the sheer volume and variety of bodies under departmental sponsorship often makes ministerial responsibility something of a myth. In recent years the size and complexity of departmental work has seriously eroded the concept of ministerial responsibility even for their own departments (pp. 229–32). How much more tenuous must it therefore be for non-departmental bodies operating at arm's length from ministers, and which 'for most of the time . . . rub along without much awareness of the Minister and his officials' (Johnson, 1982, p. 213).

(ii) *Relations with Parliament.* Because non-departmental bodies operate at arm's length from government, and ministers are not constitutionally responsible to Parliament for all of their work, accountability to Parliament is limited. Johnson (1982, p. 213) observes that MPs 'may attempt ingeniously to get at the activities of governmental bodies through the questioning of Ministers, but . . . it is not something attempted very regularly and, when it is, the attack focuses on policy and resources rather than on particular decisions'. The dilemma, he adds, is that 'reinforcement of the parliamentary accountability of these organisations would also entail a strengthening of ministerial control over them', so destroying the arm's length relationship with all its attendant advantages.

Nevertheless, some important instruments of accountability to Parliament can be identified, although most apply to some quangos and not all. For example, some come within the jurisdiction of the Ombudsman (pp. 250–6), some have their accounts audited by the Comptroller and Auditor-General and reported to the Public

Accounts Committee (pp. 225–6), some present annual reports to Parliament, and so on. In fact, no general pattern is discernible, except that almost all stop short of full accountability to Parliament. In 1979, however, accountability was strengthened with the advent of the fourteen new Commons select committees (pp. 235–9), each of which has power to examine the expenditure, administration and policy of the main government departments 'and associated public bodies'. While this represents an important development in Parliament's powers of scrutiny, non-departmental bodies account for only a small part of the work of these committees which are quite unable to exercise anything like detailed oversight.

(iii)   *Relations with the courts.*   The legal accountability of quangos also poses considerable difficulty. Because their legal status and powers are confused, judicial control of their activities lacks coherence. For example, remedies available against one body may not be available against another; procedures or standards applied by one quango may be legally sound but if utilised by another they may not, and so on. In Johnson's view (1982, p. 215), 'The confusions affecting legal accountability and the availability of enforceable remedies are one of the most serious aspects of the haphazard development of governmental bodies'.

While accountability problems are found throughout British public administration, with non-departmental bodies they are particularly acute. Clearly, orthodox ministerial responsibility could not be extended to them without undermining the arm's length principle. Several changes short of this, however, have been proposed: requiring greater disclosure of information; extending jurisdiction of the Comptroller and Auditor-General and Public Accounts Committee to more bodies; and clarifying the authority, powers and legal status of all such organisations (see, for example, Outer Circle Policy Unit, 1979; and Pliatzky Report (1980), pp. 18–23). Changes of this kind would standardise and strengthen accountability without destroying the arm's length arrangement. In view of the importance and extent of quasi-government they perhaps deserve serious consideration.

In 1981 a tentative move in this direction occurred with the publication of a government guide (*Non-Departmental Public Bodies: A Guide for Departments*) laying down ground rules on the future nature of quangos and their relationships with departments. Departments are now obliged to review from time to time the bodies they sponsor, and have received instructions that – whatever the precise degree of independence – the minister is answerable to Parliament for whether the body is working efficiently and economically. Greater financial accountability, particularly for bodies utilising government funds at a level of 50 per cent or more, was also envisaged and the establishment of new non-departmental bodies would, it was promised, involve negotiating more hurdles than hitherto.

Patronage

Considerable concern about non-departmental bodies has focused on patronage – the number of appointments in the gift of ministers. Promotion by merit rather than political influence has long characterised the British civil service, but outside the civil service ministers still exercise considerable patronage. In November 1978, for example, 'seventeen ministers had within their gift over 8,000 paid appointments and 25,000 unpaid ones at a total cost of £5m. a year' (Outer Circle Policy Unit, 1979, p. 47). One department alone was responsible for nearly 1,000 appointments. Parliamentary influence over these appointments is minimal, the matter being almost entirely one of ministerial discretion. Party political factors are frequently to the fore; indeed, 'many people ... have claimed to perceive a resurgence of eighteenth-century jobbery' (Hood, 1978, p. 40).

Whether or not patronage is used in a party political manner, the non-departmental sector nevertheless 'affords the opportunity for government by co-option rather than by election or by merit appointment' (Hood, 1978, p. 41). Additionally, once a person is appointed, not only need the minister never account for the choice, but the likelihood is that he or she will never have to justify it on performance grounds.

The Outer Circle Policy Unit study (1979, p. 48) emphasised three major areas for concern about appointments of this kind:

(i)   *Efficiency* – does patronage result in the best available people being appointed?
(ii) *Power* – does patronage give ministers too much power to influence supposedly independent organisations?
(iii) *Privilege* – does it enable elite groups to dominate patronage jobs?

Although these are legitimate grounds for unease, solutions are far from straightforward because of the diversity of quangos. Some appointments could be on a representative basis where there are sectional interests, but in other cases the wider public interest would need to be safeguarded.

Holland and Fallon (1978, p. 25) argue that several reforms are necessary:

(i)   Nomination should be much more open, with ministers more accountable to Parliament for each appointment.

(ii) The number of paid public appointments that can be held by a single individual should be limited.

(iii) All full-time paid appointments should be advertised and the appointment confirmed by a relevant parliamentary committee.

(iv) Appointments on solely political grounds should cease.

In summary, any reforms to the system of ministerial patronage should aim to reduce secrecy, encourage competition, control the power of ministers, introduce accountability for appointments made, and provide for assessment of performance. It is important, however, not to underplay the political dimension of patronage; it offers a means of securing the co-operation of key pressure groups and ensuring party discipline – hence ministerial 'resistance' to drastic pruning.

Exit Non-Departmental Public Bodies?

The Conservative government elected in 1979 promised a drastic purge of quasi-governmental organisations as part of its wider strategy of reducing public expenditure. Immediately following Pliatzky the government decided to reduce: a) the number of executive bodies by thirty; b) the number of advisory bodies by 211; c) the number of individual tribunals by six. In December 1980 the government announced that a further 192 non-departmental bodies were to be wound up by 1983, bringing the total savings up to about £23m. a year by 1983. In February 1982 the Prime Minister announced a third round of cuts: the abolition of 112 executive non-departmental bodies and 500 advisory ones. Philip Holland, MP, observed: 'That nearly one-quarter of the executive quangos and nearly one-third of the very large number of advisory bodies, as defined by Pliatzky and inherited by this Government, are scheduled for abolition after only $2\frac{1}{2}$ years is a quite remarkable achievement by any standards' (*Daily Telegraph*, 11 March 1982).

This theme was highlighted by the 1983 Conservative Party Manifesto which maintained (p. 36) that the 1979–83 government had 'abolished 500 Quangos'.

The significance of these cuts, however, should not be exaggerated. The Pliatzky cuts, for example, were more apparent than real. As Hood (1981, p. 102) notes, against 7 million or so public sector employees and public spending of £70,000m. per year, a cut of 250 permanent staff and £11.6m. per year following Pliatzky was scarcely a massive blow for retrenchment. In any case by late 1980 the Pliatzky cuts had been eroded by the creation of some thirty *new* non-departmental bodies, many of them major organisations with large budgets. The second round of cuts in late 1980 was also largely cosmetic with many of the savings achieved by amalgamations rather than closures. Even the 1982 measures, while far more substantial, were far from a total purge. As Hood (1981, pp. 120–1) argues, non-departmental bodies are too useful for politicians to abolish them too readily. There are, he adds, at least four potential political uses which make them unlikely to disappear:

(i)   Government will presumably always need bodies from which it can distance itself in sensitive areas;
(ii) There will presumably always be value in having temporary organisations outside the permanent government service that can be scrapped when chances permit;
(iii) The use of such bodies as an administrative means of by-passing other public organisations, along with the patronage dimension, continues to attract politicians;
(iv) Advisory committees are useful as political 'window dressing'. For these reasons, if for no others, quangos seem unlikely to become extinct.

Conclusions

Non-departmental public bodies (quangos) have arisen to no pattern or plan. They display a variety of structures, powers, modes of finance, methods of selection, degrees of discretion and types of staff. The main problems they pose are the excessive patronage they confer on the politicians and officials who establish them and make appointments to them, 'their frustration of the implementation of public policies, their financial irresponsibility and their erosion of democratic accountability and control' (Jones, 1982a, p. 924). Jones further argues that if central government believes it cannot or should not perform a particular public function, 'it would be better if it decentralised not to technocratic quangos but to directly elected local governments'. Less radically, Johnson (1979, pp. 393–4) argues that some order could be introduced into chaos by the creation of a Standing Advisory Commission on Administrative Organisation (another quango?). This would conduct a continuing survey of administrative structures with two purposes in mind: a) to produce information and thereby increase openness; b) to carry out inquiries and offer advice to central government and other public authorities.

Whatever the merits of such reform proposals it is a mistake to see quangos as wholly self-contained. As Hood (1979, p. 20) points out, government agencies are increasingly operating 'in multiple and dense networks of cross-cutting territorial, functional and hierarchical relationships, and within an overall context of ... government by grants and by indirect administration rather than by the older pattern of directly hired bureaucrats at the centre'. Inter-organisational and inter-agency relationships have become increasingly complex; quangos are only part of this complex administrative and political environment – an environment which the operations of quangos themselves influence.

In recent years the discrediting of quangos has become a popular political pastime. According to Dunsire (1982, p. 15), 'quango-hunting' has since 1979 'become a Conservative blood-sport, under the illusion that they are nothing but wasteful "empire-building" '. In practice, however, quangos often deal with specialised tasks in a way which both central government departments and local authorities would find difficult. They are also incredibly diverse; there is little justification for derogatory generalisations. Without denying the accountability/control/patronage problems which accompany this form of governmental organisation, the survival of the species suggests that governments (however reluctantly) themselves see a continuing role for non-departmental public bodies. As Hill (1983, p. 124) observes, the 'attacks on Quangos have obscured, rather than illuminated, the serious issue of how ministerial patronage might be replaced by alternative selection procedures, and how these bodies might be made more accountable, without losing that very semi-independence which was a major reason for establishing them in the first place'.

11 ADMINISTERING PUBLIC OWNERSHIP

Quasi-government in Britain extends to public ownership. While some publicly owned commercial or industrial undertakings are administered through orthodox central and local government institutions, such enterprises often require greater managerial and financial flexibility than organisations of this kind normally allow. Consequently, the arm's-length approach typical of quasi-government is an important feature of British public ownership. This is especially true of the nationalised industries with which this chapter is largely concerned.

Terminology and Ambiguity of Public Ownership

Public ownership typifies the ambiguity and complexity inherent in British public administration. It exists in various forms, offers a bewildering range of relationships with the wider political and administrative system, and presents complex problems of accountability and control. The very term 'public ownership' is ambiguous. Technically a vast range of assets – roads, schools, hospitals, libraries etc. – are in public ownership, and in this sense the boundaries of public ownership might be regarded as coterminous with the public sector, or even the state itself. Usually, however, in Britain the term 'public ownership' applies to commercial and industrial undertakings. Although this narrows the scope considerably, ambiguity nevertheless remains. Does public ownership, for example, include undertakings in which the state has only a minority holding (such as British Petroleum)? And what precisely is a 'commercial' or 'industrial' undertaking? The water industry is largely in public hands, and yet, unlike gas and electricity, is not usually regarded as a nationalised industry, and is rarely included in discussions of public ownership.

Some writers attempt to resolve these ambiguities by focusing on particular types of public ownership. The term 'nationalisation' – 'a process in which private assets ... are transferred into national ownership' (Steel, 1978, p. 110) – is, for example, quite widely used. Nevertheless, 'nationalisation' itself presents major terminological problems. One is that it need not apply to purely industrial or commercial concerns: for example, it is technically 'correct to talk of the nationalisation of the hospitals' (Steel, 1978, p. 110). Secondly, some nationalised industries (e.g. the postal services) are 'not in fact the end-product of nationalisation' having never been privately owned. Thirdly, nationalisation represents only part of public ownership: for example, it excludes bodies in municipal ownership. Nevertheless, despite these difficulties, the term 'nationalised industries' is capable of fairly precise definition, and considerable agreement exists about the industries to which it refers (see Table 11.1, p. 186).

Another approach is to focus on perhaps the most important form of public ownership, the 'public corporation'. This, however, is also fraught with problems. Public corporations embrace an even smaller part of public ownership than 'nationalisation' and, more problematically, there is 'little agreement as to the essential characteristics of a public corporation' (Steel, 1978, p. 110); hence, defining or describing one, other than in general terms, poses serious problems.

Terms such as 'public ownership', 'nationalisation', and 'public corporations' must, therefore, be used with caution. Confusion is compounded, moreover, because different authorities use the terms, and draw the boundaries between them, differently. Thus Tivey (1973a, pp. 67–9) includes atomic energy as a 'major nationalized industry', whilst the McIntosh Report (1976, App. Vol., p. 4) and Pliatzky Report (1980, p. 182) exclude it. Similarly, McIntosh (App. Vol., p. 5) includes regional water authorities in its list of public corporations, whereas Pliatzky excludes them (p. 183) arguing that they are 'more in the nature of a public service of the kind provided by local authorities' (p. 31). Even where consistent definitions are used, undertakings may be reclassified. Thus the Royal Mint and the Property Services Agency (Supplies Division) were officially reclassified from central government to the public corporation sector in the mid-1970s on being 'established as trading funds under the Government Trading Funds Act 1973' (Briscoe, 1981). It is, therefore, far from clear, not only how different forms of public ownership can be delineated, but even where the boundary should be drawn between 'public ownership' and the wider machinery of central and local administration.

The Development of Public Ownership

Public ownership is not exclusively a modern phenomenon. The Post Office, for example, has been publicly owned for centuries, and during the nineteenth century municipal gas and water undertakings were quite widespread. During the twentieth century, however, public ownership has undergone enormous expansion, mainly with regard to nationalisation (where the state – as opposed to local authorities – owns the assets).

Until the Second World War nationalisation was of only peripheral economic importance – the main nationalised undertakings being the Forestry Commission, the British Broadcasting Corporation (BBC), the Central Electricity Board, and the London Passenger Transport Board. After the war, however, the Attlee government massively extended public ownership by nationalising several basic industries: coal, iron and steel, electricity, gas, road transport, rail, inland waterways, and civil aviation.

Until 1979 Conservative governments – although partially denationalising iron and steel and road transport in the 1950s, and selling minor undertakings to private enterprise in the 1970s (e.g. Thomas Cook Ltd, and State Management Pubs and Breweries) – were generally disposed to leave Attlee's legacy intact. Indeed, in some respects they extended it: for example, the Heath government nationalised Rolls Royce and Upper Clyde Shipbuilders. There were also further acts of nationalisation by Labour governments in the 1960s and 1970s. Iron and steel was re-nationalised in 1967, and shipbuilding and aerospace nationalised in the 1970s. Major instruments were also established to channel public money – usually in return for state shareholdings – into industrial companies, the most important being the Industrial Reorganisation Corporation (1966–71) and the National Enterprise Board (established in 1975).

While the economic impact of public ownership is difficult to evaluate, it is clearly considerable. In 1978 a White Paper (*Nationalised Industries*, 1978, para. 52) stated:

> The nationalised industries ... employ about 1,700,000 people, or 7% of the country's total labour force. Their total investment this year and next is about £3,500 million at 1977 prices, and in 1976 they accounted for 14% of total fixed investment ... In 1976 they contributed about 10% of the total output of the U.K. economy. They dominate four strategic sectors of economic activity: energy, public transport, communications and iron and steel.

Despite subsequent contraction, public ownership in general – and the nationalised industries in particular – remain of major economic importance: in 1981–2, for example, the eighteen largest nationalised industries (including British Leyland and Rolls Royce) still employed over 1.6 million workers and had a combined annual turnover of £42.7 bn (*The Times*, 18 July 1983).

1979 probably marks the peak in the expansion of public ownership, for the Thatcher government embarked on a major programme of 'privatisation'. This took two forms: a) *Breaking public monopolies*: By 1982 steps in this direction had occurred in the bus, gas, postal, and telecommunication industries (Steel and Heald, 1982, pp. 334–5); b) *Denationalisation*: (selling nationally-owned assets to the private sector). Between 1979 and 1982 assets totalling £1½ billion were disposed of, and further sales of about £2 billion over the following three years were anticipated (*Economic Progress Report*, No. 145, HMSO, May 1982). As these developments suggest, the relative consensus of the postwar period had broken down by 1979, posing fundamental questions about the relative merits of public ownership and privatisation.

Public Ownership and Privatisation

The relationship of publicly-owned enterprises to the wider political and administrative system cannot be understood without reference to the arguments for and against public ownership.

(A) THE REASONS FOR PUBLIC OWNERSHIP

These are numerous, often being geared to the pragmatic needs of particular industries. Several seminal influences can, however, be identified:

(i) *Ideological influences.* The main ideological thrust towards greater public ownership has come from the Labour party, which is committed by clause IV of its constitution to securing

> for the workers by hand or by brain the full fruits of their industry and the most equitable distribution thereof that may be possible upon the basis of the common ownership of the means of production, distribution, and exchange, and the best obtainable system of popular administration and control of each industry or service.

Part of the wider socialist goal of a more egalitarian society, public ownership was to enable industry to serve the interests of workers and the community. To achieve this, industries would be placed under 'popular administration and control', a phrase generally taken to mean 'that public ownership was likely to . . . be State and municipal' – i.e. administered by politicians and public administrators – rather than controlled by 'workers themselves' (Taylor, 1980, p. 10).

(ii) *Monopoly arguments.* In some industries (e.g. post, gas, electricity) competition has generally been regarded as wasteful and unnecessary. In such cases statutory monopolies have usually been created, albeit public (rather than private) monopolies where workers and consumers can be protected by democratic controls.

(iii) *Modernisation and industrial efficiency.* Where industries require major capital or 'high risk' investment, or where costly industrial re-structuring is necessary, private finance may not be available. In such cases governments may inject public money in return for a stake in the industry. In recent years a major role in effecting such investments has been taken by such bodies as the Industrial Reorganisation Corporation (1966–71) and the National Enterprise Board (NEB) established in 1975.

(iv) *Industrial rescues.* From the 1960s successive governments used public ownership as a means of rescuing private companies facing liquidation. Such action was justified by the need to save jobs, protect the balance of payments, and maintain vital industries. Notable examples include Rolls Royce (nationalised by a Conservative government in 1971) and British Leyland (rescued by Labour in 1975).

(v) *Economic management.* All recent governments have been concerned with economic management, to which end have been used various combinations of fiscal and monetary measures, physical controls, and instruments of indicative planning (such as the National Economic Development Council and Regional Economic Planning Boards). In addition, the postwar expansion of nationalisation provided governments with a major economic tool for controlling wages, prices, investment, and so on, in strategic industries. Although in practice this has tended to be used more for crisis economic management than for economic planning, it is a tool to which Labour and Conservative postwar governments alike have made frequent use.

The above are not the only reasons for public ownership, but all have been important influences. The thread linking them together is the concept of industry serving the community: that, while goods and services should be produced efficiently, the wider public interest must be considered. The non-socialist arguments have been particularly crucial, for they alone explain the expansion of public ownership during a period often dominated by Conservative governments. Until 1979 successive Conservative governments generally accepted the more pragmatic arguments for public ownership, although party pronouncements and rank-and-file sentiment were often hostile. In 1979, however, a shift occurred, with the Thatcher government pursuing a policy of privatisation.

(B)   THE REASONS FOR PRIVATISATION

These have been identified by Steel and Heald (1982, pp. 337–44) as four in number: (i) Privatisation enhances economic freedom; (ii) it increases efficiency; (iii) it eases the problem of public sector pay; (iv) it reduces public sector borrowing. While some of these arguments are questionable, they must be seen against the increased emphasis placed on monetarist economic policies by British governments since the late 1970s. Monetarism sees economic wellbeing best promoted by money supply controls (i.e. manipulating interest rates and regulating the printing of money). As such it de-emphasises the need for physical controls and this – coupled with monetarist stress on market disciplines – reduces, theoretically at least, the significance of nationalised industries as instruments of economic management.

Forms of Public Ownership

The aims of public ownership are reflected in the forms in which it exists. A common theme, as already observed, is that industries should operate in the public interest; consequently, it is generally accepted that public control mechanisms are necessary to ensure that the public interest is pursued. It is also generally accepted that, as elsewhere within the public sector, those running public industries should be accountable. At the same time, however, such industries are usually felt to require a measure of independence from politicians. In some cases (e.g. broadcasting) this is deemed necessary to ensure political neutrality. More generally, however, it is justified as conducive to efficient management. Although profit is not the overriding goal, public enterprises must be efficiently managed; indeed, precisely because the profit and loss 'discipline' is often absent, high priority must be given to appropriate business and management skills. Because civil servants and politicians rarely possess such skills, experienced managers often have to be employed, and usually need to be given some independence from political intervention. Hence the justification for some relaxation of traditional control and accountability mechanisms.

Of course, once traditional forms of accountability 'are abandonded, many degrees of control and many special relationships become possible' (Tivey, 1973a, p. 29). In fact, various forms of public ownership are discernible, each offering in different measure the twin desiderata of public control and accountability on the one hand, and managerial independence on the other. In particular, four main forms can be identified: a) Central government trading bodies; b) Local authority trading bodies; c) State shareholding; and d) Public corporations.

(A) CENTRAL GOVERNMENT TRADING BODIES

Some public commercial and industrial enterprises are administered as part of central government. Although varying arrangements are found, the 'pure' form is administration by government department (along the lines of the Post Office which functioned – until 1969 – as a department of state with a minister directly responsible for its activities to Parliament). Before the twentieth century the application of the departmental model to the few state trading concerns which existed seemed logical; the advantage which it offered – full ministerial control and parliamentary accountability – squared well with traditional constitutional principles. However, being run by civil servants and ministers, and with the Treasury exercising financial control, it offered little managerial independence. Consequently, other forms of administration have been applied to most of the undertakings brought into public ownership in the twentieth century, while existing undertakings administered on orthodox departmental lines have mostly either been reconstituted as public corporations (e.g. the Post Office), or, particularly in recent years, delegated to departmental agencies (e.g. ordnance factories, royal dockyards). Today no major industrial or commercial undertakings are administered as part of central administration, suggesting that as the twentieth century has progressed managerial freedom has received increasing emphasis – albeit at the expense of public accountability and control – as a desirable feature of public ownership.

(B) LOCAL GOVERNMENT TRADING BODIES

With this form of public ownership, sometimes known as municipalisation, services are provided by local authorities. Seen by early socialists as the best means of controlling public utilities, many gas, water, and electricity services were developed under municipal control until well into the twentieth century. Subsequently, numerous municipal restaurants, theatres, transport undertakings and so forth appeared, as well as a host of less conventional enterprises including a racecourse (Doncaster), a bank (Birmingham), a telephone system (Hull), and – in the early 1980s in a small number of county councils – local enterprise boards. While many such enterprises are still thriving, municipalisation has nevertheless declined since the 1930s as services such as gas and electricity have been transferred to forms of public ownership capable of administering them on regional or national bases. Moreover, in the early 1980s several, mainly Conservative-controlled, local authorities have engaged in privatisation of particular services (e.g. refuse collection). This trend, which has been encouraged by the Thatcher government, seems likely to further reduce the extent of municipal trading activities.

(C) STATE SHAREHOLDING

An increasingly important form of public ownership is the limited company in which the state holds shares. This arrangement allows maximum managerial independence: companies operate within the Companies Acts and have boards responsible to shareholders, the state's position being like that of any other shareholder. Where the government has a majority holding it may appoint directors, and lay down financial targets and so forth, although usually it does not intervene in commercial or managerial decisions. With British Petroleum, for example, in which there has been a large state shareholding since the First World War, it was claimed in 1968 that, although the government had a veto over company affairs, this had never been used. The government's relationship was identical to that with other oil companies except that it was notified whenever dividend declarations were imminent and held consultations with the company 'if new capital or new financial structures ... [were] under consideration' (Tivey, 1973b, p. 180).

The managerial independence which state shareholding allows is, of course, achieved at the expense of public control and accountability. This was particularly apparent with the NEB, which not only enjoyed substantial independence from ministers in its dealings with firms but, in turn, allowed the management of subsidiaries considerable discretion in running their companies. While this secured extensive managerial freedom, confusion and friction developed between the NEB and ministers, and Parliament experienced difficulty even in obliging the Board to explain its investment decisions (Mitchell, 1982). Subsequently, the Thatcher government brought the Board's investment programme under greater ministerial control, and required the British Leyland and Rolls Royce boards to report directly to ministers (rather than, as before, through the NEB). Nevertheless, the problems of accountability and control associated with state shareholding seem unlikely to disappear.

State shareholding has proliferated in recent years – for three main reasons:

(i) *It offers political advantages.* State share purchases do not usually require specific enabling legislation. Hence they are 'cheap' in parliamentary time, and present limited opportunities for parliamentary criticism.

(ii) *It is appropriate for industrial rescues and restructuring.* State shareholding is relatively swift and simple to implement, and enables 'rescued' companies to maintain existing management structures, avoid excessive ministerial and civil service control, and retain the goal of profitability.

(iii) *It is a by-product of privatisation.* The post-1979 emphasis on privatisation ironically seems likely to expand state shareholding. Essentially the disposal of public assets has taken two main forms. First, selling state shareholdings in limited companies: in addition to NEB disposals totalling £122m., sales of other government holdings by 1982 included just under 50 per cent of government shares in Cable and Wireless Ltd; a 24 per cent holding in the British Sugar Corporation; and 10 per cent of the state holding in BP. Secondly, converting public corporations into limited companies and disposing of shares: by 1982 this process had occurred with British Aerospace (51.6 per cent of shares sold in 1981), the National Freight Corporation (sold in 1982 to an employees and managers consortium), and the exploration and production side of the British National Oil Corporation (transferred to Britoil, 51 per cent of whose shares went on public sale in 1982). Significantly, in many of these cases substantial state shareholdings were retained (see Steel and Heald, 1982), the effects of which will be to increase the importance of state shareholding as a form of public ownership, and to blur still further the boundary between the public and private sectors.

(D)   PUBLIC CORPORATIONS

Arguably the most significant form of public ownership is the public corporation. Public corporations are important to the study of quasi-government generally. Tivey (1973a, p. 29) has observed that 'there lies behind the public corporation a theory and a fairly definite set of principles; the other autonomous bodies have developed in a much more confused and pragmatic way, with little background of deliberate principle'. The theory referred to is the reconciliation, within a single institution, of the twin desiderata of public control and accountability on the one hand and managerial independence on the other. It is strongly associated with (Lord) Morrison whose view, expressed most clearly in *Socialisation and Transport* (1933), was that nationalised industries required considerable freedom from political control if they were to operate efficiently. Hence their running should be entrusted to industrialists (rather than civil servants) whose discretion would extend to managerial and commercial matters. Each corporation would be financially self-supporting, and thereby escape Treasury control. Ministers would be limited to appointing board members and chairmen, and to issuing directives on general matters. In exercising these powers (but not for commercial and managerial matters which were the boards' responsibility) ministers would be accountable to Parliament.

The main prototypes of the public corporation are the British Broadcasting Corporation and the Central Electricity Board (both formed in 1926). The former owed much to the Crawford Report on Broadcasting (1926) which, drawing heavily on the ideas of (Lord) Reith, recommended the administration of public broadcasting by a 'Public Commission operating in the national interest'. Although several other public corporations were created in the interwar years, it was only after the Second World War that the model became firmly established, being used by the Attlee government to administer such industries as coal, steel, gas, electricity, rail, road transport, waterways, and civil aviation (the latter having been partially nationalised in 1939). Subsequently the model was extended to the Post Office, aerospace, and shipbuilding. The NEB is also a public corporation (once again illustrating the administrative complexity surrounding public ownership) as also are a host of regulatory and promotional non-departmental public bodies (see Chapter 10).

Because of its diversity of functions and forms the public corporation is difficult to define. However, according to Tivey (1973a, pp. 33–4) it has five main features:

(i)   It is a 'corporate body' (i.e. a legal entity which can trade, own property, sue and be sued etc.).
(ii) 'It is a statutory body; its constitution, powers and duties are prescribed by law and can be modified only by legislation.'
(iii) 'It is publicly owned.'
(iv) 'There is some degree of Government control. This normally includes the appointment of a corporation's governing board, and may include by statute various policy and financial matters.'
(v)   'The corporation is independent in respect of its actual operations and management ... Its personnel are not civil servants, and its finances are separate from those of the Government.'

Not every public corporation with these features is concerned with public ownership, nor strictly is public control and composition of boards always a matter for central government. Passenger Transport Executives and Port Authorities are both public corporations and yet their membership may wholly or partially be appointed by local authorities. Nevertheless, a group of the larger public corporations are normally regarded as constituting 'the nationalised industries'. Identified largely 'by the degree to which they are engaged in sale of goods and services and the extent to which revenue is derived directly from their customers' (McIntosh Report, 1976, App. Vol., p. 3), those nationalised industries existing in 1983 are shown in Table 11.1.

Public Corporations in Action

While public corporations have developed from their interwar origins into a major form of public ownership, their postwar operations owe little to Reith's concept of public corporations

Table 11.1 *Nationalised Industries 1983*

Name of corporation	Sponsoring department
British Airports Authority	Trade and Industry
British Airways Board	Trade and Industry
British Gas Corporation	Energy
British National Oil Corporation	Energy
British Railways Board	Transport
British Shipbuilders	Trade and Industry
British Steel Corporation	Trade and Industry
British Telecom	Trade and Industry
British Waterways Board	Environment
Electricity Council (plus Central	Energy
Electricity Generating Board and Area	
Electricity Boards for England and Wales)	
National Bus Company	Transport
National Coal Board	Energy
North of Scotland Hydro-Electric Board	Scottish Office
Post Office	Trade and Industry
Scottish Transport Group	Scottish Office
South of Scotland Electricity Board	Scottish Office

Source: McIntosh Report (1976) (App. Vol., p. 4); *The Times*, 18 July 1983.

acting as trustees for the public interest. Although considerable differences exist between corporations, several common problems can be identified which have made the Reith/Morrison concept largely unattainable.

Five main 'problem areas' have characterised postwar public corporations: *(a)* Administrative Structure; *(b)* Financial Arrangements; *(c)* Ministerial Control; *(d)* Accountability to Parliament; *(e)* Consumer Representation.

(A) ADMINISTRATIVE STRUCTURE

Public corporations exhibit a variety of administrative structures. Until the 1950s centralised structures were normally preferred, being considered most likely to attract the best managers, and to maximise potential for national economic planning. In the light of experience, however, centralisation was seen to present serious problems; industries were too large for effective management, and boards became remote and bureaucratic. Consequently, several industries (notably inland transport) underwent major decentralisation. As this indicates, administrative structures do not remain static: they change in response to new circumstances and to experience of running the industries. Moreover, different industries require differing structures; for example, while electricity, like inland transport, experienced substantial postwar decentralisation, the gas industry – to meet technological problems arising from North Sea gas discoveries – underwent a major centralising reorganisation in the 1970s.

Common to all public corporations is their management by a publicly appointed board, in the case of nationalised industries appointments being made by a 'sponsoring minister' designated by statute. This is a fundamental feature of public corporations: experienced industrialists manage the industries as public trustees and at arm's length from politicians. Each enabling Act confers upon the board management responsibilities, and usually also stipulates numbers and qualifications of appointees. Most boards have about ten members, some of whom may be part time, and most of whom have appropriate business or industrial experience. Normally neither the board nor its employees are civil servants; consequently, wages, conditions, and so forth can be geared to the industry's requirements.

In practice many of the anticipated advantages of this arrangement have not materialised. Partly this is because remuneration of board members and chairmen compares unfavourably with the private sector, which has sometimes inhibited recruitment. Partly also, however, it stems from the 'haphazard' method of appointment, whereby board members 'have limited terms of appointment and no promise of reappointment'. Thus of twenty-four chairmen in post in January 1978, fourteen had left within three years, only two through retirement. Some industries had as many as three chairmen during the period. While such insecurity 'destroys ... continuity of experience, knowledge and commitment' at board level (Barlow, 1981, pp. 31–2), it also reflects the boards' relationships with the wider political system and especially with sponsoring ministers.

(B)   FINANCIAL ARRANGEMENTS

Theoretically, public corporations enjoy financial autonomy. Expenditure is met from operating revenue; surpluses are retained (not surrendered to the Treasury) to finance investment and build reserves; and borrowing is permissible within statutory limits. Sponsoring ministers usually also have financial powers: to appoint auditors, approve capital investment programmes, and determine the form of the accounts. These powers are theoretically conferred on ministers to ensure that boards exercise proper stewardship of public assets, while having sufficient financial freedom to operate commercially.

These theoretical arrangements have not materialised. Since the 1950s, government control over capital finance has been imposed by requiring loans to nationalised industries to be raised from the Treasury. There have also been various government attempts to impose investment criteria: for example, in 1967 an 8 per cent test discount rate was recommended for new investment projects (*Nationalised Industries: A Review of Economic and Financial Objectives* (1967), para. 10); and in 1978 a 5 per cent real rate of return on new investment (*Nationalised Industries*, 1978, para. 61). While such targets have rarely been obtained, more stringent control has been achieved by the imposition since 1975 of Treasury-determined cash limits. Often influenced primarily by global public sector borrowing considerations, these have had serious effects upon some corporations, disrupting 'investment planning' and causing delays in 'profitable investment projects' (Knight, 1982, p. 31).

With revenue finance, governments have also attempted to impose guidelines. The 1961 White Paper *(Financial and Economic Obligations of the Nationalised Industries*, para. 19) recommended that revenue surpluses 'should be at least sufficient to cover deficits on Revenue Account *over a 5-year period*'. In 1967 another White Paper (*Nationalised Industries: a Review of Economic and Financial Objectives*) suggested that prices should be related to marginal costs, financial objectives geared to prices, and – where social considerations required departure from commercial principles – corporations should receive government compensation. While this latter provision had some influence in the case of British Rail (which subsequently received compensation for uneconomic passenger services) it was difficult to implement. In any event the long-run marginal cost rule proved largely unattainable, and in 1978 another White Paper (*Nationalised Industries*) was issued, requiring prices to be geared to financial targets set for each industry. It seems unlikely, however, that these guidelines will prove any more successful than earlier ones. (See Redwood and Hatch, 1982, esp. p. 9.)

As these White Papers suggest, the original 'break even' concept of public corporations has now largely been abandoned in favour of more sophisticated financial targets. In practice many nationalised industries, far from breaking even, have made large losses and have needed 'bailing out' by increased borrowing or deficit grants from government departments. Others have made healthy profits, the most notable recent example being British Gas. While this mixed record is partly due to differences in market and operating conditions, it also partly reflects different patterns of ministerial intervention. Sponsoring ministers intervene in nationalised industries' financial affairs far more than either theory or statute suggests. For example, prices, wages, and industrial relations are all technically board matters; however, ministers are usually consulted informally about significant price increases (*Financial and Economic Obligations*, para. 31) and some ministers deal directly with union leaders. Again, Treasury-determined cash limits seriously constrain the boards' commercial freedom, with shortfalls in external financing often necessitating plant closures, price increases, or wage restraint.

Such interventions not only prevent boards from pursuing their commercial judgement but also largely explain their persistent failure to meet the government's own financial targets. Whatever the theory, government control of nationalised industry finance is extensive – so much so as to have totally undermined the concept of financially autonomous corporations operating at arm's length from ministers.

(C)   MINISTERIAL CONTROL

Each enabling Act creating a public corporation confers explicit powers on the designated sponsoring minister. The reasons for conferring such powers have long been controversial. The initial rationale was that ministers should be responsible for 'general policy' and boards for 'day-to-day administration', although this subsequently tended to be replaced by a distinction between 'national interest' and 'commercial' responsibilities. In fact, both distinctions are somewhat artificial and difficult to apply in practice. In 1968 the Select Committee on Nationalised Industries (SCNI) (1967/8, I, para. 74) suggested a different rationale. Two basic purposes, it suggested, justified ministerial control: first, securing 'the wider public interest', and secondly, overseeing and 'if possible' ensuring 'the efficiency of the industries'. Although not universally accepted, this analysis nevertheless offers a useful starting point for examining the position of sponsoring ministers.

(i)   *In securing 'the wider public interest'* the minister's role is to relate corporation activities to wider social and economic considerations. The main instrument provided by statute for discharging this function is the general directive, which may be issued to a board 'on the exercise and performance of its functions in relation to matters which appear to the Minister to affect the national interest'. Once issued, general directives must be obeyed.

(ii)   *The ministers' efficiency powers* involve both oversight and the laying down of performance standards. To this end ministers have extensive statutory powers: appointment and dismissal of board members; financial powers; approval of research programmes, training, education and pension schemes; and requiring returns of accounts and information.

In practice, the functional division between ministers and boards is far more ambiguous than the above might suggest, an ambiguity heightened by four main factors:

1   *There are several sponsoring departments.*   The sixteen national-ised industries listed in Table 11.1 were sponsored by five different departments, co-ordination between which has often been inadequate (see Select Committee on Nationalised Indus-tries (1967/8), I, paras 335–43). The allocation of industries to departments, moreover, owes as much to haphazard political and departmental factors as to logic. As Barlow (1981, p. 35) asks, 'Why is the Post Office in the Industry portfolio? Why are the airlines with Trade and not Transport?' These arrangements not only impair co-ordination within industrial sectors (e.g. transport) and between different industries, but – because board/sponsoring department relationships may vary – also produce inconsistency between Whitehall and the nationalised industries.

   The situation is further confused because non-sponsoring departments, particularly the Treasury, are also frequently involved in nationalised industry affairs. The precise role of these departments is often obscure and, as the McIntosh Report (1976, p. 25) observed, 'opportunities' for boards to establish 'direct contact' with them have been 'limited'.

2   *There are frequent changes of personnel.*   Not only boards, but also sponsoring ministers and departmental officials are subject to frequent changes of personnel. This prevents 'adequate understanding ... and ... essential personal relationships' from developing (McIntosh Report, 1976, p. 40), and means that board/department relationships are continually changing.

3   *Statutory obligations vary between industries.*   The statutory obligations of ministers and boards vary from industry to industry. While these differences are usually unimportant, there

are exceptions (e.g. the 1974 Railways Act gives ministers particularly extensive powers over British Railways), and their existence further complicates ministerial/board relationships.

4 *Ministers enjoy extra-statutory influence.* In practice ministers have more control over nationalised industries than even the most liberal interpretation of enabling legislation would suggest. One investigation (McIntosh Report, 1976, App. Vol., p. 136) found that boards frequently complained of ministers acting 'without . . . statutory backing'. Ministers, in fact, have often intervened in commercial matters (such as prices, equipment purchases, and plant closures) and in managerial issues (wages, redundancies, liaison with unions etc.). Usually they have been inspired not by a desire to lay down firm policy guidelines, but by short-term political or economic expediency. Consequently the theoretical position has largely been reversed, with ministers giving 'very little guidance in regard to . . . policies' but becoming 'closely involved in many aspects of management' (Select Committee on Nationalised Industries, 1967/8, I para. 877).

Significantly, ministerial interventions have rarely been effected by the statutory remedy, the general directive, which has been used only twice on major matters since the war (in 1951 to the Iron and Steel Corporation as a prelude to partial denationalisation, and in 1952 to the British Transport Commission over rail fares). Instead there has appeared the 'lunch-table directive', a reference to the 'informal relationships between Ministers and board chairmen and between departmental officials and public corporation staff' which today exist in most industries (Johnson, 1978, p. 126). Often, of course, ministers appoint chairmen and members sympathetic to their policies, in which case boards may need little persuasion to accept ministerial views.

Ministerial influence should not, of course, be exaggerated. Sponsoring departments cannot be perfectly informed about every aspect of corporation affairs, and information moves in both directions during informal exchanges. Ministers' powers to hire and fire board members, moreover, are seriously circumscribed in practice; chairmen usually have contracts, and their low remuneration relative to private industry often presents difficulties in finding replacements. Boards, moreover, often contain high calibre members, who are unlikely to meet ministerial interference simply with passive resistance. In recent years they have been prepared to ally with unions and/or consumer councils against perceived political threats, and even to organise with other industries. Particularly significant was the emergence in the 1970s of the Nationalised Industries Chairmen's Group (NICG) which meets regularly with ministers; indeed, to some extent it has by-passed sponsoring departments by dealing direct with Treasury ministers, the 'real source' of many government initiatives affecting nationalised industries (see Tivey, 1982a).

Even so, while ministers have to accept 'give and take' when dealing with boards, in the final analysis they are usually able to prevail. Even without resort to directives, they possess considerable powers. Significantly these are powers technically concerned more with overseeing efficiency than with public interest considerations. They include the ministers' financial powers – e.g. power to approve investment and borrowing – and the ultimate power of dismissal. The latter is not unknown, but happens rarely; boards usually realise that they are unlikely to prevail against determined ministers, while ministers prefer to work 'behind the scenes' – by encouragement, persuasion, even threats – in the knowledge that boards usually give way, and that the short-term nature of most board appointments will eventually provide an opportunity to rid themselves of 'unco-operative' members without resort to dismissal.

The extent of ministerial control, of course, has repercussions not only for corporations, but also for sponsoring departments, which sometimes become overburdened with what are nominally board functions. Equally significant are the implications for accountability, for where ministers intervene informally, responsibility to Parliament may be avoided.

(D) ACCOUNTABILITY TO PARLIAMENT

Nationalised industry boards control sizeable public assets and should, therefore, be accountable for their actions. Early advocates of public corporations, however, feared that detailed parliamentary scrutiny might inhibit managerial freedom, and consequently normal conventions of ministerial responsibility do not apply to public corporations.

The theoretical position regarding accountability is described by Tivey (1973a, p. 139) as 'simple and logical'. He explains:

The Minister had certain powers over the corporations. For the exercise of these powers he was answerable to Parliament, just as he was answerable for all his other powers. On those matters where the Minister exercised no powers, there was no accountability.

Thus a minister issuing a general directive, dismissing a chairman, withholding capital investment approval (or failing to do any of these things) could be held accountable. However, on matters within the board's jurisdiction the minister was not statutorily responsible, and was, therefore, not accountable to Parliament. The boards, for their own part, were required to present accounts and annual reports to ministers, who in turn placed them before Parliament. They also had to act within any general directives or other statutory controls imposed by ministers. Otherwise, however, they were to operate free from parliamentary scrutiny.

In practice this 'simple and logical' arrangement has not worked, partly because of the blurred division of responsibilities inherent in enabling Acts, and partly also owing to the growth of informal ministerial intervention. Not only can ministers technically deny responsibility for matters falling within the boards' jurisdiction, but the degree of accountability for informal intervention inevitably depends largely on whether ministerial actions are public knowledge. Nevertheless, parliamentary opportunities to call sponsoring ministers to account have increased since the 1940s. MPs have become adept at framing parliamentary questions which obtain answers (e.g. asking if the minister *intends* to issue a general directive) while adjournment debates are frequently raised on matters for which ministers are not technically responsible (see Coombes, 1971, pp. 77–8). Since 1949, moreover, it has been customary to debate the reports and accounts which corporations submit annually to Parliament, while in addition any modification of enabling Acts, or any extension of borrowing limits, usually requires legislation. Generally, however, such debates are conducted along party lines and provide little opportunity for detailed scrutiny.

Partly to overcome these deficiencies the House of Commons in the mid-1950s established a *Select Committee on Nationalised Industries* (SCNI), which subsequently gained wide acceptance both within Parliament and the nationalised industries. Normally it investigated one or two industries each year, and its reports undoubtedly made MPs better informed about nationalised industries and even had some small influence on government policy. Nevertheless, it lacked the professional staff to perform financial or efficiency audits, or even to continuously monitor particular industries (see Coombes, 1966; and 1971, pp. 79–84). In any event the

SCNI disappeared in 1979 with the reorganisation of Commons Select Committees (see pp. 235–9), and the task of scrutinising nationalised industries is now fragmented between several different specialist committees. While these arrangements mean that industries can now be investigated by committees 'well versed' in the work of sponsoring departments, the disappearance of 'a forum for discussion of common problems' and of a 'group of MPs with considerable expertise' in nationalised industry matters may well prove detrimental to the industries' long-term interests (Redwood and Hatch, 1982, pp. 37–8).

The public accountability of nationalised industries remains problematical. Because they required substantial managerial independence, public corporations were initially given considerable freedom from both ministerial control and parliamentary accountability. In practice, ministers have acquired more control over the industries than was initially envisaged. The problem for Parliament is that there has not been a *commensurate* increase in ministerial accountability, with the result that ministers – by dealing informally with boards rather than using formal powers – can often escape full accountability for their actions.

(E) CONSUMER REPRESENTATION

With many nationalised industries, provision for consumer representation exists in the form of nationalised industry consultative or consumer councils (NICCs). In 1981 forty-four NICCs, some with regional and local networks, were in existence. Almost all were statutory bodies, their general function being 'to consider any matters raised by consumers, Ministers or the industries themselves concerning the service and facilities provided by their respective industries' (Department of Trade, 1981, p. 2). Traditionally two main roles have been distinguished: a consumer complaint-redressing role, and a policy-influencing role. While considerable differences exist from one NICC to another, the complaints role has become increasingly significant, with some 70,000 complaints annually being dealt with by the early 1980s.

NICCs, Tivey (1982b, p. 144) explains, 'originated as devices to check the impact of the monopoly status' of nationalised industries. Although their impact varies from industry to industry, dissatisfaction with their work has frequently been expressed. Three main criticisms have usually been levelled against them:

(i) *NICCs are not widely enough known.* One inquiry by the National Consumer Council (1976, pp. 31–2) found that 'the proportions of people who knew about [NICCs]', despite steps to publicise them, was 'still very low'.

(ii) *NICCs are not sufficiently independent.* As Tivey (1982b, p. 145) explains, 'the NICCs began in close association with the nationalised industries themselves, sometimes sharing premises and using the industries' own staff on secondment'. Moreover, although consisting largely of nominees from bodies deemed to represent consumers, actual appointments have usually been made by sponsoring ministers.

(iii) *NICCs are largely ineffective.* They have too few staff, too little money, and insufficient expertise to challenge boards. As the McIntosh Report (1976, App. Vol., p. 86) observed, 'All the councils had powers to consider any matter affecting consumers but very little authority to do anything about it'. Significantly, the Thatcher government sought to supplement the protection to consumers offered by NICCs by subjecting industries to regular investigation by the Monopolies and Mergers Commission (see Garner, 1982).

Such criticisms, while undoubtedly in many respects still valid (see Department of Trade, 1981, pp. 5–8), nevertheless have lost force over time. For example, while public awareness remains a problem, in some industries – notably gas and electricity – NICCs appear today to be quite widely known (Tivey, 1982b, p. 148). NICCs also appear to have developed greater independence: few NICC staff are now recruited or seconded from the industries, NICC chairmen no longer normally sit on corporation boards, and financing now comes from sponsoring departments rather than the industries themselves. Effectiveness has also improved: in a 'majority of cases' NICCs now have 'some success' in redressing consumer complaints (Tivey, 1982b, p. 146), while on a number of policy matters their influence can be detected. Generally these have concerned 'medium' rather than 'high' level policy: codes of practice, tariff structures, trading practices etc. rather than, say, general price levels or investment policies. Occasionally, however, there have been spectacular successes: in 1982, for example, planned telephone charge increases were deferred immediately following criticism from the Post Office Users' National Council (*The Times*, 1 September 1982).

NICCs, clearly, have developed greater independence and effectiveness than, even now, is sometimes realised. Even so, they still face substantial problems. Some of these – e.g. responsiveness to, and representativeness of, clientele – are shared with consumer organisations generally; others – accountability, appointment, etc. – are familiar quasi-governmental problems. NICCs, however, also suffer from the political framework within which nationalised industries operate. While their relationship is nominally with the corporations, the effective determinant of policy is often the government. As observed, NICCs generally lack resources and authority to effectively challenge boards, let alone boards, sponsoring departments and the Treasury combined. In particular they often lack the expertise, the right to information, and often also the time, to mount in-depth studies in complex policy areas (Tivey, 1982b, pp. 146–7). More crucially, these deficiencies are unlikely to be rectified so long as ministers wish to retain their dominant position over the industries. Consequently, while NICCs appear likely to survive – in 1982 the government pledged itself to retain 'the essentials' of their present structure (*Hansard*, VI, vol. 34, col. 547, 22 December 1982) – their basic position seems unlikely to be significantly strengthened (see Department of Trade, 1982).

Reforming Public Corporations

Several proposals for reforming public corporations have been made. In the 1960s two broad alternatives were suggested. The first, associated with Robson (1960; Select Committee on National-ised Industries, 1967/8, II, pp. 531–7; and 1969), held that ministers should be prevented from operating informally and without statutory authority. Hanson (1961; and SCNI, 1967/8, II pp. 526–531), by contrast, recommended the removal of formal limits upon ministerial powers. Neither view, however, was wholly convincing; the postwar expansion of nationalisation has provided an impetus for ministerial intervention beyond the level originally intended by Parliament, while governments are unlikely to clarify the blurred functional division between ministers and boards so long as this works to their advantage.

In 1967/8 the SCNI in a major report *Ministerial Control of the Nationalised Industries* (Select Committee on Nationalised Indus-tries, 1967/8) suggested that sponsoring departments should dis-appear, and a new Ministry of Nationalised Industries should be responsible for ensuring the efficiency of all nationalised industries. Public interest considerations would rest with other departmental ministers, who could negotiate for corporations to depart from commercial principles in return for compensation. By adopting these arrangements, the SCNI suggested, co-ordination between industries would be enhanced, efficiency and public interest considerations be separated, and ministers made more accountable.

To the SCNI's proposal the government made a predictably negative response (*Ministerial Control of the Nationalised Industries*, 1969), and in the 1970s the debate continued. In what became known as the McIntosh Report (1976), the National Economic Development Office proposed the establishment in each nationalised industry of a policy council. Chaired by an independent president, policy councils would include officials from sponsoring departments and the Treasury, and representatives of boards, unions and consumers. Some 'independent' members would also be appointed, and an 'open seat' provided for the minister. Policy councils would determine corporate aims, monitor performance, and appoint boards; consequently, ministers would lose the right to intervene directly in board affairs. They could seek changes by agreement with policy councils, or alternatively issue formal directives (for which they would be accountable to Parliament). In this way policy councils would provide a buffer between boards and ministers, would provide more clearly defined accountability, and would enable all parties connected with the industries to become involved in developing policy.

In 1978 the government rejected these proposals (*Nationalised Industries*, 1978). Boards had generally responded unenthusiastically – fearing that policy councils would become another bureaucratic layer – and the government was unwilling to divest itself of important powers. The White Paper did concede that minister/board relationships were unsatisfactory, and proposed giving ministers power to issue directives on 'specific' as well as 'general' matters (para. 20). Significantly, however, while disavowing that ministers should become involved in 'matters of day-to-day management', it also observed that on 'many issues' the government would 'continue to ... reach agreement' with industries without issuing 'specific directions' (para. 22).

Since 1979, of course, privatisation has increasingly been seen as a possible solution to these problems. If public corporations are defective instruments for administering public ownership, one alternative is to sell the assets to the private sector. Nevertheless, public corporations seem likely to remain an important form of public ownership. For concerns inappropriate for privatisation the public corporation, for all its inherent problems, presents a convenient 'half-way house' between the central government trading body and state shareholding, allowing more managerial freedom than the former, and more accountability than the latter.

12 REGIONAL ADMINISTRATION

The Context of Regional Administration

According to Jones (1982b, p. 772) there is 'between central and local government ... a bewildering array of boards, corporations, commissions, councils, agencies, offices and associations, which constitute a tangled administrative jungle'. Elected regional *government* may be absent in Britain but regional *administration*, in a multiplicity of guises, is far from insignificant. While this chapter focuses mainly on the administration of *water* and *health* it is, however, necessary to stress the wider context of regional administration.

In Britain there is a deeply rooted tradition of dividing units by function rather than by territory (see pp. 26–8); there is no widely accepted concept of territorial administration. Nevertheless, many central government departments (e.g. Employment, Environment, Transport) maintain *regional* outposts, while others (e.g. DHSS, Inland Revenue) have extensive networks of *local* offices. Additionally, many nationalised industries organise themselves regionally (e.g. Gas, Electricity) while many non-departmental public bodies (e.g. Sports Council) have extensive regional structures.

There is, however, a lack of coherence in both the boundaries and size of such networks. Some regional networks, for example, incorporate the whole of the United Kingdom, some Great Britain, some England and Wales, while others cover only England. While, for example, the Inland Revenue divides England and Wales into twenty-three regions for valuation purposes, in 1982 the Department of Industry had only three Regional Development Grant Offices throughout England. Other public bodies exhibit similar diversity (e.g. Water Authorities (England and Wales) – ten regions; British Rail Regions (GB) – five). Not only is there diversity *between* regional public authorities but also *within* them. As Hogwood and Lindley show (1982, p. 48), the Department of the Environment (DOE) in 1979 had six separate patterns of regional administration ranging from the DOE Ancient Monument Works

Areas with seven English regions to the DOE Rent Assessment Panel Areas with fifteen. Diversity of boundaries both *between* and *within* the various agencies is, therefore, a major characteristic of regional administration. As Jones (1982b, p. 772) observes, in Britain regions are essentially 'administrative inventions of the centre, not expressions of any political community'.

This diversity of regional structures reflects the pragmatic needs of different departments and organisations. While it might appear that standardisation of boundaries would ensure greater inter-organisational co-ordination, it must be emphasised that structural diversity is paralleled by similar diversity in legal powers, lines of accountability, degrees of discretion and sources of finance. As Hogwood and Lindley (1982, p. 46) put it, 'the problems posed by differing degrees of discretion accorded to regional offices and the essentially vertical lines of control to London would still remain'.

While differences *between* regional organisations require emphasis, the distinctiveness of individual regional offices *within* a single public body needs to be explored. For example, Young (1982, p. 92) illustrates the importance of different operational styles within the DOE's regional structure: 'One of the clearest examples in the 1970s was the willingness of the DOE in Manchester or Birmingham to stretch the availability of Derelict Land Grants to the limit ... In the North West this included the demolition of derelict textile mills. However, the Leeds DOE was more conventional and consistently refused to approve applications to demolish similar structures in West Yorkshire.' Complexity, therefore, exists not only *between* but also *within* the different constituent units operating regionally.

Although the UK lacks the natural regions found in many other countries, Scotland, Wales, and Northern Ireland do, however, offer distinctive territorial units as a basis for administrative organisation. The *Scottish Office* consists of five departments covering Economic Planning, Development (housing and roads), Home and Health (hospitals, child care, police and education), Education, Agriculture and Fisheries. Other central government functions in Scotland are administered by appropriate (UK) departments, which have offices in Scotland and work closely with the Scottish Office.

The *Welsh Office* has full responsibility in Wales for ministerial functions relating to health and personal social services, housing, local government, education (except universities), new towns, water and sewerage, roads and agriculture plus other minor functions. It works closely with UK government departments concerned with economic and industrial affairs. While the head-quarters of the Welsh Office is in Cardiff, there are branches throughout Wales and a small ministerial office in London.

In his analysis of *Northern Ireland* Hogwood (1982, p. 3) points to the scrapping in 1972 of the Stormont system, under which 'a separate Northern Ireland Government and Parliament legislated on and administered most aspects of domestic policy'. Since 1972, however, many of the more important functions, such as education and social services, have been transferred to area Boards and other bodies which are effectively the agencies of Whitehall departments.

While regional administration in the UK lacks coherence, it is nevertheless crucially important. Inevitably a text such as this cannot give comprehensive treatment to the subject. As separate chapters deal with departments (Chapter 2), quangos (Chapter 10), and nationalised industries (Chapter 11), all of which exhibit some instances of regional administration, this chapter focuses upon two important services administered regionally which have not pre-viously been discussed. These services, water and health, are both extremely important in terms of their expenditure, manpower, and political significance.

The Water Industry

The Pliatzky Report (1980, p. 31) notes that the water industry in Britain 'has some of the features of a nationalised industry but in other respects it is more in the nature of a public service of the kind provided by local authorities'. Indeed, prior to reorganisation in 1974 many water-based services were provided by local authorities, as is still the case in Scotland.

The Water Act, 1973, established nine regional water authorities (RWAs) in England plus the Welsh Water Authority. These ten authorities have overall responsibility for every aspect of water usage in England and Wales: water resources; water treatment; distribution and supply; pollution control; sewerage and sewage treatment; river management; land drainage; sea defences; recrea-tion; and fisheries. Prior to 1 April 1974 these functions had been divided amongst a number of organisations, both private and public: a) water was supplied by 187 separate water undertakings; b) sewerage and sewage treatment was in the hands of 1,393 local authorities; c) water conservation and land drainage was the responsibility of twenty-one river authorities.

Reorganisation, therefore, saw 'the replacement of locally based, fragmented, and often conflicting policies for water resources with an approach based upon hydrological and regional factors' (Gray, 1982, pp. 143, 145). Despite an apparently neat administrative solution to the operational problems of the water industry, confusion and complexity remain. Size and resource differences are indicated in Table 12.1. Additionally, under a concession negotiated with the government, district councils continued after 1974 to undertake certain sewerage functions on a 'controlled agency' basis for RWAs (Richardson and Jordan, 1979, p. 112); and in 1981 some 7,212 local authority employees were employed on this function. Likewise, twenty-eight private water companies (e.g. South Staffs Waterworks Co.), employing some 8,641 staff, supplied water to a quarter of the population. Confusion is compounded since in Scotland local authorities still carry out most water functions.

Richardson and Jordan (1979, p. 47) maintain that the impetus for reform was organisational, namely a desire to rationalise the multiplicity of bodies providing water services. The boundaries of the ten new RWAs established in 1974 'were hydrologically determined and reflected natural water sheds and not local government or other administrative boundaries'. Each of these ten authorities was given responsibility for *all* water activities within its area so that, following the 1973 Act, 'functions were administered within large, managerially orientated, integrated organisations instead of small-scale, uncoordinated units. This change was as radical a policy switch as can be cited in post-war Britain.'

The situation in *Scotland*, however, was different. The Local Government (Scotland) Act, 1973, which came into force in May 1975, was the product not of a desire to reorganise water management but rather of a desire to reform local government. The Royal Commission on Local Government in Scotland (Wheatley Report, 1969) had called for the disbandment of river purification boards and water boards and for the return of their functions to local authorities. The report, in other words, argued that Scotland should move in a completely opposite direction to water management in England and Wales. In the event intensive opposition was aroused to the proposal to dispense with river purification boards, and it was ultimately agreed to retain a reduced number. However, similarly strong opposition could not be mounted in favour of the water boards; consequently, the thirteen catchment-based regional boards were abolished and their functions returned to local government.

Why were two such clearly differing approaches to water management adopted? If the arguments for bringing all the functions

Table 12.1 Regional Variations Between Water Authorities: 1980/81

	Thames	Severn-Trent	North West	Anglia	Yorkshire	Southern	Welsh	North-umbria	Wessex	South West
Population (000s)	11,545	8,177	6,928	4,872	4,517	3,801	3,015	2,638	2,285	1,392
Land area (sq. miles)	5,058	8,301	5,732	10,563	5,213	4,226	8,267	3,549	3,714	4,202
Manpower[1]	11,945	10,886	9,120	6,744	6,522	4,101	5,736	2,309	2,398	2,450
Revenue expenditure (£m.)	348	287	265	222	176	122	141	86	74	60
Capital expenditure (£m.)	88	104	96	107	80	69	38	59	28	23
Average bills[2] (£)	54.47	56.78	54.69	75.08	57.21	67.0	66.76	49.19	72.87	75.22

Source: National Water Council Annual Report and Accounts, 1980/81; National Water Council, *The Water Industry in Figures*, February 1982.

Notes: [1] Employed by Water Authorities. An additional 8,641 were employed by Water Companies and there were also 7,212 local authority agency employees.
[2] There average bills are for supplies by water authorities (and not water companies).

of the water cycle in an entire river basin under one authority were so compelling, how did a system emerge in Scotland based on totally different principles? The availability of water supplies provides some clue. England and Wales are far more populous than Scotland and it became apparent in the early 1970s that careful planning and conservation of water resources was necessary to secure water supplies on a long-term basis. In this context technical arguments, advanced by professionals, prevailed in England and Wales. In Scotland, however, water is more plentiful; hence, the focus of reform was local government rather than the water industry in particular.

ACCOUNTABILITY AND CONTROL

The regionalisation of the water industry stemmed primarily from managerial motives. As the emphasis was upon technical efficiency rather than democratic participation, and as river catchment areas did not coincide with existing administrative units, the new structure was removed from direct local government control. However, both to represent consumer interests, and because in numerous policy fields close co-operation between the new water authorities and local government would be essential, some links with local government were retained. On each board a majority of members were local authority nominees, although the chairman and other members were to be appointed by the Secretary of State. The rationale for these ministerial appointees was to give representation to particular groups – e.g. industrialists and anglers – as well as to secure the appointment of members with knowledge and experience relevant to efficient management of the industry.

These arrangements, Gray (1982, pp. 146, 151) observes, produced for the administration of water 'a form of quasi-nationalized industry'. The close links with local authorities were coupled with features similar to those of public corporations (see pp. 184–97) – the appointment of chairmen and members of RWAs by ministers, and some important ministerial controls (for example over the industry's investment programme). For the most part, however, the RWAs created by the 1973 Act were intended to be 'autonomous and executive' with 'clearly defined statutory duties' including power to determine the level of water charges. In practice, as Gray (1982, pp. 159–60) notes, these arrangements have been widely criticised 'as being neither adequately representative of the public, nor completely based upon the criteria of managerial expertise'. They have also tended 'to confuse, and obscure, where their accountability lies'. RWAs, in fact, combine both local and ministerial forms of accountability. The Pliatzky Report (1980, p. 32) observes of the system:

> It can be claimed ... that it carries with it all the accountability to Ministers, and through them to Parliament, that exists in the case of nationalised industries; and that in addition the local authority nominees provide effective representation of local interests.

In fact, ministerial accountability to Parliament 'in the case of nationalised industries' poses many problems (pp. 189–94), while in practice local authority nominees – being drawn from only a few councils within the area – have generally been regarded as remote and inaccessible. In addition, the extent of local authority representation has to some extent counteracted the original intention which was to managerialise the industry. Gray (1982, p. 161) concludes:

> The seemingly innocuous question of WA membership thus raises serious questions concerning the extent of local authority involvement in policy-making, the role of members within the industry and whether the WAs are accountable to the local, political level or to the central, ministerial level, or whether they are accountable at all.

The 1973 Water Act also established an instrument of liaison between central government and the RWAs, namely, the National Water Council (NWC). This was intended to function as a central co-ordinating, consultative and advisory body, its major task being to advise ministers on national policy and to promote efficiency within the RWAs. The Council also had responsibilities for training, industrial relations and superannuation. However, it had no *executive* powers over RWAs; indeed, neither the government nor the RWAs were obliged to accept its advice. The NWC nevertheless performed 'a vital buffer role between the WAs and the government' and provided 'a coherent voice for the water industry at the national level' (Gray, 1982, p. 152).

In 1982, however, the government published a new Water Bill intended to amend the post-1973 arrangements. Its central proposals were to dissolve the NWC and to streamline RWA boards. Under its provisions RWAs are to consist of nine to fifteen members, all appointed by ministers, thus replacing Section 3 of the Water Act, 1973, under which the majority of members were local authority appointees. It also seeks to place district council sewerage undertakings more closely under RWA control.

Why, less than ten years after the reorganisation of the water industry, were further changes proposed? The government argued that the original intention of having a majority of local authority appointees on the RWAs was to enable them to represent consumer interests. This system, it was maintained, had not worked as intended since, for example, few people knew who their representatives were on the RWA. The government also argued that many RWAs were too large – following the 1973 Act RWA membership ranged from sixteen in South-West England to sixty-two in Thames Water – leading to a proliferation of committees and bureaucracy which, it was alleged, inhibited efficient decision-making.

The 1982 Bill (which became the 1983 Water Act) needs to be seen in context. During 1980, at the government's request, the Monopolies and Mergers Commission (MMC) embarked on an in-depth investigation of the Severn-Trent WA. In its report the commission questioned a) the value and effectiveness of such a large local authority contingent on the board, and b) the size of the board itself. The MMC argued for a small board of about twelve people along similar lines to a nationalised industry; it also rejected the principle of local authority representation (see Monopolies and Mergers Commission, 1981).

In April 1982 the Welsh WA (WWA) was restructured along these lines. Whereas previously the Welsh WA board comprised twenty local authority representatives plus fifteen nominated by the Secretary of State for Wales, the new board contains only thirteen members: nine (including the chairman) nominated by the minister, two from county councils and two from district councils. Some ministerial appointees were chosen to represent consumer interests, while in addition the WWA was asked to form local consumer advisory committees covering local authority areas approximating to WWA divisions or combinations of them.

The 1983 Water Act essentially applied the principles of the Welsh reorganisation to the English regions. The government argued that a more direct relationship was necessary between government and RWAs, hence abolition of the 'buffer' NWC and the new emphasis on ministerial appointment of RWA members. In view of the alleged failure of local authority representatives to protect consumer interests, the government envisaged networks of consumer advisory committees incorporating representatives of water users in homes, offices, factories, farms, leisure complexes, and so forth.

These changes, while arguably allowing RWAs to adopt a more managerial approach, will also leave Whitehall free to do the planning and co-ordinating work of the water industry itself. Following the NWC's demise there is now no statutory body with the task of taking a complete view of future demands for water. In the context of land drainage The Ministry of Agriculture, Fisheries and Food (MAAF) remains crucially important although (in England) the dominant Whitehall department is the DOE, aided by its greater influence on the newly constituted RWAs. The change from local authority control in 1973 reduced direct public control and accountability; despite the advisory committees the 1983 Act goes further in the same direction. The quasi-nationalised industry model launched in 1973 has been replaced by one resembling more closely the working model of the public corporation, with all its inherent control and accountability problems.

The National Health Service

Although it receives scant treatment in most public administration texts, the National Health Service (NHS) is a major arm of British public administration. In 1982/3 the NHS spent over £12,050m., some 6 per cent of the gross national product, and employed about 1 million staff. Contrary to popular belief only a small proportion of these resources is devoted to administration: general administrative costs (excluding hospitals) accounts for only 2.6 per cent of the health budget compared with 7.6 per cent in Sweden and 10.8 per cent in France (Garner, 1979, p. 179). Nevertheless, the efficient administration of so large and expensive a service is of particular importance. While central government, mainly through the agencies of the Department of Health and Social Security (DHSS) and the Scottish and Welsh Offices, is responsible for overall policy and for allocating funds, since its inception the NHS has maintained a regional tier of administration and despite two recent reorganisations (1974 and 1982) this regional structure has survived. Indeed, the regional tier has been strengthened in the sense that since 1974 regional *Hospital* Boards have now broadened out to become Regional *Health* Authorities (RHAs). The DHSS and the RHAs are, however, only part of a much more extensive organisational structure which has evolved since the end of the Second World War.

THE ESTABLISHMENT OF THE NHS

The NHS is a primary ingredient of Britain's 'Welfare State'. Although it came fully into existence in 1948, the National Health Service Act (1946) which established it in fact amalgamated many services which formerly had been provided separately: its aim was to provide a free and comprehensive system of health care to the whole community. Under the Act a tripartite organisational structure was established which lasted until 1974. This consisted of:

(i) *Hospitals.* Regional Hospital Boards had strategic planning and resource allocation functions, and were accountable to the Minister of Health. Day-to-day running of hospitals was left to Hospital Management Committees.

(ii) *Local authorities.* These had responsibility for health centres, district nursing, the school health service, the ambulance service, environmental and public health.

(iii) *Executive councils.* Made up approximately half from laymen appointed by the minister and local authorities, and half from local practitioners, they administered local services provided by general practitioners, opticians, pharmacists, and dentists. Their existence reflected the resistance of many doctors and dentists, when the NHS was formed, to becoming salaried local authority or state employees.

In the late 1960s, the increasing difficulties associated with co-ordinating this tripartite service led to pressure for reorganisation. According to Brown (1975, p. 142) three major defects weakened the old system: (i) The 'absence of any single body with overall responsibility for the provision of health services'; (ii) 'the difficulty of securing effective policy co-ordination below the level of the central department'; (iii) 'the lack of any proper machinery for local medical planning'.

RESTRUCTURING THE SERVICE: 1974

In 1974 the NHS was brought into a unified administrative structure (see Figure 12.1) based in England on fourteen RHAs, ninety Area Health Authorities (AHAs) and 199 Districts. This reorganisation, however, did not extend to social services, which remained under local authority control. Given the need for an integrated health service, the retention by local authorities of

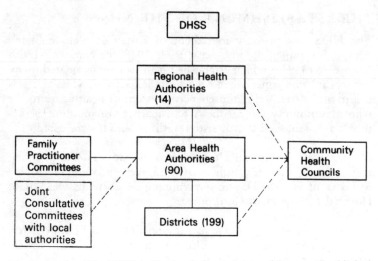

Figure 12.1   *The NHS in England: Organisational Pattern Established in 1974*

responsibility for personal social services seemed illogical from a NHS standpoint. However, from a social services perspective it made more sense; not only does efficient social service provision require close links with other local authority services – such as housing and education – but the administration of personal social services had been comprehensively reorganised under local authority control in 1971 following the recommendations of the Seebohm Report (1968). Consequently, it became necessary as part of the 1974 reorganisation to facilitate co-operation between health authorities responsible for health services and local authorities which retained responsibility for social services. As Wistow (1982, p. 44) has observed:

> So important was such collaboration considered that the boundaries of the new Area Health Authorities (AHAs) were not based upon the organisational requirements of health service administration alone. Instead, they were drawn coterminous with those of shire counties and metropolitan districts and personal social services in the restructured local government system.

The importance of collaboration, particularly in the context of *joint planning*, was emphasised in the 1973 NHS Reorganisation Act which 'provided for the establishment of formal collaboration machinery centred upon a member-level body – the Joint Consultative Committee ... composed of representatives drawn from matching health and local authorities and supported by an officer working group' (Wistow, 1982, p. 45).

The fourteen English RHAs established in 1974 were made responsible for determining regional priorities and for allocating resources to their respective AHAs. Generally they consist of twenty or so members, appointed by the Secretary of State, who have been nominated by the medical professions, local authorities, trade unions etc.

The ninety *Area Health Authorities* (abolished in 1982) consisted of about twenty members, including doctors and nurses, appointed by the Secretary of State and had a 'management' rather than a 'representative' function. They were responsible for assessing health needs and for service provision – a task often involving a good deal of liaison with local authority social services and housing departments. The ninety AHAs were divided, in turn, into 199 *Districts* which were essentially management units and were usually organised round a district general hospital incorporating a population of between 100,000 and 500,000. District management teams, consisting of six members, were allocated responsibility for day-to-day service provision. As Figure 12.1 shows, the former executive councils were replaced in 1974 by Family Practitioner Committees with similar functions and with DHA, local authority, and professional representation.

COMMUNITY HEALTH COUNCILS (CHC)

These became operative from 1974 and have survived the 1982 restructuring (albeit only against a background of DHSS pressure to abolish them), having been established as the 'representative' arm of the new look NHS, but with the clear intention of keeping representation distinct from management. One CHC was established for each health district. CHCs generally have about thirty members: half from local authorities (who need not be councillors) and the remainder from local voluntary organisations and RHA nominees. Essentially CHCs have the task of representing the public's view to those who administer the service. But, in practice, few members of the public know of their existence, let alone attend meetings. Additionally, when they do recommend changes they do not *have* to be listened to.

It is sometimes suggested that CHCs have no representativeness or legitimacy because they are not elected. As Bates (1982, p. 94) notes, the argument put forward is generally 'that CHCs are appointed, not elected bodies, and except for members who have been elected to a local authority, have no right to speak for the community or to regard themselves as representative'. The same author comments, however (p. 94), that 'representativeness in a democracy can be argued on the basis of representatives being authorized to act for someone else, or being accountable to someone, or being representative in the sense of being a microcosm of society as a whole. On none of these grounds do CHCs qualify.' On the other hand, some form of consumers' voice is essential in the NHS; CHCs at least attempt to act in this capacity. Bates (1982, pp. 97–8) concludes:

> Regardless of their legitimacy and representativeness, CHCs have clearly succeeded in turning the minds of administrators outwards to the community and to the hitherto neglected groups of patients . . . [They] are performing successfully the function of giving a voice to groups for whom no exit is possible from the NHS.

CHCs, although lacking executive power, at least enable some local people to play (or appear to play) a part in running the service by conveying suggestions and complaints to administrators, not unlike the consultative councils of the nationalised industries.

ACCOUNTABILITY AND CONTROL

The 1974 reorganisation, coinciding with the 'reform' of local government, meant that local authorities lost their remaining health functions to the newly created, non-elected health authorities, raising similar questions about accountability and control to those in the water industry. Although the new arrangements were intended to retain sensitivity to local opinion, this has barely materialised. The real influence on decision-making rests mainly with the chairmen of RHAs who, as appointees of the Secretary of State, largely owe their security of tenure to retaining the confidence of ministers and senior personnel in the authority. In fact, ministers, through the chairmen of RHAs, have a *potential* for control over most aspects of the NHS. The NHS is funded almost totally by the Exchequer, and the Secretary of State for Health and Social Security (and equivalent Welsh and Scottish ministers) have responsibility for policy developments, the allocation of funds, and general oversight.

In practice, however, ministers' ability to secure implementation of their policy objectives has been limited. According to Haywood and Elcock (1982, p. 139), RHAs have functioned 'as extensions of interests within the NHS rather than the representatives of central policy'. Decision-making is heavily dependent on expert opinion and upon the co-operation of powerful interests – consultants, teaching hospitals, etc. – to an extent that 'diminishes the effective public accountability of Ministers'. The Royal Commission on the National Health Service (1979) *Report* (ch. 19) referred pointedly to 'the inconsistency between the theoretical responsibilities for the NHS carried by health ministers, permanent secretaries and health departments, and the practical realities'. Its solution, that RHAs 'become accountable to Parliament for matters within their competence', however, was rejected by the government. Consequently, while ministers remain nominally responsible for most aspects of the NHS, their effective control over the RHAs is, in practice, somewhat limited.

While these arrangements mean that the NHS largely avoids effective public accountability or *direct* democratic control, it is not immune from scrutiny. In addition to CHCs, the 1973 Act (and the 1974 Scottish Act) established *Health Service Commissioners* empowered to investigate complaints within the NHS. However, in practice their value is limited as they cannot pass judgement in clinical matters (see pp. 257–8 for fuller discussion). In addition, MPs are able to raise issues concerning the NHS in Parliament, and since 1979 a new Social Services Select Committee has provided a useful means for further scrutiny of the health service (see pp. 235–9).

It is also important to stress that, although democratic control might not be direct, as with local authority services, local politics in the wider sense does influence NHS decision-making. MPs, councillors, pressure groups and the media frequently take up, for example, the case of a hospital about to be closed, and might thereby have some indirect influence (albeit possibly a diminishing one now that decisions increasingly have to be made in the light of economic constraints).

SLIMMING DOWN: 1982

In 1982 a slimmed down NHS came into being (see Figure 12.2), the major change being the replacement of the ninety AHAs and their 199 Districts by a single structure of 192 District Health Authorities. The rationale behind the restructuring was the reduction of bureaucracy and costs, coupled with a desire to delegate

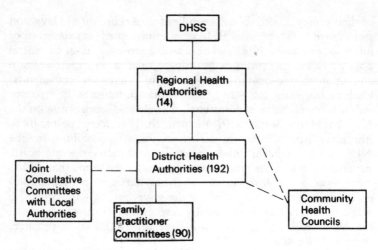

Figure 12.2   *The NHS in England: Post-1982 Structure*
Note: see Ham (1982), chapter 1, for details about structural changes in the rest of Great Britain.

more decisions to the local level. Although the existing planning procedures looked rational in theory, in practice planning had to pass through so many tiers that procedures became discredited.

The Royal Commission on the National Health Service (1979) pointed to a number of defects in the service, notably the multiplicity of management tiers and administration, and inefficiency in decision-making and use of resources. In their 1979 election manifesto, the Conservative party had talked of simplifying, decentralising and cutting back on bureaucracy, and in a Consultative Paper, *Patients First* (Department of Health and Social Security, 1979), the government asserted (p. 1): 'We have reached the firm conclusion that the structure and management arrangements of the Service introduced in 1974 do not provide the best framework for the effective delivery of care to the patients. The Royal Commission on the NHS ... has confirmed us in our view.' The government, however, rejected any radical restructuring (e.g. transferring the NHS back to local government) in favour of incremental change. The main points of the government's proposals, which came into effect on 1 April 1982, were:

(i)   Area Health Authorities were to be replaced by District Health Authorities (DHAs) following as far as possible the boundaries of existing health districts (i.e. the area tier was to be abolished). The aim was that the new district authorities should serve communities with populations up to 500,000.

(ii)   The DHAs were to have, on average, sixteen members each, four of them nominated by local authorities (this was a reduction in local authority representation from 33 per cent of the total down to 25 per cent). The chairman of a district authority was to be appointed by the Secretary of State and the other members (apart from local authority nominees) were to be appointed by the RHA, although the practice of having a consultant, a GP, a nurse, a university nominee and a trade union nominee was to continue.

(iii) Decision-making was to be brought as far as possible down to hospital and community level with a strengthening of management at that level. Each DHA was to appoint a team to co-ordinate all health service activities of the district, including policy implementation. The government also argued for the maximum delegation of responsibility to those in the hospital and community services within policies determined by the DHA.

(iv)   RHAs were to remain for strategic purposes, although the government promised a review of their functions at a future date.

(v)   Community Health Councils were to remain (one for each new district authority), but again the government promised that they were to be subject to future review, arguing that (Department of Health and Social Security, 1979 p. 14), as district authority members would 'be less remote from local services than ... [area authority] members necessarily' had been, the need for separate consumer representation was less clear than in the past. In practice, however, some new district authorities are more remote from the consumer than they had been before the 1982 reorganisation. In Leicestershire, for example, prior to 1982 there was an AHA and three districts, each with a CHC. Following restructuring there is only a single district authority (serving 836,000 people) with one CHC. Such a structure hardly facilitates administrators being 'more closely in touch with the needs of the community' as *Patients First* (p. 14) had suggested.

(vi)   While the Royal Commission recommended that Family Practitioner Committees (FPCs) should be abolished and their functions absorbed by health authorities, the government decided against this, largely because of the opposition of the medical professions. By April 1985 FPCs are scheduled to become independent bodies and given the status of employing authorities in their own right, thereby confirming the effective position they have long enjoyed. Their last remaining formal links with the districts (largely in the areas of finance and structure) will thereby disappear.

THE POST-1982 MANAGEMENT STRUCTURE

In England there are three administrative tiers in the NHS: (i) DHSS, (ii) RHAs and (iii) DHAs. Health care is still under a single organisational structure, and while the removal of a management tier has streamlined the system, much complexity remains. Indeed, in so far as local government/health authority relationships are concerned, complexity has increased. Whereas previously AHA boundaries were coterminous with social service authority boundaries, under the new arrangements 'the boundaries of two or more DHAs are combined within that of a social services authority' (Wistow, 1982, p. 59). Coterminosity has largely disappeared.

The 1982 developments need to be seen as part of the Thatcher government's desire to streamline public sector administration. A leaner, more efficient structure, with the maximum delegation of responsibility for service provision to the DHAs, was the government's professed aim, but doubts have been expressed that the new structure will actually produce more central and regional direction since the DHAs are relatively small and thereby are unlikely to carry much political weight. In addition, local authority representation has been reduced: from 1976 one-third of the membership of each RHA and AHA had consisted of local authority nominees, but since 1982 this has been reduced 'so reversing the effect of Barbara Castle's decision in 1976 to increase the local democratic accountability of the NHS' (Elcock, 1982, p. 272). At the same time there has been some evidence of attempts to exert ministerial *control* over RHAs, four chairmen of which were replaced in June 1982 by the Secretary of State's nominees after they had criticised government handling of a pay dispute within the NHS. It is unlikely, however, that this will stimulate a commensurate move towards increased *accountability*; on the contrary, as Haywood and Elcock (1982, p. 141) speculate, ministers could now 'argue that their responsibilities in practice do not extend to *all* activities but are confined to the minimal requirements of accountability – that money is spent honestly and properly, efficiently and with economy'. As with the water industry, developments in the early 1980s seem likely to move the NHS more towards the working model of the public corporation.

The new simpler structure might help to streamline the NHS, but as Brown (1982, pp. 83–4) emphasises, 'administrative reform cannot ... solve all the problems involved in delivering medical care ... [particularly] the crucial questions on objectives or priorities that medical care currently raises'. Structural change seems unlikely to be able to dislodge the medical profession from its dominance of every level within the NHS. Indeed, *Patients First* – which outlined the official rationale for the 1982 reorganisation – can be criticised for not making patients the main consideration (Department of Health and Social Security, 1979). Many people concerned with preventative and community medicine argue that the evolving of districts around hospital units will merely perpetuate the emphasis on hospital care – in line with the interests of the medical profession and other established groups – which already absorbs what they see as too large a share of NHS resources (see *Community Care*, no. 306, March 13 1980, p. 1). According to Elcock (1982, p. 276), decentralised administration 'has increased resistance to the implementation of policies that challenge established professional hierarchies and priorities within the NHS'. Public administration in the NHS is strongly influenced by a network of 'specialist' elites whose dominance it is difficult to exaggerate.

Conclusions

The postwar creation of *ad hoc* authorities to administer health and water removed these services from direct local accountability. While the ability of councillors to exert control in such technically complex fields is questionable, the proliferation of such single-purpose, non-elected, authorities has raised questions of accountability and control similar to those which in the nineteenth century prompted the creation of multi-functional, democratically-elected local authorities. In a variety of functional areas, including health and water, local authorities have been considered too small for the efficient operation of services, as well as lacking in relevant specialist resources. Nor were central government departments generally considered appropriate to provide such services, largely on the grounds that bureaucratic controls would inhibit efficiency; hence, the establishment of a confusing array of regional administrative bodies.

In Britain there are few natural regions and little regional political consciousness. From time to time political parties (notably the Liberals and the SDP) argue that a regional layer of government would represent a genuine devolution of power from the centre if it took over functions currently performed by government departments in the regions as well as those of *ad hoc* agencies. In practice, of course, the reverse could be true: a regional administrative layer could increase centralisation since it would probably control elected local government at close quarters. In any event, political regionalism remains unlikely. Untidy administrative regionalism is, however, very much a reality.

13 PARLIAMENT AND ACCOUNTABILITY

In a formal sense Parliament sets the parameters of British public administration. It lays down the functions of all public agencies and is the ultimate source of their authority. In practice, however, executive dominance over the last hundred years has transformed Parliament's role to such an extent that ministers and civil servants today 'implement their policies and act over the vast range of executive authority with little need to refer to Parliament at all' (Ryle, 1981, p. 14).

Four main aspects of Parliament nevertheless remain particularly relevant for students of public administration, and these are dealt with in this chapter: Legislation; Parliament and Public Finance; Ministerial Responsibility; Parliamentary Scrutiny.

Legislation

Parliament's legislative work has increased enormously as the role of the state has expanded. B. Jones (1982, p. 313) has observed: 'Fifty years ago Parliament produced 450 pages of legislation; now, using largely the same methods, it processed 3,000 pages plus 10,000 [pages of] Statutory Instruments not to mention the EEC regulations and directives'. Broadly speaking, two main forms of legislation can be identified: a) Primary legislation; and b) Delegated legislation. Although the former is arguably the most important, delegated legislation tends to cause more confusion for students of public administration and consequently it is given fuller treatment in this chapter.

(A) PRIMARY LEGISLATION OR STATUTE

This for the most part originates within government. In 1968 Walkland (p. 20) described the legislative process as comprising 'deliberative, Parliamentary and administrative stages, over all of which [the government was] predominant'. This predominance stems partly from the party system – in normal circumstances the government has a parliamentary majority – and partly also from the procedures of the House of Commons, the major legislative chamber. Commons procedures allow few opportunities for effective scrutiny by MPs. Detailed scrutiny of bills is possible in the committee stage, but standing committees which deal with legislation are non-investigative and (although they may contain a nucleus of party spokesmen and 'experts') essentially non-specialist (for discussion see Griffith, 1973). Commons procedure also enables the government to curtail discussion by MPs by utilising such devices as the closure and the guillotine. Even so, parliamentary time is usually scarce: there is invariably only time to enact three or four *major* government bills per session. One consequence of this is the increasing use of delegated legislation, the process by which Parliament delegates its law-making powers to ministers and administrative agencies such as public corporations and local authorities.

(B)   DELEGATED LEGISLATION

This is also known as subordinate or secondary legislation and exists in several forms, of which the most common are: ministerial and departmental regulations, regulations made by the European Commission or Council of Ministers, public corporation and local authority bye-laws, and compulsory purchase orders. Of these various forms the most important is the first: ministerial or departmental regulations, which enable ministers or their officials to issue regulations which have legal force. Alternatively, ministers may be given power to issue rules by Order in Council, a procedure usually reserved for the more important or sensitive subjects of ministerial regulation. Whichever of these two forms is adopted, however, rules or orders issued under them are commonly known as 'statutory instruments'. While statutory instruments (SIs) are nothing new (around 1,200 were issued annually at the turn of the century), the growth in the volume and complexity of government business has made them an increasingly important feature of the modern state. Today the annual total of SIs is usually nearer 2,000, and every year new Acts are passed conferring on ministers further rule-making powers.

Advantages and disadvantages. The increasing use of delegated legislation reflects its many advantages. The most important of these are:

(i)   It relieves pressure on parliamentary time by leaving some subordinate matters for regulation by ministers, local authorities, etc.

(ii) It offers technical advantages. In highly specialised fields regulation by statutory instrument – drawn up on the advice of experts – is often more appropriate than asking MPs to enact legislation.

(iii) It enables government to deal with unforeseen circumstances. When enacting legislation it is usually impossible to anticipate all the circumstances in which it will apply. Delegated legislation allows Parliament to lay down the broad framework of law, leaving ministers to fill in the details later as and when appropriate.

(iv) Speed is often necessary (e.g. to respond to outbreaks of disease, to change exchange controls, deal with war and emergencies, etc.). Delegated legislation enables ministers (or other agencies) to issue regulations with immediate effect without waiting to pilot legislation through Parliament.

(v) Circumstances change and delegated legislation provides flexibility. It would be overbearing to have to produce new bills whenever, for example, changes in hire purchase controls are required.

Despite these advantages concern is often expressed about delegated legislation. Many of its 'advantages' accrue only because normal safeguards and procedures are relaxed. For example, while the courts are able to inquire whether delegated legislation has been *infra vires*, this is not always the safeguard it might appear owing to the broad powers which (to allow maximum flexibility) have sometimes been conferred upon ministers. As Punnett (1980, p. 347) observes, 'some delegated powers are so wide as to justify almost any action by the executive, as with the wartime emergency powers, and the clause that was contained in some legislation, giving the Minister the power to make any changes necessary to put the legislation into effect'. Again, the fact that regulations can be issued with almost immediate effect, without parliamentary debate, and many years after the enabling legislation was passed, means that there is often little or no public awareness of changes in the law.

A particular problem is that, while much secondary legislation is highly technical, some SIs are extremely important. As Beith (1981, pp. 166–7) observes, what is effectively taxation can be introduced by SI: a quarter per cent increase in the national insurance contribution of all employees can be levied in this way at any time. Similarly, immigration rules, employment protection procedures, and regional development status are all determined by SIs. Matters of considerable significance, in other words, can be effected by delegated legislation, often with negligible parliamentary discussion, a fact not infrequently taken advantage of by governments desirous of introducing 'unpopular' measures with minimum public debate.

PARLIAMENTARY SCRUTINY OF DELEGATED LEGISLATION

The problem of maintaining effective parliamentary scrutiny of delegated legislation has long been recognised. It was one of the major concerns expressed by Hewart in *The New Despotism* (1929) and by the Donoughmore Report on Ministers' Powers (1932). Despite this, contemporary procedures for scrutiny are generally regarded as inadequate. With some forms of delegated legislation, notably local authority bye-laws, parliamentary scrutiny is virtually non-existent (although ministerial approval is normally a prerequisite for confirmation). Even where parliamentary scrutiny is provided for, however, as with ministerial regulations and European instruments, the position is still often unsatisfactory. This is the more disturbing because *ministerial* control over delegated legislation is generally far less effective than with primary legislation; indeed, because of the technical content of SIs, as well as their number and length, departmental civil servants, in consultation with client groups, have a largely free hand in preparing them.

The present scrutiny arrangements largely date from the end of the Second World War, when two important developments occurred:

(i) In 1944 a select committee (known since 1946 as the *Select Committee on Statutory Instruments*) was established. It had power to consider every Statutory Rule or Order laid before the Commons and to draw attention to any SIs making unusual or unexpected use of the powers conferred by the enabling statute. While performing a useful function, its lack of support staff, the immensity of its task, and the difficulty of finding parliamentary time to debate its reports, reduced its effectiveness. There was also a lack of co-ordination between this committee and the Special Orders Committee, which since 1925 had been responsible for examining affirmative instruments coming before the Lords.

(ii) *The Statutory Instruments Act, 1946* rationalised the diverse procedures governing the approval and publicising of delegated legislation. Most instruments, other than the least contentious and important, are now 'laid' before Parliament in one of two ways:

Affirmative Instruments, normally the most important, which need to be approved by Parliament within a specified time (commonly twenty-eight or forty days); and *Negative Instruments*, the most numerous, which become effective automatically unless annulled by resolution (a motion to annul is called a 'prayer'). The 1946 Act provided that all negative instruments should be open to challenge by Parliament for forty days irrespective of the period mentioned in the parent statute. Notwithstanding this rationalisation, however, major deficiencies, and some confusion, remain. Some instruments, for example, have to be laid in draft form before becoming effective; others must be complete before laying. Again, most SIs have to be laid before both Houses, but some are laid only before the Commons. Most important of all, the failure by governments to allow time for the debate of prayers within the forty days stipulated in the 1946 Act has meant that many negative instruments become effective without MPs obtaining a hearing. Largely because of such deficiencies the Brooke Committee on Delegated Legislation in 1972 (Brooke Report 1971/2) recommended the establishment of two new committees designed to strengthen parliamentary scrutiny.

(i) *Joint Scrutiny Committee (JSC)*. In February 1973 a Joint Committee on Statutory Instruments was developed out of the House of Commons Select Committee on SIs and the House of Lords Special Orders Committee. (Commons members sit separately to deal with the few SIs laid before the Commons only.) The JSC has power to investigate every instrument laid before both Houses and to draw attention to any SI on specified grounds: for example, if it imposes a charge on the public, excludes challenge in the courts, appears to be *ultra vires*, has retrospective effect, has been unduly delayed in publication, or makes unusual or unexpected use of the powers conferred by the enabling statute. As this list suggests, the committee is confined to *technical* scrutiny (i.e. it is not able to debate the merits of instruments). Even so its task is daunting, and on average it only has time to look at about one-third of all instruments.

(ii) *A Merits Committee.* A Standing Committee on Statutory Instruments was established in 1973 to consider the *merits* of SIs. This was mainly considered necessary because of the many prayers that were either not being debated or being debated out of time. The position at the moment is that prayers are debated in the Merits Committee unless twenty MPs oppose this (in which event they can be discussed in the House subject to a one-and-a-half hour time limit).

While the Merits Committee has enabled far more contentious negative instruments to be debated than hitherto, it has nevertheless attracted much criticism. Partly this is because its terms of reference allow only one and a half hours' debate on a neutral motion – i.e. it cannot reject an instrument or secure a subsequent debate in the Commons. Moreover, many less controversial affirmative instruments are now also debated in the Merits Committee (rather than, as before, on the Floor of the House). Indeed, in the two and a half years from March 1973 no less than 215 affirmative instruments were debated in the Merits Committee compared with only twenty-three prayers. The main beneficiary of the new arrangements has, therefore, been the government, which has obtained a 'useful method of saving time on the Floor', by having many affirmative instruments debated in committee, without allowing any 'noticeable corresponding increase in the time available for prayers' in the Chamber (Byrne, 1976, p. 373).

EUROPEAN SECONDARY LEGISLATION

In 1974, following British entry into the EEC, a *Select Committee on European Secondary Legislation* was established in the Commons. Possessing the usual powers of a select committee its main functions are: i) technical scrutiny of draft legislation emanating from the European Commission (prior to its submission to the Council of Ministers, the final EEC law-making body); and ii) where appropriate, recommending items for debate in the House. Generally the government acts upon such recommendations by allowing a debate on the Floor. A *Select Committee on the European Communities* performs a similar function in the Lords, although it has somewhat wider powers – being able to comment on the merits of proposed EEC instruments – and different procedures from its Commons counterpart (see Coombes, 1981, pp. 241–9; and Norton, 1981, pp. 160–4). In addition, the post-1979 Commons specialist select committees (pp. 235–9) can discuss the merits of EEC documents in their respective areas. While these various committees are able to make ministers aware of Parliament's views about EEC proposals, usually well in advance of their being considered by the Council of Ministers, it would be naive to see them as doing more than making minor inroads into an area where Parliament's influence is limited and indirect. Parliamentary opinion remains only one among very many influences upon EEC policy.

OVERVIEW

Despite these reforms, parliamentary scrutiny of delegated legislation remains inadequate. Whereas about one-third of Commons
time is spent debating government bills, under one-tenth of its time
is used to debate secondary legislation (Norton, 1981, p. 96).
Moreover, SIs debated on the Floor cannot be amended (they can
only be rejected or approved), while those referred to the Merits
Committee can be debated only on a 'take note' motion. Of course,
the majority of instruments are never debated at all; indeed, as most
are negative instruments which are not prayed against, no debate of
any kind occurs before they become effective. Even the JSC
provides an inadequate safeguard; not only does it fail to examine
two-thirds of all SIs, but it often relies heavily on advice given by
sponsoring government departments. As Alderman (1982, p. 99)
observes, 'If a department is adamant that a particular instrument is
necessary, and that no unexpected or unusual use has been made of
the powers conferred by the parent Act, the Select Committee is
unlikely to raise any objection'.

While Parliament is now able to exercise greater scrutiny over
delegated legislation than before the war, the volume of SIs is today
so extensive that detailed scrutiny of all but the most politically
contentious is out of the question. As Norton (1981, p. 99)
comments, delegated legislation 'remains a much neglected form of
legislation (except by affected interest groups and the Departments
that promulgate it) ... even more than primary legislation, [it] is
the product of consultations between Government and outside
interests, and is "made" before it reaches the House of Commons'.
Perhaps it is the extent of such consultation which explains why,
despite the inadequacy of parliamentary scrutiny, delegated legislation gives rise to relatively little litigation in the courts.

Parliament and Public Finance

Technically, Parliament holds the 'power of the purse'; parliamentary authorisation is necessary both for raising taxation and for
government spending. In reality, Parliament's role is far more
limited, partly because the huge sums involved make effective
scrutiny and control almost impossible. In the last decade public
expenditure has usually been within a few points of 50 per cent of
the Gross National Product, and although much of this is actually
spent by agencies with little or no accountability to Parliament –
local authorities, public corporations, quangos, etc. – government

departments, which are accountable to Parliament, nevertheless *control* the bulk of public spending. This, as Robinson (1981, p. 155) points out, means that 650 MPs 'of very different interests, backgrounds, training and aptitude for figures', and with 'many other functions to perform' may be responsible for 'detailed scrutiny [of] ·more than half the entire British economy'.

The inadequacy of parliamentary scrutiny of public finance stems not only from the size of the task, but also because Parliament's procedures have not adapted to the increasing demands of the job. For example, taxation and expenditure legislation is considered separately, and the huge sums involved are discussed and approved using more or less normal legislative procedures.

Essentially two main processes dominate Parliament's financial business: authorising taxation; and authorising and appropriating expenditure.

AUTHORISING TAXATION

Here the main legislative instrument is the Finance Bill, which seeks statutory authority for raising taxation in accordance with the Chancellor's budget proposals. The procedure is the same as for other public bills, except that the Committee stage is conducted partly in standing committee and partly in Committee of the Whole House. Because the budget is usually prepared in secret, without the consultations with interest groups that normally characterise the pre-legislative policy stage, attempts to alter the budget proposals are often channelled through Parliament. While government reverses during Finance Bill proceedings are not unknown, they tend to be spasmodic, and a government's main tax proposals are usually immune from defeat. 'Government backbenchers', Norton (1981, p. 177) explains, are unlikely 'to defeat a Government on the central tenet of its economic policy . . . because economic policy is at the heart of a Government's programme', and defeat would probably precipitate resignation.

AUTHORISING AND APPROPRIATING EXPENDITURE

This process also occurs annually. Each year departments present Parliament with their expenditure estimates for the following year, and these are subsequently approved by the annual Consolidated Fund and Appropriation Acts. In fact, however, Parliament has usually approved the vast sums involved virtually 'on the nod'.

Indeed, most of the time nominally devoted to expenditure business has traditionally been allotted to either backbench MPs, who have frequently used it to raise constituency items, or to the opposition, who have invariably used these 'opposition days', as they came to be called, to initiate debates on issues of political rather than financial significance. These traditional proceedings on the Floor, however, have since 1979 been supplemented by those of Commons specialist committees, each of which is able to consider the expenditure of the departments which it shadows. Since 1982, moreover, three days per session have been set aside to debate the estimates in the House, the subjects for debate being chosen by the Liaison Committee (see p. 237) after consultation with select committees. Even so, parliamentary scrutiny of future expenditure remains seriously deficient. Three days per session is totally inadequate to consider the estimates, given the huge sums involved, while the select committees' scrutiny function is blunted by resource and other constraints (see pp. 235–9). One possible reform, advocated by Edward Du Cann, chairman of the Liaison Committee, would be for select committees to play a more positive role by 'not only summon[ing] ministers and ask[ing] them to justify estimates' but also proposing and negotiating 'changes of emphasis under the major expenditure headings' (B. Jones, 1982, p. 314).

This somewhat cursory scrutiny of government financial legislation is supplemented by other parliamentary opportunities to consider public expenditure. These include debates on the annual Public Expenditure White Paper (see Robinson, 1981, pp. 162–7); and the work of the Treasury and Civil Service Committee which is able to investigate government financial and economic policy. In addition the Public Accounts Committee (PAC) provides *post hoc* control of government spending through its examination of the reports of the Comptroller and Auditor-General, whose department, the National Audit Office (NAO) annually audits the accounts of government departments. Workmanlike and useful, the PAC (Flegman, 1980) is nevertheless limited to being able to 'bolt the door after the horse has fled'. It is also limited because about half of British public expenditure – including that of local authorities and nationalised industries – is outside the Comptroller's jurisdiction (*Role of the Comptroller and Auditor-General*, 1980). In 1983 clauses in a Private Member's Bill designed to extend his jurisdiction to nationalised industries were struck out following strenuous opposition from ministers and chairmen of the nationalised industries. The final act (National Audit Act 1983) did, however, empower the Comptroller to examine whether departments are spending money economically, efficiently and effectively (not merely whether it has been spent as authorised by Parliament) and gave access to the books of certain other bodies in receipt of half their income from public funds. It also made the Comptroller a servant of Parliament rather than, as hitherto, of government. Henceforth, he will be appointed by the PAC chairman and the Prime Minister, and responsibility for staffing and running the NAO will lie with a new Public Accounts Commission of MPs. Even so, serious deficiencies in Parliament's financial control still remain. As Robinson (1981, p. 174) concludes, 'In the British tradition, whether it is appropriate in the 1980s or not, the Government governs and the House of Commons supports it'.

Ministerial Responsibility

Ministerial responsibility to Parliament occupies a crucial role in governmental accountability in Britain. Not only is *legal* responsibility for departmental work vested in ministers, but by convention ministers have *political* and *constitutional* responsibility to Parliament for all the actions of government – including those of civil servants. The convention has two main stands: a) the *collective* responsibility of ministers for the actions of the government; and b) their *individual* responsibility to Parliament both for their personal behaviour and for the work of their departments. There is, of course, some inter-linkage between individual and collective responsibility. Sometimes a matter of collective responsibility is turned into individual responsibility so that the government survives – albeit at the expense of losing one or two ministers. (An example is perhaps provided by Lord Carrington's resignation over the Falklands crisis in 1982.) Conversely, individual responsibility is sometimes made a matter of collective responsibility, that is, the government throws the shield of collective responsibility around a minister to prevent his having to resign (e.g. Strachey over the groundnuts fiasco in 1949 – see Birch, 1964, p. 143).

The convention of ministerial responsibility grew up in the nineteenth century in circumstances very different from today. This section examines its current usefulness as a vehicle of government accountability to Parliament.

COLLECTIVE RESPONSIBILITY

This has two main elements: i) if the Commons defeats the government on a motion of confidence it should resign; and ii) all members of the government – not just those in the Cabinet – are responsible to Parliament for all the work of the government. (All ministers must, therefore, publicly support government decisions; if they feel they cannot, they should resign.)

In the mid-nineteenth century, prior to the rise of strongly disciplined parties, collective responsibility provided an effective means by which Parliament could call governments to account. Between 1832 and 1867 ten governments were obliged to resign through lack of parliamentary support, but as party government became entrenched this weapon for controlling the executive lost its potency. Since 1900 only three governments have been forced to resign following parliamentary defeats (the Baldwin and Mac-Donald governments in 1924, and Callaghan's in 1979). These circumstances were, however, exceptional: no single party had an overall majority in the Commons, so a combination of minority parties was able to defeat the government. Normally modern governments have enjoyed the support of a highly organised party commanding a majority in the Commons. Consequently, even at times of major crisis, strong party discipline has usually been sufficient to secure the government's survival, however strident the opposition's calls to 'resign' might be.

It is also clear that the strand which states that all ministers share collective responsibility for all government decisions, and must defend them or else resign, is being eroded. Two points are particularly relevant in this context:

(i) *Agreements to differ.*   Prime ministers, under pressure to avoid ministerial resignation, have occasionally allowed 'agreements to differ' on contentious issues. Three such examples are: a) the National government's 'agreement to differ' in 1932 over tariff policy; b) the Wilson government's 'agreement to differ' during the 1975 referendum over Britain's EEC membership; c) Callaghan's agreement in 1977 to allow ministers who wished to vote against the government's European Assembly Elections Bill. Although 'agreements to differ' are rare, they nevertheless represent a breach of the convention of collective responsibility.

(ii) *Unattributable leaks.*   Informal leaks to the media by dis-affected ministers – whereby ministers make known to journalists their disagreement with government policy but do not resign – also weaken collective responsibility. In recent years such occurrences have been quite common.

In 1969, for example, widespread publicity was given to the opposition of the Home Secretary, James Callaghan, to the government's trade union reform proposals. Tony Benn's opposition to policies propounded by the Labour governments of 1974–9 was also widely documented. Indeed, Shell (1981, p. 159) argues that during the Thatcher government the Prime Minister herself offended against collective responsibility with her public admission over the Employment Bill that 'some of us would have liked to have gone further'.

To what extent should collective responsibility be rigorously applied? In the early nineteenth century unity was relatively easy to attain – governments were smaller, policy was simpler and there was less of it – but today it is naive to assume anything other than differences on policy among senior ministers. Moreover, as Edmund Dell (1980, p. 28) has argued, many ministers, including Cabinet ministers, are often ignorant of many government decisions until they are announced. Indeed, some 'decisions of government which are not announced remain unknown to many members of the Government, including Cabinet Ministers'. Dell's observations lead him to argue (p. 33) that collective responsibility 'is an enemy of open government'; it also confuses responsibility in that to 'make everyone responsible means in the end that no one feels responsible' (p. 39). An end to collective responsibility, he adds, would make government more open and ministers more free to speak their mind, subject only to constraints of collective purpose and tolerance. While greater discussion of the options open to ministers would clearly be welcome from a number of standpoints, it must nevertheless be recognised that governmental cohesiveness could become seriously eroded if there were too many 'agreements to differ' and ministers were even more free than at present to reveal their differences publicly.

Despite the erosion of collective responsibility, resignations have not totally disappeared from the scene. Rush (1981, p. 265) notes that between 1900 and 1976 there were sixty such resignations over specific issues or because of general disagreement with government policy. In fact, the convention provides prime ministers with a convenient way to remove dissidents and, likewise, allows dissidents who feel strongly to disassociate themselves publicly from the government. Nevertheless, ministerial differences normally stop short of resignation, and collective responsibility – by concealing those differences behind a facade of unity – serves to strengthen government. The convention of collective responsibility, therefore, survives, albeit in a form very different from 150 years ago. Then it was an instrument of accountability (i.e. strengthening Parliament against government). Today, it is an instrument for artificially strengthening government against Parliament (by making it seem more united than it really is).

INDIVIDUAL RESPONSIBILITY

There are two main elements to this doctrine: i) that the political head of a government department, and he or she alone, is answerable to Parliament for all the actions of that department; and ii) ministers must accept responsibility for their department, by explaining and defending their actions in Parliament and by resigning if serious errors are discovered.

While the constitutional principles are clear, their practical application is problematical. As with collective responsibility, the rise of strongly disciplined parties has largely eroded its punitive aspect – the party faithful invariably support ministers who are in difficulty rather than force their resignation. Additionally, the massive expansion and increased complexity of government makes it naive, if not unjust, to demand a minister's resignation over an issue in his department about which he knows little or nothing.

Under the convention of individual responsibility ministers are obliged to regularly appear and answer questions in Parliament on the work of their departments. As such, individual responsibility has traditionally been regarded as a major instrument of accountability – the means by which any act or omission within any part of central administration could be called to account in Parliament. In practice, however, many ministers are past masters at producing generalised, evasive answers when necessary; sometimes they actually refuse to answer.

Government ministers not only deal with MPs' questions; they are also expected to participate in debates on government business concerning their own departments. Thus, when a department sponsors legislation, the minister pilots it through the various legislative stages. In this context ministers are deemed to be 'answerable' to Parliament for the work of their departments; they are not now generally held 'responsible' for departmental blunders.

The resignation of ministers following major policy errors is now rare; while errors are constantly being admitted, resignations occur only infrequently. Finer (1956, pp. 377–96) found that between 1855 and 1955 only twenty ministers resigned as a result of parliamentary criticism of themselves or their departments. What distinguished these cases was not normally the gravity of the errors but the fact that ministers lost popularity within their own party. In a sense, therefore, ministers are now accountable to their party and the Prime Minister rather than to Parliament. Indeed, opposition criticism might actually help a minister to survive by rallying party support around him. Criticism from within his own party could, however, be fatal (e.g. Dugdale and Crichel Down, 1954).

Resignations can be considered under two headings: *(a)* personal indiscretions; and *(b)* administrative and policy errors.

(A)   PERSONAL INDISCRETIONS

Personal indiscretion or error by a minister is the simplest cause of resignation. A number of examples are worthy of note:

(i)   In 1947 Hugh Dalton resigned after giving budget details to a journalist before announcing them in Parliament.

(ii)   In 1962 John Profumo resigned from the War Office after admitting lying to the Commons about his relationship with Christine Keeler.

(iii)   In 1973 both Lord Lambton and Lord Jellicoe resigned following disclosures that they had consorted with prostitutes.

Bromhead (1974, p. 68) argues that such cases present no difficulty, but even this category is not entirely straightforward 'given that the dividing line between behaviour which is considered scandalous and that which is not is not always clear and changes over time' (Norton, 1981, p. 148).

(B)   ADMINISTRATIVE AND POLICY ERRORS

It is not the seriousness of an error which determines a minister's destiny, but rather whether the Prime Minister and party is prepared to support him or her. Birch (1980, p. 200) shows how blatant failures in British postwar policy 'have led to stormy debates in Parliament and to scathing comments in the press, but ... not ... to the resignation of the ministers concerned'. The failure of British policy in Palestine from 1945 to 1948; the groundnuts scheme fiasco in 1949; the 1956 Suez crisis are but three episodes cited by Birch to indicate that despite major policy errors the 'responsible' ministers were not forced to resign because they retained the support of their own party.

Until Lord Carrington in 1982, the major postwar example of resignation was that of Sir Thomas Dugdale, Minister of Agriculture, over the *Crichel Down* affair in 1954 – someone heavily criticised by his own party backbenchers. This case (see Birch, 1964, pp. 143–6) concerned land which had been acquired by the government during the war for use as a bombing range. After the war Ministry of Agriculture officials refused to honour an undertaking that the former owner should have a chance to repurchase the land. A subsequent inquiry found that civil servants had acted improperly. There was, Bromhead (1974, p. 69) notes, 'severe criticism in the press, and great indignation among Conservative [MPs]'. Dugdale resigned, largely as a result of criticism from the backbench Conservative Food and Agriculture Committee, although some accounts argue that he wanted to give the civil service a 'jolt'. Whatever the reason, Crichel Down was a relatively minor incident compared with the catalogue of errors committed by many Cabinet ministers since the war.

While resignations are very occasional, other less dramatic means of removing erring ministers exist: 'promotion' to the Lords; appointment to a public body; re-shuffling ministerial posts, are all used by prime ministers to avoid dismissals or resignations. Indeed, re-shuffles also serve to diffuse responsibility: which ministers, if any, were responsible? Today, individual responsibility no longer requires a minister to resign or accept total blame for any departmental error. While he is *answerable* to Parliament for his department's work, it is now widely recognised that he cannot be held *responsible* for decisions made in his name about which he could have had no knowledge and of which he would not have approved. The massive size of modern departments means that ministers can actually deal with relatively little departmental business.

The problems associated with size are well illustrated by the collapse of the Vehicle and General Insurance company in 1971, which left many motorists without insurance (see Chapman, 1973). A subsequent inquiry, while criticising named officials of the Department of Trade and Industry (which had responsibility for oversight of insurance companies), exonerated the relevant ministers who refused to resign. Evidence at the inquiry showed that the matter had been handled a considerable way down the departmental hierarchy over a period during which several departmental ministers had held office. The department also stated that under 1 per cent of business was referred to ministers. To expect ministers to resign in such circumstances is clearly unreasonable. Interestingly, however, the same affair shows how difficult it can be to apportion culpability between ministers and civil servants. In some quarters the inquiry's verdict was heavily criticised, on the grounds that the Secretary of State, John Davies, had considerable business experience and contacts, and should have been in a position to anticipate and handle the crisis (Baker, 1972b).

Despite the problems it presents, the doctrine of individual responsibility survives because it has benefits for both ministers and civil servants. The advantage for ministers is that they, and they alone, are the official mouthpiece of their department as well as the recipient of all departmental advice. As Mackintosh (1982, p. 169) argues:

> the public, the press and MPs are often starved of the material with which to make up a counter-argument . . . If the doctrine was broken and officials could explain their views freely in public, then ministers would have the much more formidable task of making their case against men who were seized of the key counterpoints and who knew that their arguments were accepted by many in the ministry.

The major advantage for civil servants is that the doctrine generally protects their anonymity which, in turn, is regarded as necessary if impartiality is to be maintained. It also leaves them publicly free of any repercussions arising from their advice, and this greatly increases 'their freedom and power' (Mackintosh, 1982, p. 170). As it stands, therefore, it is clearly in the interests of both ministers and civil servants to see the convention maintained. For the advocates of 'open government', however, it remains a major obstacle: civil servants are technically prevented from communicating with the public other than through the minister, and much of their power is exercised without any subsequent accountability. Significantly, the Fulton Report recommended (1968, para. 283) that both the public and central administration would benefit if civil servants were allowed greater freedom to explain 'what their departments are doing, at any rate so far as concerns managing existing policies and implementing legislation'.

THE FALKLANDS CRISIS, 1982

This crisis saw the resignation of three Foreign Office ministers, including Lord Carrington, the Foreign Secretary. The Defence

Secretary John Nott also offered to resign, but subsequently agreed to the Prime Minister's request that he should remain in office. Criticism of the government's unpreparedness for the Argentine attack upon the Falkland Islands came not only from the Opposition but from senior Conservative MPs. The three ministers resigned because of Parliament's loss of confidence in the Foreign Office, particularly in its handling of the situation prior to the invasion. In an interview Lord Carrington explained that it would have been wrong to 'behave as if nothing [had] happened' and that resignation was 'the honourable thing'. *The Times* (6 April 1982), however, described the resignation as an 'act of expiation' necessitated by parliamentary criticism of the government's unpreparedness – an interpretation suggesting that individual responsibility might have been a device to avoid involving the collective responsibility (and resignation) of the whole government (Pyper, 1983).

OVERVIEW

In 1978 Dunsire (p. 41) suggested that being 'accountable' may mean, in the context of ministerial responsibility, 'no more than having to answer questions about what has happened or is happening within one's jurisdiction'. The defeat since then of the Callaghan government, and the resignations over the Falklands crisis, serve, however, as a reminder that loss of office remains a possibility under the conventions of both collective and individual responsibility. Nevertheless, in the sense of allocating blame and requiring resignation, both conventions are likely to remain weak so long as majoritarian governments can rely on the party faithful to protect a minister, or ministry, in difficulties.

It was for reasons of *accountability* that collective and individual responsibility emerged, but they cannot really be considered entirely appropriate in this context today. Collective responsibility strengthens and shields the government in the face of parliamentary criticism, while individual responsibility presents a barrier between civil servant and MP. A civil servant, for example, may make serious errors but the minister may shield him to prevent a storm. Even worse, the minister may be misled or misinformed by his officials, and yet MPs traditionally have been able to question only the minister and not the civil servants who really have the facts. It is for such reasons that in recent years the doctrine of individual responsibility has been relaxed somewhat: for example, by allowing civil servants increasing exposure to journalists and parliamentary select committees, and by making their actions investigable by the Ombudsman (pp. 249–56). Even so, it may be premature to write off the doctrine as totally unimportant. Not only do ministers and civil servants both have vested interests in its retention, but as Johnson (1977, pp. 83–4) observes, it still serves to remind us 'about the manner in which public powers are to be established and located: it defines who is responsible for what rather than who is responsible to whom.'

Scrutiny and Redress

Parliament does not govern: its job is to scrutinise government actions and, if dissatisfied, seek redress. This role cannot be totally divorced from other parliamentary functions: debating govern-ment legislation, examining SIs, considering tax and expenditure proposals, for example, all provide opportunities for scrutiny. The government usually also provides further opportunities by initiat-ing debates on policy proposals or matters of political moment. In addition, however, a number of specific instruments of scrutiny and redress are available to MPs. These can be divided into three broad categories: *(a)* Debates and Questions; *(b)* Private Channels; *(c)* Select Committees.

(A) DEBATES AND QUESTIONS

Both the Opposition and individual MPs can raise matters in the House. The Opposition, for example, may use one of its Opposi-tion Days, or table a motion of censure (which the government must find time to debate). Individual MPs also have opportunities to initiate business, notably by tabling parliamentary questions or initiating one of the daily half-hour adjournment debates (see Borthwick, 1979).

While these opportunities can sometimes be useful for focusing public attention on issues, for raising constituency problems, or for obtaining basic information, as instruments of scrutiny and redress they are seriously deficient. They provide no opportunities for impartial, expert, or in-depth investigation of government activity, and in many respects suffer from procedural limitations. For example, only a fixed number of Opposition Days are available; question time is usually insufficient to allow oral answers to all MPs requesting them; and adjournment debates occur late at night and attract little media attention. In addition many government supporters believe 'that advancement to office is achieved by not creating difficulties for one's own Ministers' (Norton, 1981, p. 139), and consequently are often reluctant even to use the limited means available for scrutinising and influencing executive actions. As a result the 'scrutiny and influence' function, while widely acknowledged to be of vital importance, is generally conducted in a manner which many observers feel is ineffective, random, piece-meal, and unsystematic.

(B) PRIVATE CHANNELS

The opportunities available for scrutiny and redress within the House are supplemented by private channels of communication between MPs and ministers. MPs, for example, may seek information or raise grievances through correspondence or discussion with ministers. The network of party committees within Parliament also provides a vehicle for liaison; government supporters, especially, often prefer to seek concessions in these committees rather than risk embarrassing ministers in the House. Sometimes, also, the Opposition deals with government through private channels: securing information on privy councillor terms in sensitive policy areas; negotiating compromises when governments require inter-party support; and requesting concessions in return for co-operation with the parliamentary timetable. While much depends upon the issues concerned, and upon the number and standing of the MPs con-cerned, the efficiency of such channels is often contingent upon the extent to which, if necessary, they can be reinforced by formal proceedings in the House. Such proceedings, as already observed, are usually quite inadequate for exerting effective scrutiny and influence over a majority government which is unwilling to yield.

(C) SELECT COMMITTEES

In recent decades, as the scale and complexity of government has increased, traditional parliamentary procedures of scrutiny and redress have become increasingly inadequate. Consequently, several important new developments have occurred. First, the traditional procedures for securing redress have been supplemented by the establishment of the Ombudsman (pp. 249-56). Secondly, the scrutiny function has been strengthened by the development of a comprehensive system of select committees.

House of Commons *Select* Committees should not be confused with the *Standing* Committees which deal with legislation; usually they are smaller, have a more permanent membership, and are empowered to appoint advisers and 'send for persons, papers and records'. Such committees are not new: for example, the Public Accounts Committee has existed since 1861, while between 1912 and 1979 an Estimates (later Expenditure) Committee was employed examining government expenditure proposals. From the late 1960s, however, there was considerable expansion of select committee activity. Some committees were established to scrutinise the work of particular departments; others to oversee specialised areas (e.g. Race Relations, Science and Technology). Although intended to improve the House's powers of scrutiny their record was generally disappointing, not least because ministers and civil servants often saw them as a threat to departmental power (for discussion see Johnson, 1981). In 1979, however, fourteen new committees were established, each having responsibility for 'shadowing' specified departments, as shown in Table 13.1.

Table 13.1 *The Post-1979 Select Committee System in the House of Commons*

Committee	Government departments principally concerned
Agriculture	Ministry of Agriculture, Fisheries and Food
Defence	Ministry of Defence
Education, Science and Arts	Department of Education and Science
Employment	Department of Employment
Energy	Department of Energy
Environment	Department of the Environment
Foreign Affairs	Foreign and Commonwealth Office
Home Affairs	Home Office
Industry and Trade	Department of Trade and Industry
Social Services	Department of Health and Social Security
Transport	Department of Transport
Treasury and Civil Service	Treasury, Inland Revenue, Office of Management and Personnel, Customs and Excise
Welsh Affairs	Welsh Office
Scottish Affairs	Scottish Office

With this reorganisation the former Expenditure Committee and the Select Committee on Nationalised Industries both disappeared, their work having largely been absorbed by new committees. Each committee has power 'to examine the expenditure, administration and policy of the [relevant] government departments ... and associated public bodies' (*Hansard*, V, vol. 969, cols 33–4, 25 June

1979), terms of reference which include not only departments, but public corporations and other non-departmental agencies. Three committees have power to form sub-committees, while those shadowing 'sponsoring' departments of nationalised industries may set up sub-committees drawn from two or more parent committees to consider matters affecting more than one industry. The work of select committees is overseen by a Liaison Committee which includes the chairmen of the fourteen departmental committees.

In an attempt to protect the committees from arbitrary disbandment by the government, each is appointed for the duration of Parliament. Membership is kept small (between nine and thirteen) to enable them to function as effective working groups. Empowered 'to send for persons, papers and records' and to appoint specialist advisers, each committee can receive written submissions and oral evidence from not only ministers but from civil servants, pressure groups, and outside experts. Membership is bi-partisan, and Opposition members hold several chairmanships. Covering virtually the whole spectrum of government activity, these arrangements are of considerable significance. As Borthwick (1982, p. 9) observes, 'For the first time, perhaps, the House of Commons has a coherent *system* of select committees, rather than a haphazard assortment of pieces'.

A full assessment of the new committees cannot yet be made; however, some *advantages* are already apparent. Each committee chooses its own subjects for investigation, and in the first two-and-a-quarter years 150 reports on 'a wide variety of subjects attracting wide publicity and in many cases influencing government thinking and practice' were produced (B. Jones, 1982, p. 313). Some of these were short investigations; others longer and more intensive. Some dealt with policy issues (e.g. government economic strategy, overseas students' fees, selling council houses); others with 'administrative' matters (deaths in police custody; the Welsh Office's role in developing job opportunities). Possibly the most notable success was the Home Affairs Committee's inquiry into the 'sus' laws, which produced a firm recommendation favouring abolition, and a threat from committee members to introduce a repeal Bill if the government refused to act (Davies, 1980, p. 51). (The government subsequently introduced its own repeal measure.) As this example indicates, the new committees operate with some freedom from party discipline. There is also considerable enthusiasm among their members: fierce competition for places, good attendance, and low membership turnover. The media, moreover, have shown considerable interest in committee reports, and pressure groups are

increasingly using them as targets for their representations. The
new committees, in short, have emerged as an important part of
the policy community, capable of publicising, and sometimes
influencing, the less defensible aspects of governmental work. As a
result, Parliament and public are undoubtedly better informed than
previously, and the government is more accountable for its actions.

Despite their promising start, however, there are several *problems
and deficiencies* associated with the new committees. From the
governmental perspective they are sometimes criticised for impos-
ing 'excessive burdens on ministers and civil servants in the preparation of memorandums' (Riddell, 1982). An influential lobby
also argues that the new committees divert MPs away from the
Chamber into committees examining information which, Enoch
Powell (1982, p. 175) claims, 'the rest of the House . . . cannot read
and has no possibility of keeping up with'. In his view select committee members risk losing objectivity through over-exposure to
departmental briefings and civil service advice. He also adds that
committees have no 'effect except through the House' – a point
reinforced by the government's failure to allocate a fixed number of
days for debating committee reports. (During the first three years,
in fact, only five specialist committee reports were debated on the
Floor of the House, and usually these were either in opposition
time or were held 'at short notice . . . on a Friday, and in some cases
long after the Report [had] been published' (Liaison Committee,
1982/3, paras 60/5).

The new committees have no legislative or executive powers:
they can only investigate, recommend and report. Moreover, the
power 'to send for persons, papers and records' does not extend to
departmental files and records, and ministers cannot be *required* to
attend (although they usually do). Ministerial evidence, moreover,
is sometimes less than frank, while civil servants are also often
unforthcoming. Indeed, civil servants appear before committees
under restrictive conditions laid down in the so-called Osmotherly
memorandum (CSD General Notice Gen 80/38, 16 May 1980).
The convention that civil servants anonymously advise ministers
who take the final decisions pervades this memorandum: for
example, it precludes civil servants from giving evidence on advice
given to ministers, inter-departmental exchanges, and Cabinet
committees. As a result vast and ill-defined areas of government
work are excluded from the range of matters which civil servants
may discuss before select committees.

The government alone cannot be blamed for the deficiencies of
select committees. Greater backbench assertiveness, for example,

might have weakened the government's resolve and ability to limit the committees' powers. It might also have increased the resources made available to employ specialist advisers. Although committee expenditure is controlled by the House of Commons Commission, not the Treasury, the sums allocated for specialist assistance are particularly meagre. On average in 1980/1 each committee spent only £7,819 on specialist advice (Liaison Committee, 1982/3, para. 76) which, clearly, is grossly inadequate to match the expertise available to government departments.

Despite the restrictions, much valuable information nevertheless flows between government departments and select committees. While the performance of committees has inevitably been uneven, in general, as B. Jones (1982, p. 317) argues, they 'have extracted information from departments which would not otherwise have been given, and . . . provide more effective scrutiny of the government than debates and questions'. Nevertheless, further substantial development is necessary if the new committees are to become more effective as instruments of scrutiny and influence: more time to debate their reports in the Chamber, more specialist staff, and wider investigative powers. In the longer term, as *The Times* (20 January 1983) has suggested, the new committees could usefully 'take over' the legislative work of standing committees, as well as more comprehensive and 'detailed examination' of departmental estimates (see pp. 224–5). If any such developments are to occur, however, old attitudes may have to disappear. Ministers and civil servants must become more responsive to demands for 'open government'; MPs more prepared, irrespective of party, to assert themselves against government; and the House generally to accept that under modern conditions sustained questioning of ministers and civil servants in committee is invariably a more searching and effective form of scrutiny than proceedings in the Chamber. Whether, given the understandable sensitivities of government to any increase in backbench assertiveness, such changes will occur remains to be seen.

14 PUBLIC ADMINISTRATION AND REDRESS

The traditional democratic avenues of accountability through MPs and councillors have become increasingly inadequate with the growth of state activity. Not only has government bureaucracy expanded, but so have the points of contact between citizen and state. For example, the welfare state has increased people's rights to benefits; planning and compulsory purchase procedures affect property rights; government intervention in industrial matters regulates employer and employee rights; and so on. Normally such matters do not give rise to disagreement; however, some disputes inevitably occur, and often on a scale and complexity which renders traditional avenues of redress largely inappropriate. To resolve such disputes there exist numerous mechanisms through which the decisions and actions of public authorities can be challenged. Four main avenues can be identified: the courts; statutory inquiries; administrative tribunals; ombudsmen.

The Courts

Some countries, notably France, have a system of administrative law (*droit administratif*) and a separate system of courts to deal specifically with disputes between citizen and state. In Britain, this is not the case. All public bodies, however, derive their authority from statute, and thus public administrators and their political masters work within legally defined powers. Any action outside the scope of such power is *ultra vires* (beyond the powers) and may be declared unlawful by the courts. Indeed, there exists a number of judicial remedies by which public bodies can be required to fulfil their statutory obligations and unlawful decisions can be quashed or declared nullities. These remedies include injunctions, declarations, and three prerogative orders: *certiorari* (which removes decisions of administrative authorities, tribunals or inferior courts to the High Court for review); prohibition (which requires a public body to desist from unlawful – *ultra vires* – acts); and *mandamus* (issued by the High Court, and which compels public bodies to perform their statutory duties).

In recent years judicial challenges to the *vires* of official acts have increased quite sharply. In the last decade, for example, the courts have made important contributions to defining both local authority powers (see Chapter 9) and the extent of ministerial discretion (see Griffith, 1981, pp. 142–53). Since 1978, moreover, procedures for application for judicial review have been simplified, and the provision as to *locus standii* governing access to the courts relaxed (see Order 53 of the Rules of the Supreme Court; and Yardley, 1982, esp. pp. 120–7). Since *Ridge v. Baldwin* [1964] AC 40, the courts have also tended increasingly to require public authorities to respect principles of natural justice when exercising their powers. (Of course, the procedures concerned, and the availability and effectiveness of remedies, often raise complex legal points which cannot be discussed here. See, however, de Smith, 1981; and Wade, 1982.)

While the courts' role in supervising the fairness and legality of administrative actions is substantial, and increasing, litigation is often a last resort, used only when other avenues have failed to secure redress. Indeed, considerations of cost, accessibility and delay make courts generally unsuitable for securing redress, and during the twentieth century there has been a proliferation of alternative mechanisms for resolving disputes. It is upon these mechanisms that the remainder of this chapter focuses.

Statutory Inquiries

Certain ministerial decisions – notably those by the Environment Secretary on appeals against the decisions of local authorities on planning applications and in respect of compulsory purchase orders referred for confirmation where complaints are made – are only taken after a public inquiry. Such inquiries are 'an everyday occurrence in British public administration' (Wraith and Lamb, 1971, p. 13). A full investigation into the facts is conducted by an inspector, and parties are entitled to state their case. In these respects public inquiries resemble a judicial process. Indeed, since the Franks Report (1957), increasing judicialisation has entered into the handling of inquiries: inspectors' reports, for example, must be published, and reasons given for any decisions by virtue of the statutory procedural rules.

In other respects, however, the process is more like an administrative exercise. Wraith and Lamb (1971, p. 13) write: 'Public Inquiries are . . . for the most part concerned only to establish facts and to make recommendations'. The inspector is, in fact, a civil servant appointed by the minister to ascertain facts on his behalf. Since 1969 decisions in many cases (92 per cent in 1981) have actually been delegated to and decided by inspectors (Delafons, 1982, p. 259), although in the most complex or controversial cases the inspector's role is to produce a report and make recommendations with the final decision being left to the minister. (Even in such cases, of course, the decision is usually taken *in practice* by departmental civil servants rather than the minister.) From this perspective inspectors have a typically civil service role, assembling facts and recommending or taking decisions on their ministers' behalf. As Hawke (1982, p. 143) observes, 'decisions in this context are usually taken against a policy background'. Thus appeals may be decided not solely on their merits, but in accordance with policy guidelines, and ministers have the same freedom to reject inspectors' recommendations (although it happens in only a tiny percentage of cases) as to reject civil service advice generally.

Administrative Tribunals

Administrative tribunals also usually have both an administrative and judicial dimension to their work. Most tribunals contribute to the administrative process by determining the extent to which departmental policies apply in particular cases. The judicial aspect of their work normally arises because such cases involve the rights and obligations of individual citizens (or organisations) in the specialised fields of law under which such departmental policies are administered. Although their work usually has both administrative and judicial dimensions, tribunals – as the Franks Report (1957, para. 40) stated – 'are not ordinary courts, but neither are they appendages of Government Departments'. Neither are they on all fours with statutory inquiries. Their respective functions, Wraith and Lamb claimed in 1971 (p. 13), were 'fundamentally different'. Whereas inquiries essentially established 'facts' and made 'recommendations' (*before* an administrative decision was taken) tribunals were responsible for 'deciding or adjudicating in disputes' (usually *after* an administrative decision had given rise to disagreement). In practice, today, this distinction is less clear cut, particularly from the citizen's standpoint, especially since a high percentage of decisions at inquiries are now taken by inspectors.

However, another distinction drawn by Wraith and Lamb general-ly still holds good: 'Public inquiries are constituted *ad hoc* to inquire into particular matters' whereas tribunals usually have a more 'regular or permanent existence'.

During the twentieth century tribunals have proliferated. Their development has been largely piecemeal, with particular tribunals being formed as and when necessary. One effect of this is that a precise count of tribunals is impossible. In some cases a single tribunal serves the whole country, but more usually there is a regional or local network. In other cases still tribunals are consti-tuted on an *ad hoc* basis. Consequently it is safer to think less in terms of numbers of tribunals, than of tribunal systems or cate-gories. Thus the Pliatzky Report (1980, p. 2) identified sixty-seven 'tribunal systems' in the UK in 1978/9, while the Council on Tribunals (Annual Report 1980/81, HC 89, 1981, Appendix D) listed forty-one tribunal categories in England and Wales within its jurisdiction. Even these figures, however, are not definitive, for the distinction between tribunals and other non-departmental bodies is not always clear (e.g. the Monopolies and Mergers Commission, an investigative body with many tribunal-like features, is excluded from both of the above 'counts'). Nevertheless, tribunal machinery is extensive, with cases heard running at about six times the number of contested civil cases that are 'disposed of at trial before the High Court and county courts' (Williams, 1982, p. 289).

In 1957 Franks identified five main fields of public administration covered by tribunals: land and property, national insurance and assistance, NHS, military service, and transport. Today, with subsequent growth, other fields might be added, notably immigra-tion, employment, and taxation. Between them the various tri-bunal systems have two main functions:

(i) *Resolving disputes between private individuals.* The main fields involved here are land and property, and employment. Among the former are Rent Tribunals and Rent Assessment Committees, which arbitrate between landlord and tenant on rent and other matters; and, among the latter, Industrial Tribunals which deter-mine disputes between employer and employee on issues such as unfair dismissal and entitlement to redundancy payments.

(ii) *Resolving disputes between public bodies (usually government de-partments) and citizens.* Among the most important are Local Valuation Courts, which hear appeals against rateable value assess-ments (about 40,000 cases annually); Supplementary Benefit

Appeal Tribunals, which determine appeals against decisions on entitlement to supplementary benefit (45,000 cases annually); and National Insurance Local Tribunals, which dispose of about 25,000 appeals annually against decisions on a range of benefits. These all have extensive local networks (e.g. some 2,000 National Insurance Local Tribunals are constituted each year at about 180 local centres).

As should be clear, 'administrative tribunal' is a general term, incorporating a variety of boards, courts, committees, tribunals etc. Each established by statute, as and when the need has arisen, British tribunals exhibit a wide variety of procedures and constitutions. However, the reason for their prolific development is clear. As the Pliatzky Report (1980, p. 25) explains, there are two main alternatives to their use; namely, 'to make the Executive the final arbiter in disputes to most of which it is itself a party, or to transfer [their] jurisdiction ... to the ordinary courts of law'. The former course is by no means unknown; the Education Secretary, for example, decides on disputes about teachers' superannuation entitlements and the Home Secretary on naturalisation problems. Nevertheless, as Pliatzky (p. 3) adds, it is undesirable for a government department to be 'judge and jury ... in dealing with ... appeals against its administrative decisions'. The latter course, adjudication by the courts, is also arguably undesirable. Not only would the courts become heavily overburdened, but tribunals offer several *advantages over courts:*

1 *They are more specialised* – many deal with technical matters where adjudication is best discharged by persons with specialist knowledge (e.g. trade union representatives on Industrial Tribunals).
2 *They are more accessible and informal* – people are more likely to utilise tribunals because the daunting atmosphere of the courts is absent.
3 *They are more flexible* – being less bound to legal precedent and procedures than courts, tribunals are better able to allow for local or special circumstances in arriving at decisions.
4 *They are more expeditious* – largely because of their greater specialisation and flexibility.
5 *They are cheaper* – panel members are usually part-time and local, and parties rarely have legal representation.

These advantages are particularly important because of the kinds of case typically brought before tribunals. 'Ordinary' individuals claiming entitlement to benefits, or lower rents/rateable values, etc., require more informal, cheap, and speedy adjudication than the courts can provide. These 'advantages', however, can become problems if they produce judicial safeguards significantly below the standards of the courts, or if independence from the executive is compromised. In fact on both these grounds, as well as on the more theoretical one that constitutional principles such as the rule of law and separation of powers are threatened, (Hewart, 1929) administrative tribunals have been widely criticised. This is particularly evident in the main criticisms of tribunals made in the Franks Report (1957) (although see also the Donoughmore Report, 1932). Franks' main criticisms were:

(i) *Independence.* Franks felt that tribunals should be free 'from the influence, real or apparent, of Departments concerned with the subject-matter of their decisions' (para. 42). He expressed anxiety that this view was not always shared by departmental officials.

(ii) *Appointment.* Many tribunal chairmen and members were appointed by the minister concerned. While 'no significant evidence' was found that departments tried to influence tribunals, these arrangements were considered 'undesirable in principle', and a potential source of 'misunderstanding' (para. 45).

(iii) *Membership qualifications.* Although tribunal members were normally appointed from nominees of appropriate organisations (e.g. trade unions in the case of Industrial Tribunals), lack of legal qualifications was quite widespread.

(iv) *Procedural deficiencies.* Tribunal procedures varied widely. Most had 'a simple procedure, usually without the oath and sometimes with a ban on legal representation' (para. 36). Some also failed to give reasoned decisions, held hearings in secret, and provided no appeals machinery.

Most of these criticisms could be defended *either* from the administrative standpoint (i.e. that tribunals performed a primarily administrative function and hence close departmental links were desirable); *or* on the grounds that the advantages of tribunals over the courts inevitably required relaxation of normal judicial procedures. Franks' view, however, was that tribunals had been 'provided by Parliament for adjudication rather than as part of the machinery of administration' (para. 40) and that they should manifest three basic characteristics: openness, fairness and impartiality. To achieve these characteristics several recommendations were made. Reasoned decisions, public hearings, legal representation (with legal aid), and appeal to the courts on points of law, were to be the norm. Tribunal chairmen were ordinarily to have legal qualifications, and were to be appointed by the Lord Chancellor. Other members were to be appointed by a new body, the Council on Tribunals, which was also 'to keep the constitution and working of tribunals under continuous review' (para. 43).

Most of Franks' recommendations were implemented shortly afterwards, either by departmental circular or legislation. There was also a 'change in general attitude' by many tribunals 'which had not previously appreciated the full import' of the Franks 'characteristics' (Yardley, 1982, p. 199). As a result visible improvements have appeared in tribunal procedures: rights of legal representation are now generally recognised, public proceedings are the norm, and legally qualified chairmen – normally selected by appropriate ministers from panels appointed by the Lord Chancellor – are far more widespread. Many of Franks' criticisms are simply no longer valid. Indeed, the situation today is a developing one, as many of the post-Franks changes work their way through and fresh ones continue to be effected.

While these reforms have improved the fairness and impartiality of tribunals, they have also made their proceedings more legalistic. Not only are there more legally qualified chairmen, and more parties with legal representation, but attitudes to evidence and points of law are more strict. Appelate tribunals, for example, now customarily publish selected decisions and consequently case law and precedent have assumed greater importance with some tribunals. As tribunals have become more legalistic, however, many of their professed advantages over the courts – informality, flexibility, cheapness, expedition etc. – have become less visible. This, in fact, illustrates the fundamental dilemma posed by administrative tribunals: how to reconcile the need for swifter, cheaper, more flexible justice with that for adequate judicial safeguards. A balance must be struck, and in the post-Franks era the point of balance has moved markedly towards greater judicialisation.

Even so, the administrative view of tribunals – held mainly within departments – has not been abandoned, and several of Franks' more radical recommendations have been resisted by successive governments. Tribunal members, for example, are not appointed by the Council on Tribunals (departmental ministers – or in practice, their civil servants – still largely exercise this right); and 'interested' departments often still have a hand in appointing chairmen. The rights to legal representation, moreover, have been gravely undermined by the non-availability of legal aid for most tribunal hearings. Tribunal proceedings also still vary widely, and sometimes exhibit quite worrying features. (Some tribunals, for example, allow evidence which would be inadmissible in court.) In most cases departments are still responsible for finding tribunal staff and accommodation and for paying and reimbursing members. As these examples show, the conflicting demands which underlie administrative tribunals – departmental convenience and administrative flexibility on the one hand, and judicial rectitude and fairness on the other – remain problematical. Despite the advances in the twenty-five years since Franks, the haphazard pragmatic development of tribunals is still in evidence, and doubts remain about the standards of justice they dispense and about their independence from departmental influence.

Control of Tribunals and Inquiries

Control lies partly with the courts and partly with specially created machinery. Any unlawful or *ultra vires* act, or any failure to discharge statutory obligations, can be remedied through the courts by way of an application for judicial review (see pp. 240–1). In addition, appeals are usually allowed against ministers' (or inspectors') decisions following statutory inquiries, and from some (but by no means all) tribunals, on points of law. Special appellate tribunals, which hear appeals from first instance tribunals, also exist in some fields, sometimes with jurisdiction over facts, merit, and law, but in other cases only on points of law. Since Franks, judicial control of tribunals and inquiries has been strengthened substantially, although significantly not to the extent that Franks actually recommended (see Yardley, 1982, esp. pp. 196–8). In fact, considerable confusion and inconsistency persists, reflecting once again the largely piecemeal development of British tribunal machinery.

Perhaps the most significant product of the Franks Report is the *Council on Tribunals*. Established in 1958, its current functions, specified in the Tribunals and Inquiries Act 1971, are as follows:

(i)   to keep under review the constitution and workings of the tribunals specified in Schedule 1 to the Act and, from time to time, to report on their constitution and working;

(ii) to consider and report on such particular matters as may be referred to the Council under the Act with respect to tribunals other than the ordinary courts of law;

(iii) to consider and report on such matters as may be referred ...

or as the Council may consider to be of special importance, with respect to administrative procedures which involve or may involve the holding of a statutory inquiry by or on behalf of a Minister. (*Source*: Annual Report 1980/1, Appendix A)

The Council must also be consulted before new procedural rules are made for inquiries or scheduled tribunals, and may make general recommendations about membership of the latter. An independent body, the Council currently consists of fifteen members appointed by the Lord Chancellor and Lord Advocate, plus the Parliamentary Commissioner who sits ex-officio. (Some of these, plus several non-members appointed by the Lord Advocate, form the Council's Scottish Committee.)

The Council's jurisdiction is generally regarded as somewhat limited. It excludes ministerial or other administrative jurisdiction beyond the scope of tribunals and inquiries, and does not extend to Northern Ireland. Its powers are essentially advisory and consultative: it cannot award compensation, overturn decisions or hear appeals. Its membership, moreover, is part time, mostly unpaid, and its tiny staff and limited budget (1980/1 expenditure was only £200,000) are wholly inadequate for effective oversight of the several hundred thousand tribunal and inquiry proceedings occurring annually. Significantly, in 1980, the Council issued a report (Council on Tribunals, 1980) calling for increased resources and powers, notably powers to call relevant papers from tribunals and government departments, and to attend private tribunal hearings. It also requested fuller consultation by ministers, and fuller jurisdiction across the whole field of administrative adjudication. These recommendations, however, were mostly ignored by the government and the Council remains a somewhat feeble institution, largely unknown to the public.

Even so the Council has made some impact. Being consulted about new or modified rules for tribunals and inquiries, it has brought some uniformity and coherence to their procedures. Its investigations, moreover, have revealed numerous deficiencies which ministers have generally proved willing to rectify. Surprisingly, perhaps, the Council has had most impact upon statutory inquiries. Its reports into the *Chalkpit* case influenced 'a whole series' of subsequent inquiry procedure reforms (Yardley, 1982, p. 189); while its investigation into the proposed Stansted airport development in the 1960s contributed to the ordering of the Roskill Commission.

These successes, however, cannot conceal the remaining deficiencies. Notable among these is the lack of tribunal machinery in certain important fields, such as appeals against a local authority's refusal to award discretionary grants to certain categories of student, or to house allegedly homeless persons. In 1961 the Whyatt Committee (Whyatt Report, 1961) proposed the establishment of a General Tribunal to hear appeals from discretionary decisions not covered by tribunals, but this has not been implemented. No less serious is the absence of a general right of appeal from tribunals, on fact and merits as well as law. In evidence to Franks, W. A. Robson suggested forming a general administrative appeals tribunal to hear appeals both from tribunals and against other administrative decisions where no tribunal existed. Franks itself recommended that appeals on law, fact and merits should be, in most cases, to appropriate appellate tribunals; and from the latter to the courts. In 1971 there was a further suggestion (Justice, 1971) for a general right of appeal from tribunals to a new Administrative Division of the High Court. Although such arrangements would produce greater uniformity and stronger judicial safeguards, there is an obvious objection to carrying appeals from specialist to non-specialist tribunals, while the creation of a separate division of the High Court would have important legal implications. For these reasons – and also, no doubt, because of bureaucratic opposition to increased judicial control of administrative discretion – comprehensive reform seems unlikely to materialise. The piecemeal pattern which has characterised the development of tribunal and inquiry mechanisms appears likely to continue.

Introducing Ombudsmen

Despite the powers of the courts and the growth of tribunals and inquiries, many administrative actions remain immune from impartial review. A decision, for example, may appear harsh, but unless it is in a field covered by a tribunal or similar mechanism, or unless a breach of law or natural justice is involved, no appeals machinery may be available. Traditionally, in such cases, the remedy for seeking redress has been an MP or councillor. Since 1967, however, they have been supplemented by a growing band of ombudsmen.

The term 'ombudsman' is Scandinavian in origin, and can be translated as 'grievance man' or 'complaints officer'. Such an official has existed in Sweden since 1809, but during the twentieth century ombudsmen have appeared in various other countries, notably Finland (1919), Norway (1952), Denmark (1955), and New Zealand (1962). The genesis of the British ombudsman is usually attributed to the Whyatt Report (1961), although the proposal was actually implemented by the Parliamentary Commissioner Act, 1967. This innovation proved to be only a first step, and by 1983 no less than five types of ombudsman machinery could be identified in the UK:

(i)   Parliamentary Commissioner for Administration (created 1967);
(ii) Northern Ireland Parliamentary Commissioner (1969);
(iii) Commissioner for Complaints (N. Ireland) (1969);
(iv) Health Service Commissioners: England, Scotland, Wales (all 1973);
(v)   Commission(er)s for Local Administration: England, Wales (both 1974) and Scotland (1976).

Of these, the most important for students of British public administration – the Parliamentary Commissioner for Administration, the Health Service Commissioners, and the local commissioners – are examined below.

The Parliamentary Commissioner for Administration (PCA)

'Few new governmental agencies can have begun operations under a darker cloud of adverse publicity than the [PCA]' (Gwyn, 1982, p. 177). From the outset, there were claims that the PCA 'lacked teeth', particularly when compared with foreign ombudsmen. While these claims have sometimes been exaggerated, there are undoubtedly serious problems associated with the PCA, the most important of which are:

(A)   RELATIONS WITH PARLIAMENT

While the PCA exists to investigate citizens' grievances against central administration, he is a servant of Parliament. He works closely with a House of Commons committee, the Select Committee on the Parliamentary Commissioner for Administration, which receives his reports and oversees his work. This relationship with MPs (peers have no access to the PCA) has several useful aspects:

the Select Committee, for example,.can reinforce the PCA's findings and recommendations, while its support – coupled with the provision that the PCA is removable from office only by addresses of both Houses of Parliament – offers some protection from abuse or arbitrary dismissal by the executive. Nevertheless in one major respect this relationship has caused problems; namely, the requirement that complaints to the PCA must be channelled through MPs.

This provision for 'filtering' complaints through MPs was introduced for two main reasons: (i) To prevent the PCA from being 'swamped' by complaints; and (ii) to reassure MPs that the PCA would supplement, not undermine, their own role as constituency 'grievance chasers'. The first reason, while probably appropriate at the outset, is less acceptable today. On average, the PCA receives around 1,000 referrals a year from MPs, and while direct access would generate more complaints, the likely increase, in the view of the Widdicombe Committee (Widdicombe Report, 1977, paras 17–18), could be accommodated by simple organisational and procedural reforms. At present, the MP 'filter' produces serious under-utilisation of the PCA: MPs vary widely in the use they make of him, and some never refer complaints. (Forty-one MPs in the 1974–9 Parliament referred no cases.) Moreover, approximately as many complaints reach the PCA direct from the public as through MPs. Initially such complaints were returned; however, since 1978 complainants have been informed that, if they wish, their complaint will be referred to an MP. While this represents a move towards direct access, it still leaves the PCA unable to investigate cases without agreement from an MP.

The second reason for the MP filter, the need to reassure MPs, also seems unfounded today. Nevertheless, although most authorities now support direct access, the Select Committee remains unconvinced. MPs, Gwyn (1982, p. 194) observes, have managed to restrict that aspect 'of the ombudsman institution that they believe to be harmful to themselves' by preventing the PCA from establishing a direct relationship with the citizens he exists to protect.

(B) LIMITED JURISDICTION

The PCA's jurisdiction is limited in two main ways. First, several important fields of public administration are outside his terms of reference. Some initial exclusions – notably the actions of consular officials relating to UK citizens abroad – were later brought within the PCA's jurisdiction, while others (e.g. local government, and the NHS) were later placed under other ombudsmen. Even so, several controversial exclusions remain: public corporations, armed forces and civil service personnel complaints, government contractual and commercial activities, legal proceedings, and actions affecting foreign affairs. Actions pursuable through the courts or tribunals are also excluded. While this leaves a jurisdiction narrower than many foreign ombudsmen, the PCA's jurisdiction nevertheless extends to actions by both civil servants and ministers within all regular central government departments.

Secondly, the PCA is restricted to investigating complaints of alleged *maladministration* causing injustice. Although not defined in the 1967 Act, Richard Crossman (the minister responsible for it) described maladministration as 'bias, neglect, inattention, delay, incompetence, ineptitude, perversity, turpitude, arbitrariness, and so on' (*Hansard,* V, vol. 734, col. 51, 18 October 1966). Essentially, maladministration concerns defects in administrative procedures, not the merits or substance of decisions; however, successive PCAs, encouraged by the Select Committee, have widened the interpretation to include 'bad decisions', the quality of which might reasonably suggest that maladministration had been involved in taking them. Nevertheless, technically the merits of administrative decisions (e.g. their fairness) cannot be challenged so long as appropriate procedures have been followed. This presents considerable jurisdictional ambiguity, for the distinction between the merits of decisions, and actions taken in their implementation, is hardly more precise than that between policy and administration (see Chapter 1). With at least one PCA investigation (Court Line 1974/5), controversy developed precisely because of such ambiguity: 'upon the question' of whether ministerial statements in Parliament were policy matters or actions 'taken in the exercise of administrative functions' (Gregory, 1977, p. 280).

The effect of these limitations is illustrated by the fact that two-thirds of complaints forwarded by MPs are usually not accepted for investigation, mostly because they are outside the PCA's jurisdiction. In 1981, for example, more than three-quarters of complaints were not accepted: 23 per cent of these were complaints against authorities outside his scope, 41 per cent were not properly referred or were not about administrative actions, and 10 per cent concerned public personnel matters (PCA Annual Report, 1981, para. 55). Jurisdictional limitations, therefore, prevent a high proportion of properly referred complaints from being investigated.

Numerous proposals have been made for removing these exclusions. In 1977, for example, the Widdicombe Committee (Widdicombe Report, 1977, para. 67) recommended that the PCA, like the New Zealand ombudsman, should 'investigate complaints that actions, or omissions, by government departments are unreasonable, unjust or oppressive'. Nevertheless, successive governments have failed to act. One factor is that ministers have probably been concerned to prevent the PCA from challenging policy decisions, and civil servants to limit the scope of the watchdog over their own departments. Like MPs over access, civil servants and ministers have restricted the PCA's jurisdiction to limits which present least threat to themselves.

(C) APPOINTMENT AND STAFFING

Although a 'parliamentary commissioner', the PCA is appointed by government. The first three PCAs were all recruited from the civil service, as were most of their staff. While a civil service background may be useful in discharging the PCA's functions, it inevitably arouses suspicion that complaints against civil servants might not be investigated objectively. It may also explain the over-bureaucratic tendencies sometimes evident within the PCA's office: an unduly restricted interpretation (particularly by the first ombudsman) of the PCA's role, a cautious approach to the press, over-routinised investigations, and an over-reliance on the Treasury Solicitor (a government official) for legal advice. Moreover, while the PCA's salary is determined by the Commons and charged to the Consolidated Fund, the number – and conditions – of his staff require Treasury approval. As the Widdicombe Report (1977, para. 30) observed, 'this gives the Treasury power, at any rate potentially, to hamper the operation of the [PCA]'.

To rectify these deficiencies some changes have been made. For example, since 1979 the Select Committee has been consulted before the appointment of a new PCA and the choice is no longer limited to civil servants. In 1979, when Sir Idwal Pugh retired, he was succeeded – following consultation with the Select Committee – by Cecil Clothier, a lawyer and judge. Furthermore, since 1977 a small number of investigative staff have been recruited from outside the civil service, and legal advice has been obtained other than from the Treasury Solicitor. Nevertheless, scope clearly exists for allowing the PCA more independence, and more *appearance* of independence, from the executive whose activities he investigates.

(D) INVESTIGATIONS

The PCA possesses wide investigative powers, including power to examine ministers and civil servants and to inspect departmental files. Information and documents relating to Cabinet or Cabinet committee proceedings can be withheld, but this is rarely an obstacle and has only once – in the Court Line affair – aroused serious controversy. Investigations are conducted with great thoroughness: in 90–95 per cent of investigations departmental files are examined, in 40–45 per cent officials are questioned, and in about 60 per cent complainants are interviewed at home (Gwyn, 1982, p. 181). Such thoroughness, while seemingly commendable, is arguably unnecessary in routine cases. It also makes inefficient use of staff resources; consequently, the PCA completes far fewer investigations each year, and corrects considerably fewer cases of maladministration, than his foreign counterparts.

(E) REMEDIAL POWERS

As successive PCAs have widened the interpretation of maladministration, the percentage of investigations producing findings of maladministration has increased. In 1968 and 1969 it was 10 and 16 per cent, throughout the 1970s it was consistently above 30 per cent, and in 1980 and 1981 it was 48 and 46 per cent respectively. Additionally, in a number of cases (16 and 18 per cent of investigations in 1980 and 1981) departmental actions are criticised though complaints are not upheld. All told, in recent years around 110 cases of maladministration have been revealed annually and in about fifty further cases administrative actions have been criticised.

Following each investigation a report is issued to the referring MP, with a copy to the department concerned, but although the PCA may propose remedies, he cannot enforce them. In practice, however, the PCA's recommendations are usually accepted by departments, as failure to do so is likely to result in parliamentary criticism. The PCA, moreover, normally informs the Select Committee of any unremedied grievances which, in turn, may examine the departmental permanent secretary. Such procedures have, occasionally, achieved striking results. In 1979, for example, the Committee secured belated compensation for former owners of compulsorily purchased land who had been initially denied compensation because of inadequate publicity by the DOE.

The Select Committee has powers to investigate all reports from the Ombudsman, including annual reports and special reports which he is empowered to make on investigations of particular importance. Since 1972 the PCA has also published quarterly reports containing anonymised details of investigation. Nevertheless, the PCA's findings are not mandatory – his ultimate weapon is a statutory right to lay before both Houses a special report in cases where injustice has not been remedied. While most authorities accept that Parliament must ultimately hold ministers accountable, it is nevertheless widely felt that the PCA could do more to put pressure on wayward departments: for example, by making more use of press conferences. To date, departmental intransigence has not presented major problems but, as a former PCA (Pugh, 1978, p. 133) observed, if 'recommendations for remedy were ignored on any significant scale ... _the credibility of my Office would be prejudiced'. If that were to happen there would be a strong case for extending to Britain the arrangement which applies to the Northern Ireland Parliamentary Commissioner, whose reports can be used as grounds for an action for damages in the courts.

Any assessment of the PCA must take account of the above 'problem areas'. Undoubtedly, the limitations upon access and jurisdiction, as well as the PCA's cautious approach to publicity, have resulted in under-utilisation; almost all foreign ombudsmen receive more complaints per citizen than the PCA. The nature, even the existence, of his office is not widely understood among the public, and consequently many complaints do not reach him or are outside his jurisdiction. Between April 1967 and December 1980 MPs referred only 11,683 cases (under 850 per year) for investigation, and only 1,154 were upheld (under eighty-four per year). These limited results must be set against the extra workload – estimated at between one-and-a-half and five plus days per investigation (Gregory and Hutchesson, 1975, pp. 364–5) – which is created for government departments, particularly those (notably the Inland Revenue and DHSS) which attract most complaints. Moreover, the PCA's existence has probably made civil servants more cautious, with consequent extra delays and administrative costs.

The PCA, however, has not been the total failure predicted by some early commentators. Much of the first PCA's caution has subsequently been relaxed: later Commissioners have interpreted their jurisdiction more liberally, have eased access, and have discovered progressively higher incidences of maladministration. Moreover, while numbers of cases received and upheld are low by international standards, this may reflect higher standards of administrative practice in Britain. In any event, by 1980 over 4,000 complaints had been investigated – many after all other channels had been exhausted. Of the 1,154 upheld, moreover, almost all received appropriate recompense. Although many of the cases and remedies (an apology or small payment) have been relatively 'humdrum', for the complainant the outcome may nevertheless be important. There has also been the occasional *cause célèbre*, notably the 1968 Sachsenhausen case, where the PCA helped secure compensation for survivors of Sachsenhausen Concentration Camp, even though their claims had previously been rejected by three Foreign Office ministers and the Prime Minister (for discussion see Gregory and Hutchesson, 1975, esp. chs 11 and 12). Of course, even where complaints are not upheld, the PCA's investigation is not irrelevant. As the PCA observed in his 1979 Annual Report (p. 2), 'A grievance investigated is a resentment relieved, even if it be dismissed in the end'.

Many PCA investigations benefit more than just complainants. Some have brought important legislative changes: for example, the provisions in the 1974 and 1975 Finance Acts for interest to be paid on delayed tax repayments. Others have produced improved departmental practices and procedures: in 1975, for example, administrative changes introduced by the Driver and Vehicle Licensing Centre following an investigation were reported to have brought significantly reduced delays for driving licence applicants (see Gregory, 1982, pp. 57–9, 63–4). There have also been 'significant . . . changes in the attitudes of government departments to their dealings with . . . individual citizen[s]' (Pugh, 1978, p. 136). Indeed civil servants to some extent have also benefited; directly in the case of officials exonerated by the PCA, and indirectly in the sense that PCA investigations have undoubtedly improved the quality of central administration. It is important not to paint too antagonistic a picture of the PCA's relations with civil servants. His reports do more than simply keep them 'on their toes'; in many cases they have done much to acquaint ministers and senior officials with problems experienced at lower departmental levels, while cumulatively they represent a sort of guide to good (and bad) administrative practice.

The PCA, therefore, has shortcomings, but has nevertheless been a qualified success. As Gwyn (1982, p. 193) observes, 'many thousands of taxpayers, recipients of social services, property owners, automobile licensees etc. have been helped by changes in administrative practices and procedures resulting . . . from the Commissioner's investigations'.

The Health Service Commissioner

In 1973 three Health Service Commissioners were established with responsibility for investigating complaints against health authorities in, respectively, England, Scotland and Wales. Although in law separate from the PCA, all three posts have been vested in the person holding that office. Usually a single annual report is published containing information relevant to all three posts, and this is received by the Select Committee on the PCA.

Although exhibiting many common features with the PCA, two significant differences can be discerned:

(i)   The MP 'filter' does not apply. Complainants may approach the Commissioner direct provided they have first complained to the appropriate Health Authority;

(ii) The Commissioner's jurisdiction extends beyond investigating complaints of maladministration to those alleging injustice, or hardship, as a result of failure in a service provided by a Health Authority, or failure to provide a service which it was its duty to provide.

The Health Service Commissioner – like the PCA – suffers from important jurisdictional exclusions. The most significant are complaints about general medical and dental practitioners and opticians (which normally go to Family Practitioner Committees or, if professional negligence is alleged, to the courts) and complaints about clinical judgements of health service staff. Both exclusions are highly controversial and owe much to pressure from professional bodies such as the British Medical Association. Significantly, several authorities have suggested that the Commissioner should investigate clinical complaints with the help of medical assessors (the practice adopted by the PCA, who has jurisdiction over top security hospitals controlled by government departments).

Normally, the commissioner receives about 600–700 complaints annually from England, Scotland and Wales (the highest total, 712, was in 1978/9). However, a high proportion usually cannot be investigated: in 1981/2 81.8 per cent were rejected – a quarter because they concerned clinical judgement, a fifth because they had not first been referred to a health authority, and an eighth because they concerned practitioners, dentists, pharmacists, or opticians (Annual Report, 1981/2, p. 7). In fact, only about 100 complaints annually (101 in 1981/2) are fully investigated. Clearly, as with the

PCA, there is considerable under-utilisation of the Health Service Commissioner, and until his jurisdiction is widened NHS complaints procedures seem likely to remain a source of concern.

Local Commissioners for Administration

In 1974, coincident with local government reorganisation, two Commissions for Local Administration (CLAs) were established, one each for England and Wales. The English Commission consists of three local commissioners, each of whom investigates complaints in a particular part of the country, plus the PCA who sits *ex-officio* but has no investigative powers; the Welsh Commission consists of one local commissioner plus the PCA *ex-officio*. (In Scotland a single Scottish Commissioner – established in 1976 – investigates complaints without any PCA involvement.) All three institutions have similar jurisdiction, namely to investigate complaints of injustice caused by maladministration by local authorities, water authorities, joint planning boards, and police authorities (except the Metropolitan Police which is responsible to the Home Secretary). Complaints must normally be directed through a member of the authority concerned, although the commissioner may accept them direct if satisfied that a councillor/member has declined to forward it. Investigative powers are broadly similar to those of the PCA and Health Service Commissioner.

Local commissioners, like other British ombudsmen, suffer from serious limitations, the most important being:

(A) JURISDICTIONAL LIMITATIONS

Not only are local commissioners limited to investigating complaints of maladministration, but several fields of local administration are outside their jurisdiction. The most significant of these are: (i) contractual and commercial activity; (ii) certain educational matters (including curriculum, religious instruction, discipline, internal school or college management); (iii) the investigation or prevention of a crime (which since 1976 has been within the purview of the Police Complaints Board); (iv) the commencement or conduct of legal proceedings; (v) personnel matters; and (vi) actions affecting 'all or most of the inhabitants of the authority concerned' (e.g. rate levels).

(B) NO REMEDIAL POWERS

Like the PCA, local commissioners have no remedial powers. Their only course, following a finding of injustice through maladministration, is to lay a report before the authority concerned. This report must be published and considered by the authority, and the commissioner notified of remedial action proposed or taken. If the commissioner is dissatisfied with the authority's response the only remaining power is to issue a further report stating the grounds of dissatisfaction, and requiring this also to be published.

Unfortunately, unlike the PCA, local commissioners have experienced a significant minority of cases where authorities have failed to comply with recommendations. In the first five years, for example, 12.8 per cent of complaints upheld by the English Commission were the subject of second reports, and in 5.7 per cent the commissioner remained dissatisfied with the outcome (Justice, 1980, paras 114–18; and Appendix C). Even in cases with satisfactory outcomes, however, long periods may elapse between the first report and the remedy being provided: in the first nine years delays of six months or more were experienced in 25 per cent of English cases (Annual Report, 1982/3, para. 18). As a review by Justice (1980, paras 143–52) has suggested, there is a strong case for making the recommendations of local commissioners enforceable through the courts.

(C) THE REPRESENTATIVE BODY

The English and Welsh Commissions report to a Representative Body consisting of nominees of water authorities and local authority associations. (Different arrangements apply in Scotland – see Stacey, 1978, pp. 210–12.) Thus the English Representative Body receives the annual report of the English Commission as well as its annual estimates (which, if it considers them excessive, it may refer to the Secretary of State). The object of these arrangements is to make local commissioners report to bodies representative of all the authorities over whom they have jurisdiction. The effect, however, has been to give the English and Welsh Commissions a constitutional relationship, not with an independent body such as the Select Committee on the PCA, but with one representing the very authorities against whom they investigate complaints (and who meet their expenses). Not surprisingly, the English Representative Body 'appears to have performed a restrictive rather than a supportive role', reacting defensively against proposals for strengthening powers and not 'performing' anything resembling the role of the Select Committee with regard to securing redress from recalcitrant authorities (Lewis and Gateshill, 1978, pp. 54–7).

Notwithstanding these limitations, the CLA's achievements should not be ignored. Over 2,000 complaints are now being received annually in England (2,753 in 1982/3) and about 300 each in Scotland and Wales. (Most relate to planning and housing.) Complaints are investigated with great thoroughness, and in the nine years 1974–83 the English Commission alone found maladministration with injustice in 1,224 cases. Despite the problems of securing redress, an 'unsatisfactory outcome' was forthcoming in only seventy-eight of these cases (Annual Report, 1983, para. 17). Moreover, even where complaints have not been upheld, the CLA has nevertheless often managed to secure amicable settlements through informal means. Additionally, the CLA's impact on local authority procedures has been considerable, with 'very many' authorities revising administrative procedures following CLA investigations (Lewis and Gateshill, 1978, pp. 51–4).

The defects surrounding the local ombudsman system are, nevertheless, considerable. Every year, for example, many hundreds of complaints (2,045 in 1982/3) are received direct from the public without having first been sent to a councillor, and although such complaints are advised of the correct procedure only about half are subsequently referred properly. Even of complaints properly referred, only a small proportion (11 per cent in 1982/3) are fully investigated; the vast majority either have their investigations prematurely terminated, or are not accepted for investigation because they are outside the Commissioner's jurisdiction. According to Justice (1980, paras 200–25) even when complaints are investigated many complainants remain dissatisfied either with the conduct of investigations (one factor being the time taken to complete investigations – an average of forty-three weeks in 1982/3) or with the remedy obtained from the authority. Clearly, despite not inconsiderable achievements, there is substantial scope for the local ombudsman system to be improved.

Too Many Avenues?

Ombudsman machinery has been extended gradually since 1967 to cover the main layers of British public administration: central government, local government, and the NHS. That development, however, has been largely piecemeal. Not only have important

fields of public administration escaped the ombudsman phenomenon, but where ombudsmen do exist the varying provisions
relating to access and jurisdiction are bewildering. The fragmentation of ombudsman machinery also weakens its overall impact. A
single centralised ombudsman would not only carry more authority within Whitehall, but would become more prominent in the
public eye than the various individual commissioners who now
operate separately.

Despite piecemeal development, some co-operation between the
various ombudsmen does occur. The PCA is an *ex officio* member
of the English and Welsh CLAs, and the same person serves as
Health Service Commissioner for England, Scotland, and Wales.
(At various times the same person holding office as PCA has
concurrently served as the Northern Ireland PCA or as the
Northern Ireland Commissioner for Complaints.) In addition, the
English CLA regularly invites the Welsh and Scottish Local
commissioners to its meetings. Such arrangements, however, are of
little direct advantage to aggrieved citizens. Indeed, it is difficult to
avoid the conclusion that, while the establishment of ombudsmen
in Britain has extended the citizen's opportunities for securing
redress, it has not only failed to simplify the machinery and
procedures available, but has actually made them more confusing
and complex.

Access could be simplified and standardised, notably by allowing
direct access to all ombudsmen, or by allowing MPs to refer
complaints to any commissioner. However the select Committee
is unwilling to allow direct access to the PCA, and local authority
opinion generally opposes either direct access to the CLA or to
MPs concerning themselves with local authority matters.

A more comprehensive reform would be the establishment of a
single ombudsman. In 1975, the then PCA, Sir Alan Marre, noting
the proliferation of ombudsman machinery, observed: 'In the long
term it . . . will be important to consider how a more co-ordinated
total system, more directly related to the interests of members of
the public, can be brought about' (Annual Report, 1975, para. 55).
More recently Cecil Clothier has observed: 'Possibly the only way
to remove all potential inconvenience to Members and the Public
. . . would be to have a single central "Ombudsman" organisation
to which everything could be addressed' (Select Committee on the
Parliamentary Commissioner, 1979/80, p. 2). While Clothier
appears to be advocating little more than a central collection point
for complaints, the idea could be applied to a single official
performing investigative functions across the jurisdictional field of

all existing ombudsmen. Such an arrangement would not only be tidier, but would make the ombudsman more accessible and probably more effective in securing redress.

Of course, with many fields of public administration, redress lies not with an ombudsman but with other agencies. Indeed, from the citizen's standpoint, the multiplicity of agencies is a major source of confusion. In addition to agencies covered in this chapter, the following further channels can, in 1983, also be identified: MPs; Councillors ('county', 'district', or 'parish', depending on service concerned); Nationalised Industry Consumer Councils (see pp. 194–6); Police Complaints Board; Equal Opportunities Commission (deals with sex discrimination complaints); Commission for Racial Equality; Community Health Councils (represent consumer interests in the NHS); Office of Fair Trading (complaints about unfair trading practices, individual consumer rights); National Consumer Council (represent consumer viewpoints); European Commission and Court on Human Rights (in cases where public authorities breach the European Convention on Human Rights). Even this list is not exhaustive, and alternative remedies may apply in some cases.

There are today a multitude of channels through which to challenge the actions or decisions of public officials. The proliferation of agencies, however, obscures rather than clarifies the opportunities for redress available to ordinary citizens. To some extent the problems can be overcome by channelling grievances through pressure groups or the media, although to the man in the street these may not be particularly accessible. Alternatively, assistance may be provided by Citizen's Advice Bureaux, or consumer/legal/housing advice centres, which in many localities function almost as clearing houses for grievances emanating from within the local community. Such bodies, however, are only advisory, and whether redress is obtained still depends upon the efficacy of official channels.

The machinery for the redress of grievance lacks coherence. Some fields of public administration are well endowed with complaints machinery but others are not. The multitude of agencies reveals a plethora of procedures, investigative methods, remedial powers, and jurisdictional exclusions which reflects the piecemeal, haphazard pattern of their development. Proposals for rationalisation abound: the creation of something similar to the French *droit administratif*; Whyatt's proposed General Tribunal (p. 249); Widdicome's suggested extension of PCA powers (p. 253); Clothier's 'single central ombudsman' and so on. Such proposals, however, are unlikely to be implemented. A host of obstacles: the conservatism of the English legal profession, the vested interests of public officials, the threat to established institutions, bar the way to wholesale reform. The essentially piecemeal development of the past, with all its attendant complexity for citizens seeking redress, seems likely to continue into the foreseeable future.

REFERENCES

Alderman, G. (1982), 'Jews and Sunday trading: the use and abuse of delegated legislation', *Public Administration*, vol. 60, no. 1, pp. 99–104.

Alderman, R. K., and Cross, J. A. (1981), 'Patterns of ministerial turnover in two Labour Cabinets', *Political Studies*, vol. XXIX, no. 3, pp. 425–30.

Alexander, A. (1982a), *Local Government in Britain since Reorganisation* (London: Allen & Unwin).

Alexander, A. (1982b), *The Politics of Local Government in the United Kingdom* (London: Longman).

Alt, J. (1971), 'Some social and political correlates of county borough expenditure', *British Journal of Political Science*, vol. I, no. 1, pp. 49–62.

Alternatives to Domestic Rates (1981), Cmnd 8449 (London: HMSO).

Assheton Report (1944), *Report of the Committee on Training of Civil Servants*, Cmd. 6525 (London: HMSO).

Atkinson Report (1983), *Selection of Fast-Stream Graduate Entrants to the Home Civil Service, the Diplomatic Service and the Tax Inspectorate; and of Candidates from within the Service* (London: Management and Personnel Office).

Bagehot, W. (1963 edn), *The English Constitution* (London: Fontana).

Bains Report (1972), *The New Local Authorities: Management and Structure* (London: HMSO)

Baker, R. J. S. (1972a), *Administrative Theory and Public Administration* (London: Hutchinson).

Baker, R. J. S. (1972b), 'The V and G affair and ministerial responsibility', *Political Quarterly*, vol. 43, no. 3, pp. 340–5.

Barker, A. (1982), *Quangos in Britain* (London: Macmillan).

Barlow, Sir W. (1981), 'The problems of managing nationalized industries', in *Allies or Adversaries?* (London: RIPA), pp. 29–42.

Barrett, S., and Fudge, C. (eds) (1981), *Policy and Action* (London: Methuen).

Bates, E. (1982), 'Can the public's voice influence bureaucracy? The case of the community health councils', *Public Administration*, vol. 60, no. 1 pp. 92–8.

Beith, A. (1981), 'Prayers unanswered: a jaundiced view of the parliamentary scrutiny of statutory instruments', *Parliamentary Affairs*, vol. XXXIV, no. 2, pp. 165–73.

Benn, T. (1980), 'Manifestos and mandarins' in *Policy and Practice: the Experience of Government* (London: RIPA), pp. 57–78.

Benn, T. (1982), *Arguments for Democracy* (Harmondsworth: Penguin).

Binder, B. J. A. (1982), 'Relations between central and local government since 1975 – are the associations failing?', *Local Government Studies*, vol. 8, no. 1, pp. 35–44.

Birch, A. H. (1964), *Representative and Responsible Government* (London: Allen & Unwin).

Birch, A. H. (1980), *The British System of Government* (London: Allen & Unwin).

Boaden, N. (1971), *Urban Policy Making* (Cambridge: Cambridge University Press).

Borthwick, R. L. (1979), 'Questions and Debates', in *The House of Commons in the Twentieth Century* ed. S. A. Walkland, (Oxford: OUP), pp. 476–526.

Borthwick, R. L. (1982), 'Recent Changes in House of Commons Committees', in Robins (1982), pp. 1–14.

Bourn, J. (1979), *Management in Central and Local Government* (London: Pitman).

Bowen, G. (1978), *Survey of Fringe Bodies* (London: CSD).

Boyle, G., and Crosland, A. (1971), *The Politics of Education* (Harmondsworth: Penguin).

Boynton, Sir J. (1982), 'Local councils in confrontation: the current conflict with the centre', *Policy Studies*, vol. 2, pt. 4, pp. 199–216.

Bridges, Lord (1964), *The Treasury* (London: Allen & Unwin).

Briscoe, S. (1981), 'Employment in the public and private sectors, 1975–1981', *Economic Trends*, no. 338 (December), pp. 94–102.

Bromhead, P. (1974), *Britain's Developing Constitution* (London: Allen & Unwin).

Brooke Report (1971/2), *Report of the Joint Committee on Delegated Legislation*, HL 184 and HC 475.

Brown G. (1972), *In My Way* (Harmondsworth: Penguin).

Brown, M. (1982), *Introduction to Social Administration in Britain* (5th edn) (London: Hutchinson).

Brown, R. G. S. (1970), *The Administrative Process in Britain* (London: Methuen).

Brown, R. G. S. (1975), *The Management of Welfare* (London: Fontana).

Brown, R. G. S., and Steel, D. (1979), *The Administrative Process in Britain* (London: Methuen).

Bruce-Gardyne, J., and Lawson, N. (1976), *The Power Game* (London: Macmillan).

Bulpitt, J. (1967), *Party Politics in English Local Government* (London: Longman).

Butler, D., and Sloman, A. (1980), *British Political Facts 1900–1979* (London: Macmillan).

Byrne, P. (1976), 'Parliamentary control of delegated legislation', *Parliamentary Affairs*, vol. XXIX, no. 4, pp. 366–77.

Byrne, T. (1981), *Local Government in Britain* (Harmondsworth: Penguin).

Castle, B. (1980), *The Castle Diaries 1974–76* (London: Weidenfeld & Nicolson).

Central Policy Review Staff (CPRS) (1977), *Relations Between Central Government and Local Authorities* (London: HMSO).

Chapman, R. A. (1973), 'The Vehicle and General affair: some reflections for public administration in Britain', *Public Administration*, vol. 51, no. 3, pp. 273–90.

Chapman, R. A. (1982), 'Civil service recruitment – bias against external candidates', *Public Administration*, vol. 60, no. 1, pp. 77–83.

Chapman, R. A. (1983), 'The rise and fall of the CSD', *Policy and Politics*, vol. 11, no. 1, pp. 41–61.

Chester, Sir N. (1979), 'Fringe bodies, quangos and all that', *Public Administration*, vol. 57, no. 1, pp. 51–4.

Civil Service Commission (1979), *Report of the Committee on the Selection Procedure for the Recruitment of Administrative Trainees* (London: Civil Service Commission).

Civil Service Department (1978), *Report of the Administration Trainee Review Committee* (London: CSD).

Civil Service Department (1980), *The Civil Service: Introductory Factual Memorandum Submitted to the House of Commons Treasury and Civil Service Committee* (London: CSD).

Clark, A. (1977), 'Ministerial supervision and the size of the Department of the Environment', *Public Administration*, vol. 55, no. 2, pp. 197–204.

Clarke, Sir R. (1971), *New Trends in Government* (London: HMSO).

Clarke, Sir R. (1975), 'The Machinery of Government', in Thornhill (1975), pp. 63–95.

Cockburn, C. (1977), *The Local State* (London: Pluto Press).

Collins, C. A., Hinings, C. R., and Ranson, S. (1978), 'The officer and the councillor in local government', *Public Administration Bulletin*, vol. 28, pp. 34–50.

Conservative Central Office (1983), *The Conservative Manifesto* 1983 (London: CCO).

Coombes, D. (1966), *The Member of Parliament and the Administration* (London: Allen & Unwin).

Coombes, D. (1971), *State Enterprise: Business or Politics* (London: Allen & Unwin).

Coombes, D. (1981), 'Parliament and the European Community', in Walkland and Ryle (1981), pp. 236–59.

Council on Tribunals (1980), *Special Report, The Functions of the Council on Tribunals*, Cmnd 7805 (London: HMSO).

Cousins, P. F. (1982), 'Quasi-Official Bodies in Local Government', in Barker (1982), pp. 152–63.

Cousins, P. F. (1983), 'Local quangos – or how to make local government more confusing', *Teaching Public Administration*, vol. III, no. 1, pp. 1–16.

Crawford Report (1926), *Report of the Broadcasting Committee*, Cmd 2599 (London: HMSO).

Crossman, R. H. S. (1963), 'Introduction', in Bagehot, W., *The English Constitution* (London: Fontana).

Crossman, R. H. S. (1975), *The Diaries of a Cabinet Minister*, vol. 1 (London: Hamilton & Cape).

Daalder, H. (1975), 'Cabinet Reform Since 1914: Major Trends', in Herman and Alt (1975), pp. 242–76.

Davies, A. (1980), *Reformed Select Committees: The First Year* (London: Outer Circle Policy Unit).

Davies, B. P. (1968), *Social Needs and Resources in Local Services* (London: Joseph).

Davies, B. P. (1972), *Variations in Children's Services among British Urban Authorities* (London: Bell).

de Smith, S. A. (1981), *Constitutional and Administrative Law* (Harmondsworth: Penguin).

Dearlove, J. (1973), *The Politics of Policy in Local Government* (Cambridge: Cambridge University Press).

Dearlove, J. (1979), *The Reorganisation of British Local Government* (Cambridge: Cambridge University Press).

Delafons, J. (1982), 'Working in Whitehall: changes in public administration 1952–1982', *Public Administration*, vol. 60, no. 3, pp. 253–72.

Dell, E. (1980), 'Collective responsibility: fact, fiction or facade?', in *Policy and Practice* (London: RIPA), pp. 27–48.

Department of Health and Social Security, (1979), *Patients First* (London: HMSO).

Department of Trade (1981), *Consumers' Interests in the Nationalised Industries: A Consultative Document.*

Department of Trade (1982), *The Nationalised Industry Consumer Councils: A Strategy for Reform.*

Derbyshire, J. D., with Patterson, D. T. (1979), *An Introduction to Public Administration* (Maidenhead: McGraw Hill).

Doig, A. (1979), 'The machinery of government and the growth of governmental bodies', *Public Administration*, vol. 57 (Autumn), pp. 309–31.

Donoughmore Report (1932), *Report of the Committee on Ministers' Powers*, Cmd 4060 (London: HMSO).

Draper, P. (1977), *Creation of the DOE* (London: HMSO).

Dugdale, W. (1982), 'The ten-month chairman', *Water Bulletin*, no. 37, (10 December), pp. 5–6.

Duke, V., and Edgell, S. (1981), 'Politics of the Cuts', paper presented at PSA Urban Politics Group.

Dunleavy, P. (1980a), *Urban Political Analysis* (London: Macmillan).

Dunleavy, P. (1980b), 'Social and Political Theory and the Issues in Central–Local Relations', in *New Approaches to the Study of Central–Local Government Relationships*, ed. G. W. Jones (Farnborough: Gower), pp. 116–36.

Dunleavy, P. (1982), 'Is there a radical approach to public administration?', *Public Administration*, vol. 60, no. 2, pp. 215–25.

Dunsire, A. (1956), 'Accountability in local government', *Administration* (Dublin), vol. 4, pp. 80–8.

Dunsire, A. (1973), *Public Administration: The Word and the Science* (London: Martin Robertson).

Dunsire, A. (1978), *Control in a Bureaucracy* (Oxford: Martin Robertson).

Dunsire, A. (1982), 'Challenges to public administration in the 1980's', *Public Administration Bulletin*, no. 39 (August), pp. 8–21.

Eckstein, H. (1960), *Pressure Group Politics* (London: Allen & Unwin).

Efficiency and Effectiveness in the Civil Service: Government Observations on the Third Report from the Treasury and Civil Service Committee Session 1981–82, HC 236 Cmnd 8616 (London: HMSO).

Elcock, H. (1982), *Local Government* (London: Methuen).

Expenditure Committee (1977), *The Civil Service*, Eleventh Report, and Volumes of Evidence, 1976/7, Vols I–III, HC 535 (London: HMSO).

Financial and Economic Obligations of the Nationalised Industries (1961), White Paper, Cmnd 1337 (London: HMSO).

Finer, S. E. (1956), 'The individual responsibility of ministers', *Public Administration*, vol. 36, no. 4, pp. 377–96.

Flegman, V. (1980), *Called to Account: The Public Accounts Committee of the House of Commons 1965–6/1977–8* (London: Gower).

Fletcher, P. J. (1967), 'Public Administration', in *Political Science*, ed. H. V. Wiseman (London: Routledge & Kegan Paul), pp. 51–77.

Franks Report (1957), *Report of the Committee on Administrative Tribunals and Inquiries*, Cmnd 218 (London: HMSO).

Friend, J. K., Power, J. M., and Yewlett, C. J. L. (1974), *Public Planning: The Intercorporate Dimension* (London: Tavistock).

Fulton Report (1968), *The Civil Service, Vol. I: Report of the Committee*, Cmnd 3638 (London: HMSO).

Garner, L. (1979), *The NHS: Your Money or Your Life?* (Harmondsworth: Penguin).

Garner, M. R. (1979), 'The White Paper on nationalized industries: some criticisms', *Public Administration*, vol. 57 (Spring), pp. 7–20.

Garner, M. R. (1982), 'Auditing the efficiency of nationalized industries: enter the Monopolies and Mergers Commission', *Public Administration*, vol. 60, no. 4, pp. 409–28.

Garrett, J. (1972), *The Management of Government* (Harmondsworth: Penguin).

Garrett, J. (1980), *Managing the Civil Service* (London: Heinemann).

Goodin, R. E. (1982), 'Rational politicians and rational bureaucrats in Washington and Whitehall', *Public Administration*, vol. 60, no. 1, pp. 23–41.

Gordon Walker, P. (1972), *The Cabinet* (London: Fontana).

Government Observations on the Eleventh Report of the Expenditure Committee (1978), Cmnd 7117 (London: HMSO).

Gray, A., and Jenkins, B. (1982), 'Policy analysis in British central government: the experience of PAR', *Public Administration*, vol. 60, no. 4, pp. 429–50.

Gray, C. J. (1982), 'Regional Water Authorities', in Hogwood and Keating (1982), pp. 143–67.

Greater Manchester Council (1982), *Greater Manchester, Facts, Figures and Finance, 1982/83* (Manchester: Metropolitan County Council).

Green, D. G. (1981), *Power and Party in an English City* (London: Allen & Unwin).

Greenwood, J. R. and Wilson, D. J. (1980), 'How to train new councillors', *Local Government Chronicle* (21 March).

Greenwood, J. R., and Wilson, D. J. (1982), 'Councillor/officer relationships: case material for simulation', *Teaching Politics*, vol. 11, no. 3, pp. 263–71.

Greenwood, R. (1982), 'The politics of central–local relations in England and Wales, 1974–81', *West European Politics*, vol. 5, no. 3, pp. 253–69.

Greenwood, R., Walsh, K., Hinings, C. R., and Ranson, S. (1980), *Patterns of Management in Local Government* (Oxford: Martin Robertson).

Gregory, R. (1977), 'Court Line, Mr. Benn and the ombudsman', *Parliamentary Affairs*, vol. 30, no. 3, pp. 269–92.

Gregory, R. (1982), 'The Select Committee on the Parliamentary Commissioner for Administration, 1967–1980', *Public Law*, no. 1 (Spring), pp. 49–88.

Gregory, R., and Hutchesson, P. G. (1975), *The Parliamentary Ombudsman* (London: Allen & Unwin).

Griffith, J. A. G. (1966), *Central Departments and Local Authorities* (London: Allen & Unwin).

Griffith, J. A. G. (1973), *Parliamentary Scrutiny of Government Bills* (London: Allen & Unwin).

Griffith, J. A. G. (1981), *The Politics of the Judiciary* (London: Fontana).

Gwyn, W. B. (1982), 'The ombudsman in Britain: a qualified success in government reform', *Public Administration*, vol. 60, no. 2, pp. 177–95.

Gyford, J. (1976), *Local Politics in Britain* (London: Croom Helm).

Hague, D. C., Mackenzie, W. J. M., and Barker, A. (1975), *Public Policy and Private Interests* (London: Macmillan).

Haines, J. (1977), *The Politics of Power* (London: Cape).

Haldane Report (1918), *Report of the Machinery of Government Committee*, Cd 9230 (London: HMSO).

Ham, C. (1982), *Health Policy in Britain* (London: Macmillan).

Hanson, A. H. (1961), *Parliament and Public Ownership* (London: Cassell).

Hanson, A. H., and Walles, M. (1980), *Governing Britain* (London: Fontana).

Hawke, N. (1982), 'Administrative Justice and the Protection of Individual Rights', in Robins (1982), pp. 141–51.

Haynes, R. J. (1980), *Organisation Theory and Local Government* (London: Allen & Unwin).

Haywood, S. C., and Elcock, H. J. (1982), 'Regional Health Authorities: Regional Government or Central Agencies?', in Hogwood and Keating (1982), pp. 119–42.

Headey, B. (1974), *British Cabinet Ministers* (London: Allen & Unwin).

Headey, B. (1975), 'Cabinet Ministers and Senior Civil Servants: Mutual Requirements and Expectations', in Herman and Alt (1975), pp. 121–39.

Heath, E., and Barker, A. (1978), "Heath on Whitehall reform',

Parliamentary Affairs, vol. 31, no. 4, pp. 363–90.

Heaton/Williams Report (1974), *Report on Civil Service Training* (London: CSD).

Herbert Report (1960), *Report of the Royal Commission on Local Government in Greater London*, Cmnd. 1164, (London: HMSO).

Herman, V., and Alt, J. E. (eds) (1975), *Cabinet Studies: A Reader* (London: Macmillan).

Hewart, Lord (1929), *The New Despotism* (London: Benn).

Hill, D. M. (1967), 'Leeds', in *Voting in Cities*, ed. L. J. Sharpe (London: Macmillan), pp. 132–64.

Hill, D. M. (1983), 'Decisions, decisions . . .', *Parliamentary Affairs*, vol. 36, no. 1, pp. 121–5.

Hogwood, B. W. (1982), 'Introduction', in Hogwood and Keating (1982), pp. 1–20.

Hogwood, B. W., and Keating, M. (eds) (1982), *Regional Government in England* (Oxford: Clarendon Press).

Hogwood, B. W., and Lindley, P. D. (1982), 'Variations in Regional Boundaries', in Hogwood and Keating (1982), pp. 21–49.

Holland, P. (1979), *Quango, Quango, Quango* (London: Adam Smith Institute).

Holland, P. (1982), 'Shooting sitting quangos', *Daily Telegraph* (11 March).

Holland, P., and Fallon, M. (1978), *The Quango Explosion* (London: Conservative Political Centre).

Hood, C. (1978), 'Keeping the centre small: explanations of agency type', *Political Studies*, vol. 26, no. 1, pp. 30–46.

Hood, C. (1979), 'The world of quasi-government', paper presented to PSA Annual Conference.

Hood, C. (1981), 'Axeperson Spare that Quango', in Hood and Wright (1981), pp. 100–22.

Hood, C., Dunsire, A., and Thompson, K. S. (1978), 'So you think you know what government departments are . . .', *Public Administration Bulletin*, no. 27, pp. 20–32.

Hood, C., and Dunsire, A. (1981), *Bureaumetrics* (Farnborough: Gower).

Hood, C., and Wright, M. (eds) (1981), *Big Government in Hard Times* (Oxford: Martin Robertson).

Hoskyns, Sir J. (1983), 'Whitehall and Westminster: an outsider's view', *Parliamentary Affairs*, vol. 36, no. 2, pp. 137–47.

Jennings, R. E. (1982), 'The changing representational roles of local councillors in England', *Local Government Studies*, vol. 8. no. 5, pp. 67–86.

Johnson, N. (1971), 'The reorganizing action of central government', *Public Administration*, vol. 49, no. 1, pp. 3–6.

Johnson, N. (1977), *In Search of the Constitution* (London: Pergamon).

Johnson, N. (1978), 'The Public Corporation: An Ambiguous Species', in *Policy and Politics*, ed. D. E. Butler and A. H. Halsey (London: Macmillan), pp. 122–39.

Johnson, N. (1979), 'Editorial: quangos and the structure of British government', *Public Administration*, vol. 57 (Winter), pp. 379–95.

Johnson, N. (1981), 'Select Committees as Tools of Parliamentary Reform: Some Further Reflections', in Walkland and Ryle (1981), pp. 203–36.

Johnson, N. (1982), 'Accountability, Control and Complexity: Moving Beyond Ministerial Responsibility', in Barker (1982), pp. 206–18.

Jones, B. (1982), 'Select committees and the floor of the House: Du Cann vs. Kilroy-Silk', *Teaching Politics*, vol. 11, no. 3, pp. 312–20.

Jones, G. W. (1965), 'The Prime Minister's powers', *Parliamentary Affairs*, vol. 18, no. 2, pp. 167–85.

Jones, G. W. (1969), *Borough Politics* (London: Macmillan).

Jones, G. W. (1973), 'The functions and organisation of councillors', *Public Administration*, vol. 51, pp. 135–46.

Jones, G. W. (1975), 'Development of the Cabinet', in Thornhill, (1975), pp. 31–62.

Jones, G. W. (1976), 'The Prime Minister's Secretaries', in *From Policy to Administration*, ed. J. A. G. Griffith (London: Allen & Unwin).

Jones, G. W. (1980), *The Prime Minister's Aides* (Hull: University of Hull Occasional Papers in Politics, No. 6).

Jones, G. W. (1982a), 'Running those mysterious quangos to ground', *Local Government Chronicle*, no. 6013 (20 August).

Jones, G. W. (1982b), 'The regional threat', *Local Government Chronicle*, 9 July, p. 772.

Jones, G. W., and Stewart, J. D. (1982), 'The Layfield analysis applied to central–local relations under the Conservative government', *Local Government Studies*, vol. 8, no. 3, pp. 47–59.

Jordan, G. (1976), 'Hiving-off and departmental agencies', *Public Administration Bulletin*, no. 21, pp. 35–51.

Jordan, G. (1978), 'Central co-ordination: Crossman and the Inner Cabinet', *Political Quarterly*, vol. 49, no. 2, pp. 171–80.

Justice (1971), *Administration Under Law* (London: Justice).

Justice (1980), *The Local Ombudsmen: A Review of the first five Years* (London: Justice).

Kellner, P., and Crowther-Hunt, Lord (1980), *The Civil Servants: An Inquiry into Britain's Ruling Class* (London: Macdonald).

Kimber, R., and Richardson, J. J. (eds) (1974), *Campaigning for the Environment* (London: Routledge).

Knight, Sir. A. (1982), 'The control of nationalised industries', *Political Quarterly*, vol. 53, no. 1, pp. 24–34.

Layfield Report (1976), *Local Government Finance: Report of the Committee of Enquiry*, Cmnd 6453 (London: HMSO).

Lee, M. (1981), 'Whitehall and Retrenchment', in Hood and Wright (1981), pp. 35–55.

Lewis, N., and Gateshill, B. (1978), *The Commission for Local Administration* (London: RIPA).

Liaison Committee (1982–3), *The Select Committee System*, First Report,

HC 92.

Likierman, A. (1982), 'Management Information for Ministers: the MINIS in the Department of the Environment', *Public Administration*, vol. 60, no. 2, pp. 127–42.

Local Government Finance (1977), Cmnd 6813 (London: HMSO).

Local Government in England: Government Plans for Reorganisation (1971), Cmnd 4854 (London: HMSO).

Local Government Reform in England (1970), Cmnd 4276 (London: HMSO).

Lowe, P., and Goyder, J. (1983), *Environmental Groups in Politics* (London: Allen & Unwin).

Macdonald, J., and Fry, G. K. (1980), 'Policy-planning units – ten years on', *Public Administration*, vol. 58, no. 4, pp. 421–37.

Mackenzie, W. J. M., and Grove, J. W. (1957), *Central Administration in Britain* (London: Longman).

Mackintosh, J. P. (1977), *The British Cabinet* (London: Stevens).

Mackintosh, J. P. (1982), *The Government and Politics of Britain* (London: Hutchinson).

Mair, R. (1977), 'Civil Service Training and the Civil Service College', in Rhodes, (1977), pp. 41–9.

Maud Report (1967), *Committee on the Management of Local Government*, vol. I: Report (London: HMSO).

McIntosh Report (1976), NEDO, *A Study of UK Nationalised Industries* (and Appendix Volume) (London: HMSO).

Michael, J. (1982), *The Politics of Secrecy* (Harmondsworth: Penguin).

Miliband, R. (1973), *The State in Capitalist Society* (London: Quartet Books).

Ministerial Control of the Nationalised Industries (1969), Cmnd 4027 (London: HMSO).

Mitchell, D. (1982), 'Intervention, control and accountability: the National Enterprise Board', *Public Administration Bulletin*, vol. 38, pp. 40–65.

Monopolies and Mergers Commission (1981), *A Report on Water Services Supplied by the Severn Trent Water Authority and its Companies* (London: HMSO).

Morrison, H. (1933), *Socialisation and Transport* (London: Constable).

Morrison, H. (1959), *Government and Parliament* (2nd ed) (Oxford: Oxford University Press).

National Consumer Council (1976); *Consumers and the Nationalised industries* (London: HMSO).

Nationalised Industries: A Review of Economic and Financial Objectives (1967), Cmnd 3437 (London: HMSO).

Nationalised Industries (1978), White Paper, Cmnd 7131 (London: HMSO).

Neustadt, R. E. (1966), 'White House and Whitehall', *Public Interest*, vol. 2, pp. 55–69.

Newman, O. (1981), *The Challenge of Corporatism* (London: Macmillan).

Newton, K. (1976), *Second City Politics* (Oxford: Clarendon Press).

Newton, K. (1979), 'The Local Political Elite in England and Wales', in *Local Government in Britain and France*, ed. J. Lagroye and V. Wright (London: Allen & Unwin), pp. 105–13.

Nigro, F. A., and Nigro, L. G. (1973), *Modern Public Administration* (New York: Harper & Row).

Non-Departmental Public Bodies: A Guide for Departments (1981) (London: HMSO).

Norton, P. (1979), 'The Organisation of Parliamentary Parties', in *The House of Commons in the Twentieth Century*, ed. S. A. Walkland (London: Oxford University Press), pp. 7–68.

Norton, P. (1981), *The Commons in Perspective* (Oxford: Martin Robertson).

Norton, P. (1982), *The Constitution in Flux* (Oxford: Martin Robertson).

Norton, P. (1983), 'Party committees in the House of Commons', *Parliamentary Affairs*, vol. 36, no. 1, pp. 7–27.

Outer Circle Policy Unit (1979), *What's Wrong with Quangos?* (London: OCPU).

Page, B. (1979), 'Labour's culture of illusions', *New Statesman* (29 September,) pp. 446–8.

Painter M. J. (1980), 'Policy co-ordination in the Department of the Environment, 1970–1976', *Public Administration*, vol. 58, no. 2, pp. 135–54.

Parris, H. (1969), *Constitutional Bureaucracy* (London: Allen & Unwin).

Paterson Report (1973), *The New Scottish Local Authorities: Organisation and Management Structures* (London: HMSO).

Peele, G. (1983), 'Government at the Centre', in *Developments in British Politics* ed. H. Drucker, P. Dunleavy, A. Gamble, and G. Peele, (London: Macmillan), pp. 83–105.

Pitt, D., and Smith, B. (1981), *Government Departments* (London: Routledge & Kegan Paul).

Pliatzky Report (1980), *Report on Non-Departmental Public Bodies*, Cmnd 7797 (London: HMSO).

Plowden Committee (1961), *The Control of Public Expenditure*, Cmnd 1432 (London: HMSO).

Plowden, W. (1981), 'The British Central Policy Review Staff', in *Policy Analysis and Policy Innovation: Patterns, Problems and Potentials*, ed. P. R. Baehr and B. Wittrock (London and Beverly Hills: Sage), pp. 61–91.

Pollitt, C. (1974), 'The Central Policy Review staff, 1970–1974', *Public Administration*, vol. 52 (Winter) pp. 375–92.

Pollitt, C. (1980), 'Rationalizing the machinery of government: the Conservatives 1970–1974', *Political Studies*, vol. 28, no. 1, pp. 84–98.

Pollitt, C. (1982), 'The CSD: a normal death?', *Public Administration*, vol. 60, no. 1, pp. 73–6.

Poole, K. P. (1978), *The Local Government Service* (London: Allen & Unwin).

Powell, E. (1982), 'Parliament and the question of reform', *Teaching Politics*, vol. 11, no. 2, pp. 167–76.

Pugh, Sir I. (1978), 'The ombudsman – jurisdiction, powers and practice', *Public Administration*, vol. 56, no. 2, pp. 127–38.

Punnett, R. M. (1980), *British Government and Politics* (London: Heinemann).

Pyper, R. (1983), 'The F. O. resignations: individual ministerial responsibility revived?', *Teaching Politics*, vol. 12, no. 2, pp. 200–10.

Rates: Proposals for Rate Limitation and Reform of the Rating System (1983), White Paper, Cmnd 9008 (London: HMSO).

Redwood, J., and Hatch, J. (1982), *Controlling Public Industries* (Oxford: Blackwell).

Regan, D. E. (1977), *Local Government and Education* (London: Allen & Unwin).

Regan, D. E. (1983), 'Central-local relationships in Britain: applying the power-dependence model', *Teaching Politics*, vol. 12, no. 1, pp. 44–53.

Reorganisation of Central Government (1970), White Paper, Cmnd 4506 (London: HMSO).

Rhodes, R. A. W. (ed.) (1977), *Training in the Civil Service* (London: JUC).

Rhodes, R. A. W. (1979), 'Research into Central–Local Relations in Britain: A Framework for Analysis', unpublished paper, University of Essex, Department of Government.

Rhodes, R. A. W. (1981), *Control and Power in Central–Local Government Relations* (Farnborough: Gower).

Rhodes, R. A. W., Hardy, B., and Pudney, K. (1981), 'Public interest groups in central–local relations in England and Wales', *Public Administration Bulletin*, no. 36, pp. 17–36.

Richardson, J. J., and Jordan, A. G. (1979), *Governing Under Pressure* (Oxford: Martin Robertson).

Riddell, P. (1982), 'Select committees two years on', *Financial Times*, 16 February.

Ridley, F. F. (ed.) (1979), *Government and Administration in Western Europe* (Oxford: Martin Robertson).

Robins, L. (ed.) (1982), *Topics in British Politics* (London: The Politics Association).

Robinson, A. (1981), 'The House of Commons and Public Expenditure', in Walkland and Ryle (1981), pp. 154–74.

Robinson Report (1977), *Remuneration of Councillors*, Vol. 1: Report, Cmnd 7010; *Remuneration of Councillors*, Vol. 2: The Surveys of Councillors and Local Authorities (London: HMSO).

Robson, W. A. (1960), *Nationalized Industry and Public Ownership* (London: Allen & Unwin).

Robson, W. A. (1966), *Local Government in Crisis* (London: Allen & Unwin).

Robson, W. A. (1969), 'Ministerial control of nationalised industries', *Political Quarterly*, vol. 39, no. 1, pp. 103–12.

Role of the Comptroller and Auditor-General (1980), Cmnd 7845 (London: HMSO).

Rose, R. (1980), Contributions in *Presidents and Prime Ministers*, ed. by. R. Rose and E. Suleiman (1980) (Washington DC: American Enterprise for Public Policy Research).

Royal Commission on the National Health Service (1979), *Report*, Cmnd 7615, (London: HMSO).

Rush, M. (1981), *Parliamentary Government in Britain* (London: Pitman).
Ryle, M. (1981), 'The Commons Today – A General Survey', in Walkland and Ryle (1981), pp. 11–38.
Saunders, P. (1980), *Urban Politics* (Harmondsworth: Penguin).
Saunders, P. (1981), 'The Crisis of Central–Local Relations in Britain', University of Melbourne (Issues in Contemporary Planning Seminar Paper).
Saunders, P. (1982), 'Why study central–local relations?', *Local Government Studies*, vol. 8, no. 2, pp. 55–66.
Sedgemore, B. (1980), *The Secret Constitution* (London: Hodder & Stoughton).
Seebohm Report (1968), *Report of the Committee on Local Authority and Allied Personal Social Services*, Cmnd 3703 (London: HMSO).
Select Committee on Nationalised Industries (SCNI) (1967/8), *Ministerial Control of the Nationalised Industries*, First Report, HC 371 (3 Vols).
Select Committee on the Parliamentary Commissioner for Administration (1979/80), Second Report, *The System of Ombudsmen in the United Kingdom*, HC 254.
Seymour-Ure, C. (1974), *The Political Impact of Mass Media* (London: Constable).
Sharpe, L. J. (1970), 'Theories and values of local government', *Political Studies*, vol. 18, no. 2, pp. 153–74.
Sharpe, L. J. (ed.) (1981), *The Local Fiscal Crisis in Western Europe, Myths and Realities* (London: Sage).
Shell, D. R. (1981), 'The British constitution in 1980', *Parliamentary Affairs*, vol. XXXIV, no. 2, pp. 149–64.
Shell, D. R. (1982), 'The British constitution in 1981', *Parliamentary Affairs*, vol. XXXV, no. 2, pp. 118–35.
Simon, H. A., Smithburg, D. W., and Thompson, V. A. (1971), *Public Administration* (New York: Knopf).
Skelcher, C. (1983), 'Towards salaried councillors? – the special responsibility allowances', *Local Government Studies*, vol. 9, no. 3, pp. 10–15.
Smith, B. L. (1969), 'The Justification of Local Government', in *Politics and Government of Urban Canada: Selected Readings*, ed. L. D. Feldman and M. D. Goldrick (Toronto: Methuen), pp. 332–47.
Smith, B. L. (1976), *Policy Making in British Government* (London: Martin Robertson).
Smith, B. L. (1977), 'The Development of Central Training in the Civil Service', in Rhodes (1977), pp. 30–40.
Stacey, F. (1978), *Ombudsmen Compared* (Oxford: Oxford University Press).
Stanyer, J. (1976), *Understanding Local Government* (London: Fontana).
Stanyer, J., and Smith, B. (1976), *Administering Britain* (London: Fontana/Collins).
Steel, D. R. (1978), 'Nationalisation and Public Ownership', in *Trends in British Politics since 1945*, ed. C. Cook and J. Ramsden (London: Macmillan), pp. 109–31.

Steel, D. R. (1979), 'Britain', in Ridley (1979), pp. 18–66.

Steel, D. R., and Heald, D. A. (1982), 'Privatising public enterprise: an analysis of the government's case', *Political Quarterly*, vol. 53, no. 3, pp. 333–49.

Stephenson, H. (1980), *Mrs Thatcher's First Year* (London: Jill Norman).

Stevens, A. (1978), 'The role of the Ecole Nationale d'Administration', *Public Administration*, vol. 56, no. 3, pp. 283–97.

Stewart, J. D. (1974), 'The politics of local government reorganisation', in *The Year Book of Social Policy 1973*, ed. K. Jones (London: Routledge).

Strauss, A., Schatzman, L., Ehrlich, D., Bucher, R., and Sabshin, M. (1971). 'The hospital and its negotiated order', reprinted in *Decisions, Organizations and Society*, ed. F. G. Castles, D. J. Murray, and D. C. Potter (Harmondsworth: Penguin, in association with Open University Press), pp. 103–23.

Taylor, I. (1980), 'Ideology and Policy', in *The Labour Party*, ed. C. Cook and I. Taylor (London: Longman) pp. 1–31.

Thornhill (1975), *The Modernization of British Government* (London: Pitman).

Tivey, L. (1973a), *Nationalization in British Industry* (London: Cape).

Tivey, L. (1973b), *The Nationalized Industries Since 1960* (London: Allen & Unwin).

Tivey, L. (1982a), 'Nationalized industries as organized interests', *Public Administration*, vol. 60, no. 1, pp. 42–55.

Tivey, L. (1982b), 'Quasi-Government for Consumers', in Barker (1982), pp. 137–51.

Treasury and Civil Service Committee Report (1980): *The Future of the Civil Service Department*, First Report, 1980/81, HC 54.

Wade, H. W. R. (1982), *Administrative Law* (Oxford: Oxford University Press).

Waldo, D. (1955), *The Study of Public Administration* (Garden City, New York: Doubleday).

Walker, S. D. (1982), 'Managing a government department', *Management in Government*, vol. 37, no. 4, pp. 251–9.

Walkland, S. A. (1968), *The Legislative Process in Great Britain* (London: Allen & Unwin).

Walkland, S. A., and Ryle, M. (eds) (1981), *The Commons Today* (London: Fontana).

Wheatley Report (1969), *Report of the Royal Commission on Local Government in Scotland*, Cmnd 4150 (London: HMSO).

Whyatt Report (1961), *The Citizen and the Administration* (London: Justice).

Widdicombe Report (1977), *Our Fettered Ombudsmen* (London: Justice).

Williams, D. G. T. (1982), 'The Donoughmore Report in retrospect', *Public Administration*, vol. 60, no. 3, pp. 273–92.

Williams, M. (1972), *Inside Number 10* (London: Weidenfeld & Nicolson).

Williams, S. (1980), 'The Decision Makers', in *Policy and Practice: The Experience of Government* (London: RIPA), pp. 79–102.

Wilson, D. J., and Woodhead, N. (1982), 'Public administration', *Teaching Politics*, vol. 11, no. 2, pp. 210–20.

Wilson, Sir H. (1977), *The Governance of Britain* (London: Sphere).

Wistow, G. (1982), 'Collaboration between health and local authorities: why is it necessary?', *Social Policy and Administration*, vol. 16, no. 1, pp. 44–62.

Wood, G. (1981), 'Examining statistics on the higher civil service', *Public Administration*, vol. 59, no. 3, pp. 473–80.

Wraith, R. E., and Lamb, G. B. (1971), *Public Inquiries as Instruments of Government* (London: Allen & Unwin).

Wright, M. (1977), 'Public expenditure in Britain: the crisis of control', *Public Administration*, vol. 55 (Summer), pp. 143–70.

Wright, M. (ed.) (1980), *Public Spending Decisions* (London: Allen & Unwin).

Yardley, D. C. M. (1982), *Principles of Administrative Law* (London: Butterworths).

Young, H., and Sloman, A. (1982), *No, Minister* (London: BBC Publications).

Young, S. (1982), 'Regional Offices of the Department of the Environment: their Roles and Influence in the 1970s', in Hogwood and Keating (1982), pp. 75–95.

INDEX

References in **bold characters** denote chapters that are wholly concerned with the subjects to which they refer.